WHOLE FOOD
VEGETARIAN
COOKBOOK

WHOLE FOOD
VEGETARIAN
COOKBOOK

135 Recipes *for* Healthy, Unprocessed Food

IVY STARK

Photography by
DARREN MUIR

ROCKRIDGE
PRESS

For general information on our other products and services or to obtain technical support, please contact our Customer Care Department within the United States at (866) 744-2665, or outside the United States at (510) 253-0500.

Rockridge Press publishes its books in a variety of electronic and print formats. Some content that appears in print may not be available in electronic books, and vice versa.

TRADEMARKS: Rockridge Press and the Rockridge Press logo are trademarks or registered trademarks of Callisto Media Inc. and/or its affiliates, in the United States and other countries, and may not be used without written permission. All other trademarks are the property of their respective owners. Rockridge Press is not associated with any product or vendor mentioned in this book.

Interior and Cover Designer: John Calmeyer
Art Producer: Megan Baggott
Editor: David Lytle
Production Editor: Emily Sheehan
Photography © 2020 Darren Muir.
Author photo courtesy of Dillon Burke.

ISBN: Print 978-1-64611-884-7 |
eBook 978-1-64611-885-4

R0

In memory of my dear friend Viejo.
You brought so much laughter and joy to my life . . .
Cierro los ojos y aún te escucho sonreír.

CONTENTS

INTRODUCTION   ix

CHAPTER ONE
Whole Foods & A Plant-Forward Lifestyle   1

CHAPTER TWO
Your Whole Food Kitchen   15

CHAPTER THREE
Staple Recipes & Snacks   27

CHAPTER FOUR
Condiments, Sauces & Dressings   55

CHAPTER FIVE
Breakfast   75

CHAPTER SIX
Sandwiches & Handhelds   97

CHAPTER SEVEN
Bowls, Salads & Sides   123

CHAPTER EIGHT
Soups & Stews   149

CHAPTER NINE
Dinner Mains   175

CHAPTER TEN
Drinks & Desserts   221

MEASUREMENT CONVERSIONS   241

RESOURCES   242

REFERENCES   243

INDEX   245

As the owner of a vegetarian/vegan restaurant, I'm often asked if I'm a strict vegetarian, and the answer is "most of the time." Although the majority of the food I eat is plant based, as a professional chef, I find it essential to taste the food I prepare in my work setting, which includes other types of restaurants. I make sure that the meats and fish I serve are from cruelty-free, humane, and sustainable sources. I also enjoy sushi occasionally.

From the time I left home and began cooking for myself, I've leaned toward a more plant-rich diet for many reasons. When I was in college in California, the abundance of extraordinary fresh produce was something I'd never seen before while growing up in Colorado. The first asparagus I had ever eaten was from a jar. As a typical student, money was tight and meat was a luxury, so plant-based meals were the norm. These days, I find that even though I can buy meat every day, I'd rather have a big bowl of satisfying grains spiked with beans, veggies, and herbs.

Recently, chefs have spearheaded the concept of beautiful vegetables as the stars of a dish and are forgoing the meat portion altogether. Besides being delicious and ultimately healthier, eating less meat can save thousands of dollars a year in groceries. Plant-based eating also benefits our planet's ecosystem by reducing the use of endangered natural resources like water and reducing packaging waste.

In this book I share my passion for cooking plant-forward food with you from a healthy perspective. Whole foods—including seasonal fruits and vegetables, grains and legumes, pulses, nuts, seeds, herbs, and spices—drive the recipes in this book. This book provides not just recipes but also a road map for making intelligent and thoughtful choices for eating nutritious food without feeling like you're on a "diet." You picked up the book because you are looking to reap the benefits of eating more veggies, and I am here to help you eat veggies in a smart, delicious, and easy way. Do I have a lot of time to spend cooking for myself every day? Absolutely not! All the recipes are designed with this in mind, and whenever appropriate, I include prep-ahead advice that can save time. Along with the recipes, I share some tips for using leftovers and how to be flexible with ingredients and use what is available. In this way, we can reduce waste, which helps Mother Nature as well as our pocketbooks.

CHAPTER ONE

WHOLE FOODS &
A PLANT-FORWARD
LIFESTYLE

The term *plant-forward* is my way of describing clean eating, a concept that stresses healthy, whole, unprocessed foods. It may include small portions of animal protein if you are not a strict vegetarian, or if you're cooking for a non-vegetarian who wants to increase their consumption of nutrient-dense veggies. The plant-forward approach to eating and living well can maximize energy and optimize your health. It's not a diet at all but a lifestyle with a ton of flexibility, meaning that it can be adapted to fit everyday life. Let's look at how exactly one follows a plant-forward diet, and what makes it healthy.

A Variety of Vegetarians

A plant-forward diet consists of eating whole foods and plants—fruits, vegetables, whole grains, legumes, pulses, nuts, and seeds. One of the best things about this eating style is that it can be flexible. It doesn't necessarily mean plants only. For some people, a plant-based diet does exclude all animal products (vegan diet). For others, it's a flexible choice, which means most of your foods are derived from plants and occasionally from animal sources (flexitarian diet). Others do not consume animals but still choose to eat dairy and eggs (lacto-ovo vegetarian). Pescatarians include fish in their plant-forward meals. Many of the recipes in this book are dairy-free, and in the cases that dairy is included, there are tips to show where the dairy products may be eliminated or replaced with non-dairy equivalents. We live in a world where excellent substitutes can be purchased, and I include recipes for non-dairy basics like butterless butter, non-dairy yogurt, and eggless mayo. All the recipes can be adjusted to add animal protein as you desire, but you will want to keep the portions small. You will feel full and satisfied and will not miss the large portions of meat that are part of the mainstream diet. In fact, you may find yourself eliminating meat altogether.

Daily Nutritional Needs

It's not complicated to make shifts in your current diet to move toward healthier whole food eating, and it doesn't require you to give up all the foods you love.

A whole food plan can include a wide variety of vegetables, fruits, whole grains, beans, legumes, fish, skinless poultry, nuts, and fat-free/low-fat dairy products. It should limit sugary drinks, sweets, fatty or processed meats, solid fats, and salty or highly processed foods. Eliminate the poultry, fish, and meat, and by making smart choices you have a whole food vegetarian pattern that still offers variety.

The recommended numbers of daily or weekly servings of each food type are provided here, based on eating a total of 2,000 calories per day. Your calorie needs may be different, depending on your age, activity level, and whether you are trying to lose, gain, or maintain your weight.

The vegetarian's plate would contain the following foods and number of servings. The following are a few examples of what represents one serving of each category of food:

VEGETABLES

5 servings per day

Fresh, frozen, and canned are all excellent choices. Frozen vegetables are frozen quickly after picking and retain all their nutritional value.

EXAMPLES

- 1 cup raw leafy greens—the darker the greens, the more nutrients they have
- ½ cup raw or cooked vegetables
- ¼ cup sun-dried tomatoes

FRUITS

4 servings per day

Fresh, frozen, canned, and dried

EXAMPLES

- 1 medium whole fruit such as an apple or an orange
- ½ cup cut-up fruit like pineapple
- ¼ cup 100 percent fruit juice, freshly squeezed juice when possible
- ¼ cup dried fruit—look for fruit dried without chemicals

GRAINS

6 servings per day

Whole grain and high in dietary fiber

EXAMPLES

- ½ cup cooked brown rice or pasta
- ½ cup cooked quinoa or barley
- 1 corn tortilla
- ½ cup popped popcorn

DAIRY AND EGGS (*IF DESIRED*)

3 servings per day

Low-fat and fat-free

EXAMPLES

- 1 cup milk
- 1 cup Greek yogurt
- 1½ ounces cheese
- 1 or 2 egg whites

NUTS, SEEDS, BEANS, AND LEGUMES

5 servings per week

EXAMPLES

- 1 tablespoon peanut butter
- 2 tablespoons nuts or seeds
- ¼ cup cooked beans

FATS AND OILS

3 servings per day

Unsaturated

EXAMPLES

- 1 tablespoon vegetable oil (canola, corn, olive, soybean, safflower)
- 1 tablespoon low-fat or vegan mayonnaise
- 1 tablespoon salad dressing

Plant-Based Proteins

One of the typical questions people have when considering a plant-based diet is "But how will I get enough protein?" Protein is composed of essential amino acids that support every part of our bodies and are crucial for maintaining energy, healthy tissues, and a healthy brain. By eating a wide variety of plant-based foods, you can get all the essential nutrients, although some plants contain more protein than others.

Quinoa: This ancient Peruvian grain is an excellent source of protein and other nutrients like fiber and magnesium, which support healthy bones. Quinoa is quick and easy to cook and provides a complete source of protein on its own. I always have it on the menu in one form or another because it is so versatile for making bowls, salads, soups, and stews, and it's even great for baking.

Tofu and Tempeh: Both tofu and tempeh are made from soy and high in protein; both also contain a decent amount of calcium, which is a crucial nutrient that needs to be gotten from other sources if you do not consume dairy. Tofu gets a bad rap because of its lack of flavor and texture, but its ability to absorb other flavors makes it ideal for marinating and for the cooking techniques that create different textures. This book contains several recipes that show you how to prepare this protein-rich plant food in delicious ways. Tempeh has a distinctly nutty flavor and can be used to replace tofu in any recipe; it is especially useful for making items like plant "bacon" because of its meaty texture.

Lentils, Chickpeas, and Beans: These are all great sources of plant-based proteins, and this book shows how to use these legumes in your daily cooking. As with tofu and tempeh, they are mostly interchangeable, so use the type you like best.

A Vegetarian's Plate

A simple way to create a balanced vegetarian diet is to use the plate method by dividing your plate into quarters:

½ fruits and vegetables

¼ grains

¼ plant proteins

If you are following a vegan diet, calcium and protein sources such as fortified soy milk should be a part of your daily eating plan.

The Quandary of Animal Rennet in Cheeses

Most cheeses are made with animal rennet; however, more cheese makers have begun producing excellent cheeses with vegetarian solidifiers, as well as some surprisingly good dairy-free cheeses using nut or soy bases. Not all cheeses contain animal rennet: soft cheeses like ricotta and cream cheese are traditionally made with whey and are a safe choice for vegetarians. Many specialty cheese shops, Whole Foods, and Trader Joe's label their cheeses as suitable for vegetarians, and if you are still unsure a cheese is vegetarian, check the nutrition label for "animal enzymes" or "animal rennet."

What Are Whole Foods?

There as many different diets and eating styles based on tradition, religion, or spiritual or social philosophy as there are people in the world. Not many adhere to the all-processed junk food style. The first thing to understand about eating the natural way is that whole foods are the most nutritious. What are whole foods? You might know they are clean, authentic, and good for you, but what are some examples and why are they so important?

Simply put, whole foods are as close to their natural form as possible.

FRUITS

Eating fruit is a great way to improve your overall health and reduce the risk of many diseases. Fruits are one of the best sources of essential vitamins and minerals, as well as being high in heart-healthy fiber. Fruits also provide a wide range of health-boosting antioxidants, including anti-aging flavonoids. Whether you choose fresh or frozen, make it your goal to get more fruit into every meal. Add mixed berries or a banana into break-fast oats and throw an apple or orange in your bag for an energy-boosting afternoon snack. Use avocado to top a salad at dinner, and enjoy sweet pineapple for dessert. Just choose whole, natural fruits from the produce or freezer section and check the labels for added sugar and unwanted ingredients. Nutritionists recommend about 2 cups of fruit per day to get all the benefits. No matter how you do it, eat more fruit to benefit your healthy lifestyle.

VEGETABLES

To keep your body and mind healthy, the more vegetables the better: aim for at least 3 cups of vegetables a day. Vegetables come in all the colors of the rainbow, and the various colors represent different nutrients that benefit your body. Be sure to choose veggies from the full spectrum of the rainbow. Red vegetables like peppers and chiles contain vitamin C, vitamin B_6, and folic acid, which help the immune system, nervous system, and metabolism. Orange veggies like carrots, squash, and sweet potatoes have vitamin A, a form of beta-carotene, which is important for maintaining our vision. Green vegetables provide a huge variety of nutrients such as folic acid, which helps our immune response and combats fatigue. Kale, broccoli, and green beans contain high concentrations of vita-min K, which is important for maintaining healthy bones. Dark leafy veggies like spinach and Swiss chard are high in calcium and iron, which we need for supporting our bones and circulatory system.

NUTS

Nuts are seed kernels that are used in cooking or eaten as a snack. They contain a hard outer shell that is typically cracked open to get the edible flesh inside. Luckily, we can buy most nuts shelled and ready to eat. Though nuts can be high in fat, the fat they contain is a healthy type. Most of the fat in nuts is monounsaturated fat, as well as omega-6 and omega-3 polyunsaturated fat, which are necessary and beneficial to heart health. Nuts are also good sources of fiber and protein. The suggested amount of nuts to eat to reap the health benefits is 4 to 5 ounces per week, and the type of nuts doesn't matter. Most nuts are generally healthy, although some do have more nutrients than others. For example, walnuts contain particularly high amounts of omega-3 fatty acids. Almonds, macadamia nuts, hazelnuts, and pecans also fall into the healthy category. And peanuts, though technically not a nut but a legume, are also relatively healthy.

LEGUMES

Legumes are a staple food in many cultures. They include beans, peas, and lentils and are some of the most nutritious whole plant foods on the planet. Legumes are typically low in fat, have zero cholesterol, and are high in folic acid, potassium, iron, and magnesium. They also contain heart-healthy omega fats and fiber, and are one of the best plant-based sources of protein. Both supermarkets and health food stores stock a wide variety of dried and canned legumes. Dried beans and legumes, like chickpeas and black beans, generally require soaking overnight, which rehydrates them for quicker, more even cooking. You can skip this step, but your beans will take longer to cook. Lentils, split peas, and black-eyed peas don't need to be soaked. Canned legumes are a great time-saver and can be added to dishes that don't require extended simmering. Just be sure to check the labels for added sodium and other preservatives or chemicals, and rinse them before use. Beans can be added to many dishes that you probably already eat. Chickpeas and other types of beans are fabulous in soups and stews or pureed into a creamy dip. Try swapping the beef in your chili for beans or stuffing beans into corn tortillas with some scrambled eggs and salsa for breakfast tacos.

TUBERS

Tubers have been eaten for thousands of years in healthy diets. Also known as root vegetables, tubers are an edible variety of plants that grow underground and include common foods such as potatoes and carrots. Tubers sometimes get a bad rap because of the low-carb diet trend, but nourishing starches are an important part of our human ancestral diet. Root vegetables are low in calories and high in antioxidants, and each one contains a wide variety of vitamins and minerals. Turnips, rutabagas, and parsnips are not the most beautiful foods on the produce shelf, but they're superstars in terms of plant-forward eating and whole food cooking. You can use every part of these vegetables, including the tops, stems, and skins. Do you really need to peel carrots? No, not at all; just give them a good scrub and save the tops for salads or a delicious pesto. Sweet potatoes, one of the most nutrient-dense tubers, can be a bun substitute for a veggie burger or a tasty container for a hearty chili. Tubers are especially important in winter when they are plentiful and it's harder to find fresh veggies.

WHOLE GRAINS

All types of grains are a good source of complex carbohydrates and essential vitamins and minerals, but the healthiest kinds of grains are whole grains. Whole grains, also known as cereals and grains, are the seeds of grasses that have been cultivated for food. Whole grains come in many varieties, from popcorn to quinoa. Whole grains are naturally high in fiber and therefore filling, which helps when trying to maintain a healthy body weight. Whole grains are also linked to a lower risk of heart disease and diabetes. According to the United States Department of Agriculture and the Department of Health and Human Services, Americans should get at least half of all the grains in their diet from whole grains. You can find whole-grain versions of rice, bread, cereal, flour, and pasta at most grocery stores. Many whole-grain prepared foods, including some bread and pasta, are ready to eat, but always check the label to make sure whole grains appear first in the ingredients list. Replace white rice with quinoa, brown rice, wild rice, barley, or bulgur, and add these whole grains to soups, stews, casseroles, and salads as well. Use rolled oats as a replacement for bread crumbs in recipes.

ANIMAL PROTEINS

Protein provides our get-up-and-go energy and supports our brain functions. It's an essential nutrient, needed for maintaining healthy tissues, cells, and organs in our bodies. Although protein is in many of the foods that we eat every day, most protein sources are animal-based, like meat, poultry, fish, eggs, and dairy. That doesn't mean you have to eat animal products to get your protein. By eating a range of plant-based sources every day, you can ensure that your body gets all the protein it needs. Eating small amounts of egg and dairy is relatively common among plant-forward eaters; just avoid overly processed dairy, like flavored yogurt. Beans, legumes, tofu, and nuts are good sources of plant-based proteins for those who don't eat dairy or eggs. Protein bars don't fall into the category of whole foods and often contain sugar and chemical preservatives, so skip them. If you are vegan and have trouble getting enough protein in your diet, try a scoop of soy protein in a fruit smoothie or over your breakfast oats.

Health Benefits of Whole Foods and Vegetarian Eating

Plants are healthy. This is common knowledge, but most of us don't eat enough fruits, veggies, and grains. Taking the step to make most or all of your diet plant rich is a healthy choice. Produce and grains are packed with vitamins, minerals, antioxidants, and fiber. Fiber is one of the most vital nutrients, and it has tons of health benefits. It is excellent for maintaining your waistline, helping your heart, supporting digestion, and balancing blood sugar.

Science has shown that people's overall health is usually better when they follow a vegetarian or vegan diet. They also tend to have lower body mass indexes (BMIs) compared to omnivores. People who use a vegetarian diet to lose weight have more success not only shedding unwanted pounds but also keeping them off.

Eating a vegetarian diet can lower the risk of cardiovascular disease and can positively impact other risk factors for heart disease, such as lowering blood pressure and cholesterol as well as improving blood sugar. Eating plant-based foods helps reduce inflammation and promotes healthy arteries, further reducing the risk of heart disease.

Regardless of weight or BMI, eating a plant-based vegetarian or vegan diet lowers your risk of diabetes. Recent studies show that plant-based diets result in higher insulin sensitivity, which is important for maintaining healthy blood sugar levels.

Research also shows that the consumption of an abundance of fruits, veggies, legumes, and grains is associated with lower cancer risk. Plants and whole foods contain disease-fighting phytochemicals that have been shown to prevent cancer.

Whatever your reason for making a diet change to plant-based foods, the benefits will come both from eating more plants and from replacing unhealthy foods with whole plant foods.

Put Down the Processed Foods

According to the USDA, *processed food* is defined as any raw agricultural commodity that has been subjected to washing, cleaning, milling, cutting, chopping, heating, pasteurizing, blanching, cooking, canning, freezing, drying, dehydrating, mixing, packaging, or other procedures that alter the food from its natural state. This may include the addition of other ingredients to the food, such as preservatives, flavors, nutrients, and other food additives or substances approved for use in food products, such as salt, sugars, and fats. Some are healthy, like precooked whole grains, Greek yogurt, nut butters, organic stock, tofu, frozen vegetables, and unsalted canned beans. When shopping for groceries, read ingredients labels and look for items like high-fructose corn syrup, hydrogenated oil, and aspartame. These ingredients indicate that the item is chemically processed and not something you could produce in your own kitchen. Many condiments are filled with sodium, sugar, preservatives, gums, stabilizers, artificial colors, and artificial flavors. Packaged breakfast cereals are almost all highly processed, as are commercially produced breads and crackers. Make informed choices and you will stock your kitchen with clean, unprocessed foods.

Here are the worst of the worst processed foods and ingredients to be avoided when reading the Nutrition Facts section on anything you buy prepackaged. Even if the label on the front may claim that the food is "natural" or "healthy," be aware that harmful ingredients such as these can lurk in the ingredients list.

Artificial Colorings: Used to make food more attractive, they can cause all kinds of serious health problems, from asthma to cancer.

Artificial Sweeteners: Aspartame/Equal, sucralose/Splenda, and saccharine/Sweet'N Low are just a few of these products. They can trick us into thinking that sweet things mean no calories and encourage us to crave more sweets.

BHA and BHT: These are chemical preservatives in many processed foods that are believed to cause certain cancers.

High-Fructose Corn Syrup: This is sugar in disguise and can increase bad fats in the body and drive the hormones that cause us to overeat. This one is absolutely a no-go, zero-tolerance item, and it is in almost all processed foods.

Palm Oil or Any Type of Shortening or Hydrogenated Oil: Legally, items containing so-called "trans fats" can't be served in New York City. They are your heart's worst enemy. They can cause blood clots and plaque buildup in arteries, leading to heart disease.

Recombinant Bovine Growth Hormone (rBGH): This is a cancer-causing GMO hormone created to boost milk production. Make sure you always purchase hormone-free milk and dairy products.

Sodium Nitrites and Nitrates: These are commonly found in processed lunch meats and are linked to diseases like colon cancer and diabetes.

White Bread: The germ and bran are removed in the processing of white bread to increase both its shelf life and digestibility. Guess what is removed in this process? All the fiber and nutrients. Choose a whole-grain bread instead and read the label carefully.

CHAPTER TWO

YOUR WHOLE FOOD KITCHEN

A well-stocked whole food kitchen includes plant-based ingredients, so preparing nutrient-packed meals at home is easy and fast. In this chapter, we explore how to cleanse your kitchen of unhealthy processed foods, thus increasing the likelihood that you will stick with whole foods and a plant-rich eating plan. By stocking the pantry with whole food staples, you will save time and money because the ingredients to make simple meals will be at your fingertips. No more last-minute trips to the grocery store. These staples are found in the recipes throughout this book, and a well-stocked kitchen is the first and most important step to preparing creative and healthy dishes. Imagine fresh fruits, veggies, and herbs alongside whole grains and spices, and a refrigerator full of homemade tofu, dairy-free nut milk, and yogurt. This is now your kitchen, your whole food kitchen.

Stocking Your Pantry

With a well-stocked whole food pantry, you will be able to whip up a delicious meal on a busy weeknight in a flash or create a special night's dinner, saving time and money. Here are lists of basic "must-haves" and "nice-to-haves," which may become must-haves for you, in addition to the staples. I find that storing my pantry items in glass jars is the best way to see and use what I have, as well as a way of simplifying my shopping list. Jars of all sizes can be used, and they are inexpensive to purchase in bulk on Amazon or from Costco. Recycling used mustard or olive jars is an ideal way to both store condiments and reduce waste.

MUST-HAVES

Black Beans or Any Type of Beans: These are a great way of supplementing a quick dinner salad with additional protein, and they are incredibly heart-healthy. Black beans are an excellent source of fiber, potassium, folate, vitamin B_6, and phytonutrients.

Brown Rice: This is one of the healthiest of all the whole grains, containing a high content of B vitamins, essential amino acids, and close to 80 antioxidants.

Chia Seeds: These have high omega-3 fatty acid content. When mixed with water, they form a filling gel that can be flavored and consumed. As a natural thickener, they are a great addition to smoothies, soups, and desserts.

Chickpeas: These have more vitamin C than any other legume and, when cooked right, are creamy and delicious on their own. Many recipes in the book use this versatile staple ingredient.

Goji Berries: These berries are one of the most nutrient-dense foods you can eat. They are packed with beta-carotene, antioxidants, minerals, and amino acids, and they are a natural immune booster. They can be baked into cookies and added to oatmeal and salads. In powdered form, they are a powerhouse addition to smoothies or tea.

Lentils: These are one of the best sources of legume-based protein. They make amazing soups, stews, and chilis, and can also be added to salads to boost the protein.

Naturally Fermented Organic Vinegars: Unpasteurized apple cider vinegar is a versatile everyday vinegar and, in its unpasteurized form, is an immune booster and weight regulator; it can also balance the body's alkaline/acid system. Balsamic vinegar is rich and sweet and can be drizzled over everything from French fries to berries to add a burst of flavor.

Nuts: Walnuts are high in omega-3 fatty acids and are good for reducing inflammation. I love them toasted and crushed and sprinkled on just about anything. Almonds are high in calcium and iron and can alkalinize the blood. Almonds are great for adding to breakfast cereals and salads and, of course, for using in baking.

Quinoa or Any Whole Grain: An ancient grain from South America, quinoa contains all the essential amino acids, making it a complete protein. It also has more calcium than milk, which is particularly important if you are following a vegan diet.

Rolled Oats: These are naturally gluten-free, and they can help reduce cholesterol, regulate weight, and soothe the nervous system. Eating rolled oats at breakfast is an excellent way to start the day.

Spices and Condiments: These are a personal choice, but good-quality seasonings will add variety to your meals, and many have nutritional benefits as well. Some suggestions are:

- *Bay leaves*
- *Red pepper flakes*
- *Cinnamon*
- *Dried herb blends*
- *Freshly ground black pepper*
- *Mustard*
- *Sea salt*

Unrefined Oils: Extra-virgin olive oil is an excellent source of vitamin E. Its yummy, fruity flavor makes it an easy flavor boost for vegetables and salads. It can withstand high heat and is good for sautéing. Coconut oil is antiaging, antibacterial, and dense with antioxidants. Its delicate flavor is not damaged by heat, and it can add a wonderfully coconutty touch to sautéed vegetables.

NICE-TO-HAVES

Bee Pollen: This ingredient, which contains all the nutrients needed for human health, has been used for centuries as a vitality tonic. I put 1 teaspoon in my breakfast smoothie or oatmeal every day.

Flaxseed: Flaxseeds have the highest plant-based content of omega-3 fatty acids. They are great in cereal and for baking and, when mixed with water, can replace eggs in vegan baking.

Pumpkin Seeds: These are high in iron and omega-3 fatty acids and are great for snacks, salads, and yogurt.

Rice Vinegar: This is my favorite light vinegar; it makes an excellent seasoning for grain dishes and vegetables.

Sesame Oil: This oil can be used to add flair to dressings, marinades, or stir-fries. Drizzle it over the top of some steamed vegetables and rice to create a quick and creative dinner.

Sesame Seeds: These have a rich, nutty flavor and are great sprinkled over steamed vegetables, dips, and salads.

Sunflower Seeds: These have a light, sweet flavor and are high in protein. Sunflower seeds add texture and crunch to grain dishes and are a handy snack.

Whole Rye Berries: Besides being delicious, rye is packed with nutrients and loaded with fiber and magnesium. It can also help regulate weight and balance blood sugar.

Kitchen Cleanse

Processed foods have a long shelf life due to the addition of excess sugar, salt, and chemical preservatives. When processed, they're often stripped of their existing nutrients or are nutrient-free in the first place. As a result, eating processed foods can take away your opportunity to nourish your body with whole foods and possibly do damage instead. The following items should be removed from your kitchen and diet to start your plant-forward eating journey:

Sugar-sweetened beverages: soda, sports drinks, sweetened tea, energy drinks

Processed meats: bacon, cold cuts

Frozen snacks/convenience meals

Salty processed snack foods: potato chips, pretzels, some crackers, microwave popcorn

Sweets: cookies, cakes, brownies, ice cream, candy

Refined and processed grains: packaged bread, white pasta, instant noodles, white rice

Highly sweetened granola bars

Condiments: store-bought ketchup, store-bought pickle relish, mayonnaise, and "light" salad dressings

Stocking Your Refrigerator

Keeping an assortment of longer-lasting fresh vegetables will allow you to throw together something quick and easy, even if you haven't had time to shop. The magic of leftovers and a few "pantry vegetables" can be a lifesaver after a long day.

MUST-HAVES

- **Apples** are packed with nutrients, equally fabulous in both sweet and savory dishes, and fantastic in salads. Their high fiber makes them very filling and perfect for a low-calorie snack between meals.

- **Beets** have a beautiful color and sweet flavor. They are nutrient dense, high in vitamins and minerals, and low in calories. Beets are excellent for maintaining healthy blood pressure.

- **Berries** are super high in anti-oxidants, fiber, and vitamins. They are so healthy I make a point of eating some every day. Sweet and delicious, they are great in oatmeal.

- **Cabbage** is well known for cancer-fighting properties. It can be eaten raw in salads or cooked in soups or stews. I like to use a mix of both green and red for brightly colored dishes.

- **Carrots** are sweet and colorful as well as being packed with antioxidants and beta-carotene to keep our eyes healthy. They are amazing grated into a raw power salad or steamed and smashed into a hearty puree.

- **Celery** is the backbone of any good soup or stew and famously low-calorie. Aromatic and under-rated, celery is great for dipping into hummus or shaving into a salad. It also contains antioxidants that are particularly good for digestion.

- **Citrus fruits,** like lemons, limes, grapefruits, and oranges, are great flavorings for almost anything and can eliminate the need for extra salt when you are follow-ing a low-salt diet. Citrus is high in vitamin C and is a fabulous energy-boosting snack.

- **Cultured butter,** which is wonderful for baking, is lower in lactose than regular butter and can be a better choice for those who have sensitivi-ties to lactose.

Free-range organic **eggs** are a great protein source for vegetarians who choose to eat them. They can be considered a superfood because they are low in calories and contain a small amount of every nutrient you may need.

Fresh herbs have many healthy properties and were used medicinally for centuries to treat almost everything from stomach distress to fevers as well as to stimulate hair growth. Common herbs include basil, parsley, and thyme, but try experimenting with tarragon, cilantro, and others for more exotic flavors.

Garlic is one of the healthiest ingredients with numerous benefits such as lowering cholesterol and stimulating metabolism. Garlic is also antibacterial, and it makes everything taste better.

Kale can be eaten raw or cooked. It is one of the most nutrient-dense vegetables, absolutely packed with vitamins and minerals, and very low in calories.

Low-fat **milk** or fortified nut, oat, or soy milk can help meet calcium and protein needs. Both nut milk and soy milk are great sources of protein.

Onions have antioxidants and anti-inflammatory compounds. Try using red onions for raw preparations because of their mellow and sweet flavor and yellow onions for cooking because of their savory bite.

Sweet potatoes are a great source of beta-carotene that supports eye health. I often roast a sweet potato and smash it open, leaving the jacket on, and eat it with salsa or tomato sauce for a simple dinner.

NICE-TO-HAVES

Avocados can be a meal in themselves with a pinch of seasoning. This creamy, rich superfood is a nutritional powerhouse. Avocados are low in calories, cholesterol, and saturated fats while being high in healthy fats.

Ginger adds a flash of heat along with antibacterial and anti-inflammatory

properties to meals. For thousands of years, this root has had a place in traditional medicine to ease nausea, soothe sore throats, and treat the common cold.

Grapes have held an essential place in the human diet since ancient times, both as a food item and in winemaking. This sweet ingredient is high in an antioxidant called resveratrol, which is said to lower blood sugar and reduce the risk of cancer.

* **Radishes** add color, crunch, and fiber to salads and are a lovely garnish for almost anything. I love to dip them in a bit of butter and sprinkle them with Tajín seasoning. They have practically no calories and lots of vitamin C.

* **Scallions,** like onions and garlic, have antibacterial and anti-inflammatory properties. They also add interesting color and flavor to Asian-inspired dishes. A scattering of chopped scallions is a great finishing touch to any savory dish, adding a bit of texture and an elegant appearance. We do eat with our eyes as well as our mouths.

* **Squashes,** so versatile and rich, make an excellent addition to grain blends, soups, casseroles, and salads. The vivid color of squash adds visual impact to just about any dish. Squash is not only pretty but also high in manganese, which supports bone health.

* **Stone fruits** (cherries, peaches, plums), when in season, are packed with vitamins and healthy plant compounds and can be used in both sweet and savory dishes.

Stocking Up on Equipment

It is best to keep your kitchen uncluttered and austere. A good-quality knife is the first and most important thing any cook needs. Why have a garlic press taking up space, not to mention it being a pain to clean, when the back of your knife works just as well to peel and smash garlic? I'd rather have an excellent set of knives, a cutting board, a wooden spoon, mixing bowls, and a cast iron skillet than expensive gadgets and machines taking up my cupboard space. Here you will find the basic supplies, and a list of items that are nice to have, to create fabulous meals efficiently and safely.

Box Grater: A box grater is versatile, with each of the four sides having handy functions. The most-used function (the shredder/grater) can be used for shredding cheese or vegetables. There is also a smaller shredder/grater ideal for finely grating hard cheeses like Parmesan or to grate garlic and ginger. The very fine grater side is great for zesting citrus fruit and spices like whole nutmeg or cinnamon sticks. The thin slicing side makes beautiful, uniformly thin veggie slices in a snap.

Cast Iron Skillet: A well seasoned cast iron skillet serves most of your stove top, oven, and even baking needs. One or two sizes are all you need. To keep your cast iron in top shape, never, ever wash it with water; just fill it with coarse salt as soon as you're finished working with it and scrub it with a brush to remove any food residue. Coat the skillet with a thin layer of oil (cooking spray works great for this) and then wipe it with a dry towel.

Colander: I prefer a heavy-duty metal colander over plastic for sturdiness. Besides draining your pasta or veggies, it can be used for washing greens, as a steamer basket for veggies, and for draining tofu, yogurt, or soft cheese. I have colanders in several sizes, and they are real workhorses in my kitchen.

Glass and Stainless Steel Mixing Bowls: I can't have enough bowls in my kitchen, which houses an assortment including small, medium, and large. Attractive heatproof glass bowls make it easy to prepare food and serve it in the same bowl, saving cleanup time. Stainless steel bowls will last you a lifetime, and, importantly, are nonreactive and won't affect the flavor of whatever you are mixing.

Heavy Wooden Cutting Board: A heavy board will not slip and provides a superior surface for chopping; wood is more bacteria-resistant than plastic. Water is the enemy of wood. After using, wipe with a damp towel and very mild soap or do as I do: scrub it with a little lemon juice and coarse salt, and oil it once a week. Allow the board to sit overnight to soak up the oil, then wipe it with a dry cloth.

Measuring Cups (Both Liquid and Dry) and Measuring Spoons: It's important to have accurate measurements when cooking, especially for baking. Liquid and dry cups differ in how they measure; liquid cups measure fluid ounces, and dry measures vary because different ingredients have different weights (1 cup of flour equals 4½ ounces, and 1 cup of sugar equals 7 ounces). For the best results, use the appropriate measure for your ingredient. I love the OXO measuring tools because they have magnets in the handles for easy, neat storage.

Slotted Stainless Steel Spoon: A slotted spoon is important for frying items, fishing whole herbs out of soups and stews, and retrieving vegetables from boiling water. They can be used for serving stews and braised items to lift the items out of the cooking liquid.

Stainless Steel Baking Sheets (Round and Rectangular): Rimmed baking sheets are probably the most-used piece of equipment in a professional kitchen; we use them for everything, every day, for making pizzas, baking cookies, and all-around heating up of things. They are also great for cooking foods quickly, and even for storage and serving. I prefer stainless steel because they are pretty much indestructible and don't rust.

Stainless Steel Saucepans of different sizes: The better the quality of the cookware

you invest in, the longer it will last. I have used only All-Clad pots and pans in both my home and the restaurants because they take a beating and last forever, but they are a little more expensive than most. A great budget option is Cuisinart, which is great quality and has a lifetime warranty. A full set can be purchased at a reasonable price.

Wooden Spoons and Spatulas: Indispensable in my kitchen, wooden spoons and spatulas don't scratch my nonstick cookware, and they get softer and comfier in your hand the longer you own them. I feel like they add a certain soul to my cooking. They don't transfer heat from the pan to the food you are stirring, which is important when preparing temperature-sensitive items like risotto or scrambled eggs.

NICE-TO-HAVES

Blender: A blender is essential for fine textured soups, sauces, and smoothies. Newer models have adjustable speed dials that are especially helpful for blending hot liquids (to avoid spatter), emulsifying vinaigrettes, and pureeing thicker items.

Ceramic Dutch Oven for Casseroles: When I cook at home, I use my ceramic Dutch oven almost every day. I can sauté in it directly, then add ingredients for a

casserole or pasta directly to the pot and move it into the oven to finish. It produces a reliably even heat and is perfect for braising or roasting. Once my dish is done, the Dutch oven is attractive enough to serve in, and it retains the heat of the dish while it's on the table.

Food Processor: A good food processor can perform many functions like chopping, slicing, grating, and grinding, which makes it a great time-saver. Most food processors have a variety of attachments available for these functions as well as for vegetable and fruit juicing, kneading dough, and even whipping eggs. If you want to buy one small appliance for your kitchen, this is the most versatile one.

Handheld Stick Blender: A stick blender, or immersion blender, is a lightweight, portable, and inexpensive alternative to a full-size blender. It was one of the first utensils I purchased when I moved away from my parents. I like it to reduce the number of pots, pans, and containers I use in preparation, and cut down on kitchen cleaning. It can make a smoothie right in the cup you are going to drink it from, it can be used to puree a soup or sauce right in the pot, and it cleans up easily.

Instant Pot: The Instant Pot became all the rage in kitchen appliances a few years ago, with good reason. The Instant Pot is a multicooker that can take the place of several kitchen appliances, so it saves space in your kitchen. A miracle worker for whipping up dinner superfast using the pressure cooker function, it also works as a slow cooker, rice cooker, and yogurt maker.

Pressure Cooker: A pressure cooker works with steam pressure and is ideal for cooking beans, grains, and legumes because it speeds up the cooking time dramatically. The real beauty of a pressure cooker lies in its ability to keep food moist. It will make delicious moist soups, stews, risottos, and breakfast porridges. Many cooks like to bake cheesecakes in a pressure cooker because it gives the cake a superior moist texture.

Vegetable Juicer: My father gave me one of these for my birthday a few years ago, and it's one of the best gifts I've ever received. I make fresh juice three times a week, so I always have some on hand. Many models also have food processor, pasta maker, and coffee grinder attachments.

Toasted-Pepita Dip, page 40

CHAPTER THREE

STAPLE RECIPES
& SNACKS

Fresh Tofu & Soy Milk   28

Homemade Seitan   30

Basic Vegetable Stock   32

Dairy-Free Soft Cheese   33

Non-Dairy Yogurt   34

Nut Milk   35

Butterless Butter   36

Eggless Mayonnaise   37

Mediterranean-Style Hummus   38

Toasted-Pepita Dip   40

Fresh, Chunky Guacamole   41

Charred-Carrot Dip   42

Crispy Cinnamon Chickpeas   44

Quinoa Fritters   45

Power Trail Mix   47

Fruit Leather   48

Baked Vegetable Chips   51

Kale Crisps   52

FRESH TOFU & SOY MILK

DAIRY-FREE, GLUTEN-FREE

SERVES 1 or 2 //*PREP TIME* 1 hour, plus overnight to soak //*COOK TIME* 15 minutes

Is it possible to make tofu at home? Yes, it's easy and so delicious. Nigari flakes are the coagulant for the soy milk and can be purchased at most health food stores, Japanese markets, or online. If you're just making fresh soy milk, follow the recipe through step 4, and enjoy the milk. I like my fresh tofu sprinkled with some matcha powder and sea salt, but it's a great meat substitute for stir-fries or soups as well.

8 ounces dried soybeans   9½ cups water, divided   1½ teaspoons nigari flakes

1 Place the soybeans in a large bowl and cover them with 2 inches of cold water, then cover the bowl with plastic wrap and let it sit at room temperature overnight. Drain the beans in a colander and rinse with cold water.

2 Transfer 1 cup of the soybeans to a blender and add 3 cups of water. Blend on high until the mixture is smooth and turns milky white, about 1 minute. Pour the soy milk into a large, deep stockpot. Repeat with the remaining soybeans in two batches.

3 Place the stockpot over medium heat and bring the soy milk to a simmer, stirring frequently, then reduce the heat to medium-low. Continue to simmer for 10 minutes and remove the stockpot from the heat.

4 Place a fine-mesh strainer over a large bowl or pot. Line the strainer with a clean kitchen towel or a triple layer of cheesecloth. Ladle the soy milk into the strainer, letting the milk drain into the pot. Bring the edges of the towel together and twist to squeeze out as much of the milk as possible. Discard the remaining pulp.

5 Pour the strained soy milk back into the pot. Place the pot over medium-high heat and bring just to a boil, then remove from the heat. Let the milk sit for 3 to 4 minutes, stirring occasionally to prevent a skin from forming. Meanwhile, in a small bowl dissolve the nigari in the remaining ½ cup of water.

6 While stirring the pot with a wooden spoon, pour about one-third of the nigari solution into the soy milk. Continue to stir for about 15 seconds. Sprinkle another one-third of the nigari solution over the soy milk. Cover and let the mixture rest for

3 minutes. Uncover the pot. The soy milk should be curdling at this point. Sprinkle the remaining nigari solution over the top and use the spoon to gently stir it into the milk, trying not to disturb the curds. Cover the pot and let rest for another 3 minutes.

7   Uncover the pot; if the curds are separated from clear yellow liquid whey, you're ready for the next step. If you see still see milky areas in the pot, gently give them a stir, cover the pot, and let it sit for 3 minutes more.

8   While the soy milk is curdling, set up a tofu mold on a rimmed baking sheet. Line the mold with fine cheesecloth. Use a spoon to pour a bit of whey into the mold to moisten the cloth. Using a slotted spoon, gently transfer the curds to the mold, trying to keep the curds as intact as possible. Once all the curds have been moved, fold the cheesecloth over the top of the tofu. Place the lid or a plate on top of the cloth and top with a weight.

9   Let the tofu rest under the weight until it has reached the desired texture. For medium tofu, let it sit for about 15 minutes, until it has compressed to about half its original height. For firm tofu, let it sit for 30 to 45 minutes; it will compress to about one-third of its original height. Once the firmness of the tofu is correct, remove the weights, lid, and side of the mold. Let it rest, wrapped in the cloth until it has reached room temperature.

10 Unwrap the tofu and place it in an airtight container with just enough water to cover it and refrigerate until you're ready to eat it.

Storage: If you're going to store the tofu for more than a day, place some cool water in its storage container. The tofu will keep refrigerated for about 1 week.

Cooking Tip: If you plan to prepare tofu often, a tofu mold is a convenient and inexpensive purchase. However, if you don't have one, a strawberry quart container with the lid separated and turned upside down for a lid makes a nice substitute. I use a small colander with a plate as a cover for round, dome-shaped tofu.

Per serving: Calories: 1,012; Total fat: 45g; Carbohydrates: 68g; Fiber: 21g; Protein: 83g; Calcium: 628mg; Vitamin D: 0mcg; Vitamin B12: 0mcg; Iron: 36mg; Zinc: 11mg

HOMEMADE SEITAN

SERVES 1 or 2 *//PREP TIME* 15 minutes

COOK TIME 1 hour 10 minutes, plus overnight to chill

Seitan is the "meatiest" of the meat substitutes. "Wheat meat" has been around for centuries, but only recently have we come to know it as seitan. Made by rinsing the starch from wheat dough, it can be sliced, grilled, ground, and used in chili or stew or cubed for stir-fry.

1 tablespoon extra-virgin olive oil

1 large onion, diced

⅓ teaspoon sea salt

2 garlic cloves, minced

1 teaspoon paprika

½ teaspoon of your favorite seasoning blend

2 tablespoons tomato paste

1 cup vegetable stock

1 tablespoon naturally fermented soy sauce (optional, omit for soy-free)

¼ cup chickpea flour

2 tablespoons nutritional yeast

1½ cups vital wheat gluten

1 Heat the oil in a large skillet over medium heat. Add the onion and sea salt and cook for 4 to 6 minutes, stirring occasionally, until the onion is softened and translucent. Reduce the heat to medium-low and add the garlic. Cook for about 2 minutes, until the garlic is softened and fragrant. Add the paprika and seasoning blend to the skillet and cook for 1 minute, until fragrant. Remove the skillet from the heat.

2 Use a large spoon to transfer the onion and garlic mixture to a food processor. Add the tomato paste, vegetable stock, soy sauce (if using), chickpea flour, and nutritional yeast. Blend until smooth.

3 Transfer the mixture to a large bowl, fold in the vital wheat gluten, and stir until incorporated. Once combined, use your hands to knead the mixture until it becomes firmer and bouncy, about 2 minutes. The dough should be loose and moist.

4 Prepare the steamer (see Tip for a simple steamer setup) and set the water to boil. Form the dough into a loaf shape and then roll it up tightly in a piece of aluminum foil, twisting the foil ends tightly to secure. Depending on the size of your steamer, prepare two loaves if needed. Once the water is boiling, steam the wrapped dough for 1 hour, carefully turning it over with a spoon or tongs after 30 minutes.

5 When the seitan is done, remove it from the heat and let it cool to room temperature. Unwrap the loaf and place it in an airtight container or bag in the refrigerator for at least 8 hours to overnight. To keep the seitan from drying out, slice it as needed for recipes.

Storage: Store the seitan in an airtight container in the refrigerator for up to 1 week or in the freezer for up to 3 to 4 weeks.

Cooking Tip: The steamer setup is a small mesh colander placed over boiling water in a saucepot with a lid. You don't need any fancy equipment.

Per serving: Calories: 1,099; Total fat: 19g; Carbohydrates: 75g; Fiber: 15g; Protein: 151g; Calcium: 177mg; Vitamin D: 0mcg; Vitamin B12: 5mcg; Iron: 16mg; Zinc: 2mg

BASIC VEGETABLE STOCK

DAIRY-FREE, GLUTEN-FREE

MAKES **2 quarts** // *PREP TIME* **10 minutes** // *COOK TIME* **40 minutes**

Vegetable stock is a must-have in the pantry. In many commercial kitchens, there is a perpetually simmering stockpot on the back of one of the stoves creating fragrant, flavorful stock for all the recipes, vegetable or otherwise. Try to keep a basic vegetable stock like this one around to use as needed, or make a mushroom or corn-based stock for special uses like soup or risotto. The beauty of stock is that anything can be used to infuse flavor, so depending on what you have in the kitchen, the stock will be unique each time you make it.

1 large onion, cut into 1-inch chunks

2 celery stalks, including some leaves, cut into 1-inch chunks

2 large carrots, cut into 1-inch chunks

1 bunch scallions, both white and green parts, chopped

8 garlic cloves, minced

8 fresh parsley sprigs

6 fresh thyme sprigs

2 bay leaves

1 teaspoon sea salt

2 quarts water

1 Put the onion, celery, carrots, scallions, garlic, parsley, thyme, and bay leaves in a medium stockpot. Cook over high heat for 5 to 10 minutes, stirring frequently.

2 Add the salt and water and bring to a boil over high heat. Reduce the heat to medium-low and simmer, uncovered, for 30 minutes.

3 Strain the stock into another medium stockpot or container and discard the vegetables.

Storage: Store the cooled vegetable stock in a sealed container in the refrigerator for up to 1 week, or pour the stock into ice cube trays and freeze. Transfer the cubes to a freezer bag, seal, and store for up to 3 months.

Prep Tip: Making a vegetable stock is a fabulous way to use the entire vegetable and reduce waste. Save your unused trimmings (they can be frozen until needed) from onions, mushrooms, eggplant, asparagus, broccoli stems, corncobs, fennel stalks, bell peppers, pea pods, chard stems, celery root parings, marjoram stems, basil stems, thyme stems, or potato parings.

Per 1-cup serving: Calories: 13; Total fat: <1g; Carbohydrates: 3g; Fiber: 1g; Protein: 1g; Calcium: 18mg; Vitamin D: 0mcg; Vitamin B12: 0mcg; Iron: <1mg; Zinc: <1mg

DAIRY-FREE SOFT CHEESE

DAIRY-FREE, GLUTEN-FREE

MAKES 1 pound // *PREP TIME* 5 minutes, plus 8 hours to soak and 24 hours to ferment

With just a few ingredients, you can easily make vegan cheese at home. This simple, plain version can be used as a spread for toast or a bagel as well as in more complex recipes like lasagna. For a lovely treat, dress up the cheese with herbs, spices, roasted garlic, or sun-dried tomatoes for a company-worthy, elegant cheese plate.

2 cups organic raw cashews

½ cup water

2 tablespoons non-dairy yogurt

¼ teaspoon sea salt

1 Put the cashews in a medium bowl and cover with 2 inches of water, then soak them for 8 hours to overnight in the refrigerator.

2 Discard the soaking water. Put the cashews, ½ cup of water, yogurt, and salt in a food processor and process until smooth and creamy.

3 Transfer the mixture to a medium glass bowl, cover tightly with plastic wrap, and allow to rest at room temperature for 24 to 48 hours.

4 Refrigerate in an airtight container and use in recipes or as desired as a spread.

Storage: Place in an airtight container in the refrigerator for up to 2 weeks or in the freezer for up to 4 months.

Serving Tip: Fold in chopped, blanched spinach and black olives to create a Mediterranean-inspired dip that is perfect with toasted pita chips.

Per serving: Calories: 1,451; Total fat: 115g; Carbohydrates: 80g; Fiber: 9g; Protein: 48g; Calcium: 160mg; Vitamin D: 1mcg; Vitamin B12: <1mcg; Iron: 18mg; Zinc: 15mg

NON-DAIRY YOGURT

DAIRY-FREE, GLUTEN-FREE

MAKES 2 cups // *PREP TIME* 15 minutes, plus 24 hours to let rest

Coconut milk yogurt is one of my favorite all-around, versatile foods. It can be eaten on its own or scooped into a baked sweet potato or whipped as a dessert topping. Although you can purchase coconut yogurt commercially, there's nothing that compares to the taste of homemade.

1 (14-ounce) can full-fat, unsweetened coconut milk (organic when possible)

2 capsules vegan-friendly probiotics (be sure that they do not contain prebiotic fiber)

1 Shake the coconut milk, then open the can and pour the milk into a clean, sterilized, dry glass jar or bowl. You can sterilize clean jars by dunking them in boiling water and letting them dry completely.

2 Empty the probiotic capsules into the coconut milk and stir with a wooden spoon until creamy, smooth, and thoroughly combined.

3 Cover the mixture with cheesecloth or a clean kitchen towel and secure with a rubber band or kitchen twine.

4 Let the yogurt activate for at least 24 hours and up to 48 hours in a warm place. The longer it rests, the tangier the yogurt will be.

5 Once the yogurt has reached the desired tanginess and thickness, cover the jar tightly with a lid or plastic wrap and refrigerate until cold.

Storage: Store covered in the refrigerator for up to 1 week.

Serving Tip: Enjoy your delicious yogurt plain or add fruit, nuts, shredded coconut, and a bit of sweetener like maple syrup or vanilla.

Per 1-cup serving: Calories: 336; Total fat: 35g; Carbohydrates: 9g; Fiber: 2g; Protein: 3g; Calcium: 7mg; Vitamin D: 0mcg; Vitamin B12: 0mcg; Iron: 1mg; Zinc: 1mg

NUT MILK

DAIRY-FREE, GLUTEN-FREE

MAKES **2 cups** // *PREP TIME* **15 minutes, plus 12 hours to soak**

Different plant milks have become increasingly popular, and they are so simple to make it's easy to keep a supply in the refrigerator for your coffee, your cereal, or any recipe that requires a milk replacement. Oat milk can be made similarly by replacing the nuts with quick-cooking oats.

1 cup raw almonds, walnuts, or cashews (or any kind of nut)

⅛ teaspoon sea salt

1 tablespoon sweetener (agave nectar, maple syrup, honey, or stevia) (optional)

4 cups very hot water

1 Place the nuts in a large bowl and add enough water to cover them by 2 inches. Let them soak for at least 12 hours or overnight in the refrigerator.

2 Drain the nuts and discard the soaking liquid. Transfer the nuts to a blender and add the salt, sweetener (if using), and water, and puree on high speed until very smooth, about 2 minutes.

3 Strain the mixture through a fine-mesh sieve lined with cheesecloth into a medium glass mixing bowl, pressing down on the solids to extract as much milk as possible. Discard the nut pulp. Thin the nut milk with water as necessary to reach the desired consistency.

4 Transfer to an airtight container and chill until cold.

Storage: Store covered in the refrigerator for up to 1 week.

Variation Tip: Have fun experimenting with different types of nuts or combinations of nuts and sweeteners to create your own special blend. Cinnamon and vanilla can also be added for a tasty variation.

Per 1-cup serving: Calories: 373; Total fat: 30g; Carbohydrates: 20g; Fiber: 8g; Protein: 12g; Calcium: 148mg; Vitamin D: 0mcg; Vitamin B12: 0mcg; Iron: 2mg; Zinc: <1mg

BUTTERLESS BUTTER

DAIRY-FREE, GLUTEN-FREE

MAKES **1 pound** *//PREP TIME* **10 minutes, plus 4 hours to set**

This dairy-free butter is so good I've come to prefer it to regular butter. It works for sauté-ing or as a creamy spread on toast or a muffin. Top steamed vegetables with it, stir it into sauces, and even bake with it in place of regular butter. See if you can tell the difference when you taste the results.

½ to 1 cup melted refined coconut oil

½ cup soy milk or your favorite nut milk

¼ cup canola oil

½ teaspoon sea salt

2 teaspoons liquid lecithin (see Tip)

* Put the coconut oil, soy milk, canola oil, salt, and liquid lecithin in a blender and blend on medium speed for about 1 minute until completely combined. Pour the mixture into a silicone butter mold or storage container of your choice. Put the container in the refrigerator for a few hours until the mixture has hardened.

Storage: Keep the butter in the refrigerator in an airtight container for up to 3 to 4 weeks or in the freezer for up to 2 months.

Ingredient Tip: Lecithin is an emulsifying agent generally derived from soybeans. It will help mix the oil and water and prevent separation. If you can find only lecithin granules, you'll need to use two to four times the amount of the liquid lecithin called for in this recipe. For cultured butter, replace the non-dairy milk with ½ cup of plain non-dairy yogurt, or add 1 teaspoon of apple cider vinegar or lemon juice.

Per 1-tbs serving (32 per pound): Calories: 80; Total fat: 9g; Carbohydrates: <1g; Fiber: 0g; Protein: <1g; Calcium: 5mg; Vitamin D: 0mcg; Vitamin B12: <1mcg; Iron: <1mg; Zinc: <1mg

EGGLESS MAYONNAISE

MAKES **1 cup** *//PREP TIME* **5 minutes**

Technically, this is not a mayonnaise because it does not contain egg, but this tangy, creamy, and rich spread is perfect for sandwiches or salads and can be flavored with just about anything. I like to add chipotle pepper in adobo and always have a jar of it in the refrigerator for this reason. This mayo can be made in 5 minutes and used anywhere you would normally use mayonnaise.

½ cup canola oil (or any neutral-flavor oil)

¼ cup milk (or soy milk for a vegan version)

1 teaspoon apple cider vinegar

1 teaspoon Dijon mustard

½ teaspoon sea salt

⅛ teaspoon turmeric

1   Pour the canola oil, milk, vinegar, mustard, salt, and turmeric into a blender.

2   Blend on high speed for about 2 minutes, until the mixture emulsifies and turns thick and creamy.

Storage: Store in an airtight container in the refrigerator for up to 7 to 10 days.

Ingredient Tip: The seasonings in this recipe are used to add taste and more acidity. Blend in your favorite herb or combination of herbs for a delicious herb mayonnaise.

Per 1-tbs serving: Calories: 62; Total fat: 7g; Carbohydrates: <1g; Fiber: 0g; Protein: <1g; Calcium: 5mg; Vitamin D: 0mcg; Vitamin B12: <1mcg; Iron: 0mg; Zinc: <1mg

MEDITERRANEAN-STYLE HUMMUS

DAIRY-FREE, GLUTEN-FREE

SERVES 1 or 2 //*PREP TIME* 45 minutes, plus overnight to soak //*COOK TIME* 45 minutes

This may not be the olive oil-based hummus that you have enjoyed at home and in restaurants for years, but instead it is a light, creamy, and delicious authentic version from the southern Mediterranean. It's excellent as a dip with homemade pita bread or raw veggies, as a sandwich spread, or as a base for a warm stew. Cooking your own dried chickpeas might seem like a lot of work, but the finished dish is well worth the effort.

1½ cups dried chickpeas

1 teaspoon baking soda

6½ cups water

½ cup light tahini

¼ cup freshly squeezed
  lemon juice

4 garlic cloves, smashed

1½ teaspoons sea salt

⅓ cup ice water

1 tablespoon extra-virgin
  olive oil

Zest of 1 lemon

1 Put the chickpeas in a large bowl and cover them with about 4 inches of cold water. Soak them overnight at room temperature.

2 Drain the chickpeas and transfer them to a medium saucepan and add the baking soda. Place over high heat and sauté for 3 to 4 minutes. Add the water and bring to a boil. Reduce the heat to low and cook, skimming the foam occasionally, until tender, 20 to 40 minutes, depending on the freshness of the chickpeas.

3 Drain the chickpeas, transfer them to a food processor, and process until they form a thick paste. With the machine still running, add the tahini, lemon juice, garlic, and salt, and process until well combined.

4 Slowly drizzle in the ice water and continue to process for about 5 minutes, until the hummus is a smooth and creamy paste.

5 Transfer the hummus to a glass bowl, cover the surface of the hummus with plastic wrap, and let it rest at room temperature for 30 minutes.

6 To serve, make a well in the center of the hummus, drizzle in the olive oil, and sprinkle with the lemon zest.

Storage: May be stored covered in the refrigerator for 5 to 7 days.

Variations: Add roasted red peppers, cooked beets, roasted garlic, red pepper flakes, or sun-dried tomatoes after adding the ice water for different flavors of hummus. You can also use 2 (15-ounce) cans of chickpeas, drained and rinsed, to save time, but the texture of the hummus will not be as light.

Per serving: Calories: 1,945; Total fat: 96g; Carbohydrates: 226g; Fiber: 63g; Protein: 87g; Calcium: 845mg; Vitamin D: 0mcg; Vitamin B12: 0mcg; Iron: 33mg; Zinc: 6mg

TOASTED-PEPITA DIP

DAIRY-FREE, GLUTEN-FREE

SERVES 4 //*PREP TIME* **15 minutes** //*COOK TIME* **15 minutes**

Based on the Mayan dish *sikil pak*, this healthy and complex dip is amazing on a crudités plate. Pepitas are hulled pumpkin seeds and a staple of the Latin American diet. These delightful seeds are rich in fiber. They make a stellar snack all by themselves, add crunch as a salad topping, and, of course, are the star of this brilliant dish.

4 garlic cloves, roasted

1 cup hulled pepitas

3 plum tomatoes

½ medium red onion, finely chopped

1 habanero chile, stemmed, seeded, and finely chopped, divided (optional)

¼ cup finely chopped cilantro

1 tablespoon chipotle pepper in adobo, finely minced

Juice of 1 lime

Juice of ½ orange

1 teaspoon ground cinnamon

Sea salt for seasoning

1   Preheat the oven to 400°F.

2   Wrap the garlic in foil, creating a packet, and roast in the oven until soft, about 40 minutes. Remove from the oven and set aside to cool for 10 minutes.

3   Put the seeds in a small sauté pan or skillet over medium-low heat and, when the first seed pops, stir constantly until all have popped from flat to round, about 5 minutes. Once toasted, place them in a food processor and process into a smooth paste, scraping down the sides a few times with a spatula.

4   Preheat the oven to broil.

5   Place the tomatoes on a baking sheet and place it 4 inches below the broiler. Broil the tomatoes until blackened and very soft, turning once, about 6 minutes per side. Cool the tomatoes and chop finely.

6   In a medium bowl, combine the garlic, pepita paste, tomatoes, onion, half the habanero chile (if using), cilantro, and chipotle. Stir in the lime juice, orange juice, and cinnamon. Taste and season with sea salt and add more habanero, if needed.

Storage: Keep the dip in a sealed container in the refrigerator for up to 4 days.

Serving Tip: Serve with crisp vegetables like baby carrots, cucumber slices, radishes, and sliced fennel.

Per serving: Calories: 198; Total fat: 15g; Carbohydrates: 11g; Fiber: 3g; Protein: 10g; Calcium: 38mg; Vitamin D: 0mcg; Vitamin B12: 0mcg; Iron: 3mg; Zinc: 2mg

FRESH, CHUNKY GUACAMOLE

DAIRY-FREE, GLUTEN-FREE

SERVES **2** //*PREP TIME* **15 minutes**

Having cooked Mexican food in restaurants for more than 15 years, I have become a bit of an expert on guacamole. I have discovered that ripe avocado is the key. When you use the method described here, you'll be surprised how the simple technique of mashing the ingredients into a paste creates guacamole bursting with flavor. Serve this lush, colorful dip with warm corn tortilla chips or sliced cucumbers.

1 large serrano pepper, minced

1 small jalapeño pepper, minced

½ bunch cilantro, chopped

½ small onion, diced

Juice of 2 limes

1 teaspoon sea salt

3 large Hass avocados

1 plum tomato, diced

1   Place the serrano and jalapeño peppers, cilantro, onion, lime juice, and salt in a large bowl and smash with the back of a fork until you get a chunky paste.

2   Add the avocados and mash them lightly with the fork, leaving some chunks, then stir into the paste with a wooden spoon until completely combined.

3   Gently fold in the tomato and adjust the seasonings.

4   Serve immediately, or cover the guacamole with plastic wrap pressed directly on the surface and store within a few hours.

Ingredient Tip: Guacamole is all about the avocado. A ripe avocado has a dark brown, pebbly texture, and the stem end is intact and yields gently to pressure. If your avocado isn't ripe, place it in a paper bag with an apple or tomato in a warm place overnight, and it will ripen quickly.

Per serving: Calories: 469; Total fat: 41g; Carbohydrates: 31g; Fiber: 20g; Protein: 6g; Calcium: 53mg; Vitamin D: 0mcg; Vitamin B12: 0mcg; Iron: 2mg; Zinc: 2mg

CHARRED-CARROT DIP

DAIRY-FREE

SERVES 4 //*PREP TIME* 20 minutes

This Moroccan-inspired dip is one of my absolute favorites. I can eat it by the spoonful, and I mean a serving spoon, not a tablespoon! Its vibrant beauty makes it a superstar for entertaining, but it's a wonderful component for a bowl or as a side dish as well. If you'd prefer, you can substitute butternut squash, pumpkin, or sweet potatoes for the carrots. The dip will still be a lovely color with these other choices.

1½ pounds peeled carrots

2 tablespoons canola oil

1 teaspoon sea salt, plus more for seasoning

½ teaspoon freshly ground black pepper

1 tablespoon chopped pistachios

1 teaspoon sesame seeds

¼ cup light tahini

6 to 7 tablespoons extra-virgin olive oil, divided

¼ cup ice water

Juice of 1 lemon

1 tablespoon honey

½ teaspoon smoked paprika

¼ teaspoon ground coriander

¼ teaspoon ground cumin

1 large pita bread

1 tablespoon pomegranate arils

4 or 5 mint leaves, gently torn

1   Preheat the oven to broil.

2   In a large bowl, toss the carrots in the canola oil, salt, and pepper. Spread the carrots on a baking sheet and broil until tender and browned, turning once, about 10 minutes.

3   While the carrots are broiling, place a small sauté pan or skillet over medium heat and lightly toast the pistachios and sesame seeds until golden, about 1 minute. Remove from the heat and set aside.

4   Reduce the oven heat to 200°F.

5   Trim and discard the ends of the carrots. Cut the carrots into chunks, place them in a food processor, and pulse until finely chopped.

6   Add the tahini, 4 tablespoons of olive oil, ice water, lemon juice, honey, smoked paprika, coriander, and cumin. Process until smooth and creamy, scraping down the sides of the processor a few times. Taste the dip and season with more salt, honey, or lemon juice as needed.

7 Brush the pita with 1 tablespoon of olive oil, season with salt, and wrap it in foil. Place it in the oven until warmed. Remove the pita and cut it into quarters.

8 Transfer the dip to a serving bowl and sprinkle with the pistachios, sesame seeds, pomegranate, and mint, and drizzle on the remaining 1 tablespoon of olive oil.

9 Serve with the warm pita bread.

Storage: Store the dip, covered, in the refrigerator for up to 5 days.

Ingredient Tip: This dip is excellent with corn tortilla chips for a gluten-free snack. It also makes a fantastic sandwich spread.

Per serving: Calories: 585; Total fat: 38g; Carbohydrates: 55g; Fiber: 8g; Protein: 10g; Calcium: 184mg; Vitamin D: 0mcg; Vitamin B12: 0mcg; Iron: 4mg; Zinc: 2mg

CRISPY CINNAMON CHICKPEAS

DAIRY-FREE, GLUTEN-FREE

SERVES **2 to 4** //*PREP TIME* **10 minutes, plus 30 minutes drying time**
COOK TIME **45 minutes**

I love these crispy, crunchy little bites, quick and easy to make with just a few ingredients—and they are totally irresistible. Roasted chickpeas are a great addition to a Mediterranean mezze board for entertaining, they're a healthy take-along snack, and they're perfect for adding a crackly zip to your salad or veggie bowl.

2 (15-ounce) cans chickpeas, drained, rinsed, and dried

2 tablespoons canola oil

¼ cup sugar

2 tablespoons ground cinnamon

1 teaspoon sea salt

1 Preheat the oven to 400°F. Line a baking sheet with parchment paper.

2 Allow the chickpeas to air-dry for at least 30 minutes; the drier the chickpeas, the crispier they will be when baked.

3 In a large bowl, toss the chickpeas with the oil, sugar, cinnamon, and salt. Spread them on the baking sheet and bake, uncovered, stirring occasionally, for 45 minutes, or until golden brown and crunchy.

Storage: Store the cooled chickpeas in an airtight container at room temperature for up to 1 week; recrisp in the oven as needed.

Ingredient Tip: Chili powder, smoked paprika, or dried herbs are also fabulous with this crunchy snack.

Per serving: Calories: 606; Total fat: 21g; Carbohydrates: 91g; Fiber: 21g; Protein: 19g; Calcium: 201mg; Vitamin D: 0mcg; Vitamin B12: 0mcg; Iron: 3mg; Zinc: 2mg

QUINOA FRITTERS

MAKES **about 12 fritters** *//PREP TIME* **20 minutes** *//COOK TIME* **20 minutes**

I have been making these golden fritters for years and have found multiple uses for them besides as a great snack or starter. They are also delightful tucked into a corn tortilla with some salsa and avocado as a taco or rolled up into a wrap with some crispy cabbage slaw for a healthy lunch.

⅔ cup quinoa

1⅓ cups water

¼ cup all-purpose flour

¼ cup grated Parmesan cheese

¾ teaspoon sea salt

Pinch freshly ground black pepper

4 scallions, both white and light green parts, finely chopped

½ bunch Italian parsley leaves, chopped

1 large egg

1 large egg yolk

¾ cup canola oil

Lemon wedges, for garnish

Green goddess dressing (page 66), for serving

1   Wash the quinoa and drain well. Place a large sauté pan or skillet over high heat, pour in the quinoa, and toast until golden brown, shaking and stirring constantly, for 3 to 4 minutes.

2   Transfer the quinoa to a large saucepan and add the water. Bring to a boil over medium-high heat, reduce the heat to low, cover, and simmer until the water is absorbed, about 10 minutes. Spread the quinoa on a parchment-lined baking sheet to cool.

3   When cooled, transfer the quinoa to a large bowl and stir in the flour, cheese, salt, and pepper. Add the scallions, parsley, egg, and egg yolk, and stir until the ingredients are thoroughly combined and the mixture has the consistency of a soft dough.

4   Heat the canola oil in a large, deep skillet over medium heat. Working in batches, scoop out the batter using a soup spoon, taking care to create rounded mounds, and carefully slide them into the hot oil. Fry about 4 fritters at a time and avoid crowding the skillet.

CONTINUED

5 Fry until the bottoms are golden brown, about 1 minute. Turn and fry the other side until golden, about 1 minute.

6 Drain the fritters on paper towels and serve warm with lemon wedges and green goddess dressing.

Storage: The dough can be stored covered in the refrigerator for up to 1 day before shaping and frying. Or shape the dough into ovals and place in an airtight container and freeze until ready to use.

Serving Tip: Top the fritters with creamy tzatziki sauce for a Middle Eastern–inspired dish.

Per serving: Calories: 187; Total fat: 16g; Carbohydrates: 9g; Fiber: 1g; Protein: 3g; Calcium: 37mg; Vitamin D: <1mcg; Vitamin B12: <1mcg; Iron: 1mg; Zinc: 1mg

POWER TRAIL MIX

DAIRY-FREE, GLUTEN-FREE

MAKES **3 pounds** *//PREP TIME* **5 minutes** *//COOK TIME* **15 minutes**

I have found that it is infinitely easier to stay on track with healthy, plant-rich eating when you have some emergency snacks around. I always take a bag of this trail mix along when I'm traveling so I'm not tempted by hunger to consume a less healthy option. Dark chocolate is not only one of the most tempting ingredients, but it is also a powerful source of antioxidants and a natural energy lifter.

¾ cup raw walnut pieces

¾ cup raw cashews

½ cup raw sunflower seeds

½ cup raw pumpkin seeds

½ cup unsweetened, unsulfured dried cherries

½ cup unsweetened, unsulfured raisins

½ cup chopped dark chocolate

½ teaspoon ground cinnamon

¼ teaspoon sea salt

1 Preheat the oven to 350°F. Line a baking sheet with parchment paper.

2 In a large bowl, toss the walnuts, cashews, sunflower seeds, and pumpkin seeds together and spread them on the baking sheet. Toast in the oven until golden, 10 to 15 minutes. Set them aside to cool.

3 In a large bowl, stir together the cherries, raisins, chocolate, cinnamon, and salt until well mixed. Add the cooled nut and seed mixture and toss to combine.

Storage: Transfer the mixture to an airtight container and store at room temperature for up to 1 month.

Ingredient Tip: Use your favorite combination of fruits and nuts to make this recipe your own. These ingredients are my personal favorites, but dried apricots, bananas, or cranberries are also excellent choices.

Per 1-pound: Calories: 955; Total fat: 63g; Carbohydrates: 77g; Fiber: 12g; Protein: 25g; Calcium: 140mg; Vitamin D: <1mcg; Vitamin B12: <1mcg; Iron: 11mg; Zinc: 5mg

FRUIT LEATHER

DAIRY-FREE, GLUTEN-FREE

MAKES 1 (12-by-18-inch) leather sheet //*PREP TIME* 20 minutes

COOK TIME 25 minutes, plus 8 to 12 hours to dry

Fruit leather is just plain fun. It's easy to make, portable, and yummy to boot. Bake the fruit leather on parchment paper, roll it up, cut it into strips, and you have a healthy whole food snack that you can throw in a bag or lunch box. Who knew nutritious could be so delicious?

4 cups chopped fresh fruits (apricots, peaches, plums, berries, apples, pears)

½ cup water

Sugar (as needed, optional)

Juice of 1 lemon

Pinch cinnamon, allspice, or ginger (optional)

1 Place the fruit and water in a large saucepan over medium-high heat. Bring to a simmer, reduce the heat to low, cover, and let cook, stirring occasionally, for 10 to 15 minutes, or until the fruit is soft.

2 Use a potato masher or the back of a wooden spoon to mash the fruit in the saucepan. Add sugar in small amounts (if using) to the desired level of sweetness. Add the lemon juice 1 teaspoon at a time to bring out the flavor of the fruit. Add a pinch of spice (if using) to brighten the flavor.

3 Continue to simmer and stir until the fruit mash has thickened, 5 to 10 minutes more (or longer as needed). Set aside to cool enough to handle.

4 Preheat the oven to 140°F. Line a baking sheet with parchment paper.

5 Puree the mixture in a blender or food processor until it is very smooth.

6 Pour the puree onto the baking sheet and spread to about ⅛- to ¼-inch thickness in a 12-by-18-inch rectangle. Place the baking sheet in the oven and let dry for as long as it takes for the puree to dry out and form fruit leather, usually 8 to 12 hours.

7 When the fruit leather is smooth and no longer sticky, remove it from the oven, allow it to cool slightly, roll it in the parchment paper it was prepared on, and then wrap it in plastic wrap.

Storage: Store in an airtight container in the refrigerator; it can also be frozen and thawed when ready to eat.

Ingredient Tip: Have fun creating different flavor combinations by using different fruits and spices, like apple-cranberry or strawberry-rhubarb.

Per serving using apricots: Calories: 308; Total fat: 3g; Carbohydrates: 72g; Fiber: 13g; Protein: 9g; Calcium: 84mg; Vitamin D: 0mcg; Vitamin B12: 0mcg; Iron: 3mg; Zinc: 1mg

BAKED VEGETABLE CHIPS

DAIRY-FREE, GLUTEN-FREE

SERVES **2 to 4** //*PREP TIME* **20 minutes** //*COOK TIME* **40 minutes**

A brightly colored bowl of veggie chips on the kitchen counter satisfies the urge for a crunchy snack and sneaks in your veggie servings at the same time. Any type of root vegetable or potato makes a terrific chip; for a vivid selection, use purple potatoes, sweet potatoes, and taro root.

---

3 large sweet potatoes, unpeeled and scrubbed

Sea salt

Nonstick avocado oil spray

1 Preheat the oven to 300°F. Line 2 baking sheets with parchment paper.

2 Use a mandoline or vegetable peeler to slice the sweet potatoes into thin slices.

3 Lay the sweet potato slices in one layer on paper towels. Sprinkle them with salt and set aside for 5 to 10 minutes to allow them to weep out any excess moisture. Blot off the extra moisture.

4 Place the chips on the prepared baking sheets in a single layer, then spray them with avocado oil.

5 Bake for 12 to 15 minutes and rotate the pans. Bake for 12 to 15 minutes more and rotate again. Bake an additional 5 to 10 minutes, or until chips are golden and slightly crisp.

Storage: Store the chips in an airtight container in the pantry for up to 1 week.

Cooking Tip: The chips will crisp up as they cool, so don't panic if they are a bit soft when you take them out of the oven.

Per serving: Calories: 263; Total fat: <1g; Carbohydrates: 62g; Fiber: 9g; Protein: 5g; Calcium: 92mg; Vitamin D: 0mcg; Vitamin B12: 0mcg; Iron: 2mg; Zinc: 1mg

KALE CRISPS

DAIRY-FREE, GLUTEN-FREE

SERVES **2 to 4** // *PREP TIME* **10 minutes** // *COOK TIME* **20 minutes**

These kale crisps are addictive and are the ideal guilt-free snack. They are so crunchy and flavorful you will want to eat them all straight off the baking sheet. Before you know it, a whole head of iron-rich leafy greens will be consumed. Make a fresh bowl to replace your popcorn for home movie night.

1 head kale, washed and thoroughly dried	2 tablespoons extra-virgin olive oil	Sea salt

1 Preheat the oven to 275°F. Line a baking sheet with parchment paper.

2 Remove the ribs from the kale and cut or tear the leaves into 1½-inch pieces. Arrange them on the baking sheet and toss with the olive oil and season with salt. Bake the kale until crisp, turning the leaves halfway through, about 20 minutes.

Storage: Store the kale crisps in an airtight container in the pantry for up to 1 week.

Ingredient Tip: To make cheesy chips, sprinkle them with Parmesan (or vegan Parmesan); for spicy chips, sprinkle them with red pepper flakes.

Per serving: Calories: 130; Total fat: 14g; Carbohydrates: 1g; Fiber: 1g; Protein: 1g; Calcium: 80mg; Vitamin D: 0mcg; Vitamin B12: 0mcg; Iron: 1mg; Zinc: <1mg

Pickled Red Onions, page 58

CHAPTER FOUR

CONDIMENTS, SAUCES
& DRESSINGS

Flavored Oils 56

Flavored Vinegar 57

Pickled Red Onions 58

Verde Cruda 60

Roasted Tomato Serrano Salsa 60

Pico de Gallo 61

Homemade Ketchup 62

Fruit Mustard 63

Agave-Lime Vinaigrette 64

Apple & Red Chile Chutney 65

Vegan Caesar Dressing 66

Habanero Hot Sauce 67

Pomegranate Vinaigrette 68

Herb Vinaigrette 69

Orange Vinaigrette 70

Thai-Inspired Peanut Sauce 71

Coconut Curry Sauce 72

FLAVORED OILS

DAIRY-FREE, GLUTEN-FREE

MAKES **1 quart** *// PREP TIME* **10 minutes** *// COOK TIME* **10 minutes**

Homemade infused oils are much less expensive than store-bought, and you can flavor them with absolutely anything you'd like to try. They are easy to make and add something special to any recipe calling for oil. As you experiment, you might discover favorite combinations that perk up your cooking. I have a bottle of lemon-chile oil on my counter right now and probably use it more than any other oil in the pantry. These handcrafted products also make beautiful gifts.

Zest of 4 lemons   4 cups avocado oil

TO MAKE A COLD INFUSION

1 Divide the lemon zest and avocado oil evenly between 2 clean glass bottles or mason jars.

2 Seal the bottles or jars tightly, leaving a little air space at the top to prevent botulism. Let the oil sit in a cool, dark place for 2 weeks before using it. The oil will slowly infuse with the added flavoring so do a taste test every few days to check the flavor.

3 Strain out the zest and rebottle the oil once the flavor is to your liking.

Oils infused by this method should be refrigerated after straining.

TO MAKE A HEAT INFUSION

4 Heat the zest and oil gently in a large saucepan over low heat to about 180°F.

5 Remove from the heat and let the oil cool completely and then strain out the zest before bottling the infused oil. This is a quicker way of infusing the oil, and the oil does not need to be refrigerated.

Some of my favorite flavor combinations are:

- *Cilantro and jalapeños*
- *Lemon zest and dried chiles*
- *Assorted colored peppercorns (pink, black, green, etc.)*
- *Mint and lemongrass*

- *Rosemary, lemon, and garlic*
- *Fresh basil, parsley, or thyme*
- *Orange, lemon, and lime zest*
- *Sun-dried tomato and basil*

Serving Tip: If giving as a gift, you may want to add some fresh herbs or flavorings to the bottle.

Per serving: Calories: 120; Total fat: 14g; Carbohydrates: 0g; Fiber: 0g; Protein: 0g; Calcium: 0mg; Vitamin D: 0mcg; Vitamin B12: 0mcg; Iron: 0mg; Zinc: 0mg

FLAVORED VINEGAR

DAIRY-FREE, GLUTEN-FREE

MAKES 1 quart //*PREP TIME* 15 minutes //*COOK TIME* 3 to 4 weeks to infuse

Flavored vinegar adds excitement to salads, marinades, and sauces. This is barely a recipe; it takes so little effort to throw together. The 15 minutes spent creating this great pantry item is well worth it, considering the vinegar's long shelf life. Like flavored oils, these pretty bottles also make special gifts.

4 cups of sliced fruit or veggies, spices, or herbs or any combination

2 (16-ounce) bottles apple cider vinegar or distilled white vinegar

1   Place the prepared fruit or veggies, spices, or herbs in 4 (500 ml) sterilized mason jars with lids, being careful to avoid overpacking the bottles. Use 3 or 4 fresh herb sprigs, 3 tablespoons of dried herbs, or 1 cup of fruit or vegetables per pint of vinegar.

2   Pour the vinegar into a large saucepan over medium heat and bring it to just below boiling (190°F). Remove from the heat and pour the vinegar into the jars and cap tightly.

Allow to stand for 3 to 4 weeks in a cool, dark place for the flavor to develop fully.

3   Strain the vinegar through a damp cheesecloth or coffee filter one or more times until the vinegar is no longer cloudy. Discard the fruit, vegetables, or herbs.

4   Pour the strained vinegar into clean, sterilized jars. Add 1 or 2 sprigs of thoroughly washed fresh herbs or fruits. Seal the jars tightly.

Storage: Store the vinegar in a cool, dark place for up to 2 weeks or in the refrigerator for up to 6 weeks.

Ingredient Tip: Experiment with the freshest seasonal fruits and veggies and surprise a friend with a beautiful jar of peach vinegar as a thoughtful winter gift.

Per 1-tbs serving using peaches: Calories: 5; Total fat: 0g; Carbohydrates: 0g; Fiber: <1g; Protein: 0g; Calcium: 1mg; Vitamin D: 0mcg; Vitamin B12: 0mcg; Iron: 0mg; Zinc: <1mg

PICKLED RED ONIONS

DAIRY-FREE, GLUTEN-FREE

MAKES 1 cup //*PREP TIME* 20 minutes, plus 10 minutes to several hours to infuse

Pickled red onions are a staple item in my refrigerator. This bright condiment imparts a lively tang to almost everything along with a splash of color. It takes about 20 minutes to make and lasts for weeks in the refrigerator. Add these pretty pickles to sandwiches, tacos, bean dishes, and mayo-based salads like potato or egg salad. When the pickles are gone, use the remaining liquid to make a lovely vinaigrette.

1 quart water

¾ cup rice vinegar, white vinegar, or apple cider vinegar

½ teaspoon sugar

½ teaspoon sea salt

1 medium red onion, thinly sliced

Optional:

1 garlic clove, halved

5 whole black peppercorns

5 allspice berries

3 small thyme sprigs

1 small dried chile de arbol or Thai chile

1 Boil the water over high heat in a pot or kettle.

2 Put the vinegar, sugar, salt, and any optional flavorings (if using) in a large glass jar and stir to dissolve.

3 Place the sliced onion in a colander in the sink. Carefully pour the boiling water over it and let the water drain through.

4 Add the onion to the jar with the vinegar mixture and stir to combine. Allow to cool at room temperature.

5 Cover the jar and place it in the refrigerator. The pickles can be used right away but are better after a few hours.

Storage: The pickles will keep for several weeks in the refrigerator.

Cooking Tip: This pickling technique can be used with any type of vegetable. Try pickling fresh chile peppers, tomatoes, or beets to add a little extra oomph to your salads.

Per ¼-cup serving: Calories: 24; Total fat: 0g; Carbohydrates: 4g; Fiber: 1g; Protein: <1g; Calcium: 14mg; Vitamin D: 0mcg; Vitamin B12: 0mcg; Iron: <1mg; Zinc: <1mg

Roasted Tomato Serrano Salsa, page 60

SALSAS

DAIRY-FREE, GLUTEN-FREE

MAKES 1 quart // *PREP TIME* 15 minutes

Salsas are a healthy, zingy way to spice up almost any dish, from scrambled eggs to grain bowls. They take very little time and keep well in the refrigerator, and fresh salsa is free of the chemicals and preservatives often found in store-bought salsas. I offer a couple of variations here, but as always, feel free to experiment with your favorite fruits and vegetables.

VERDE CRUDA

2 pounds tomatillos (10 to 12), husked and washed

1 white onion

6 garlic cloves

1 medium serrano pepper

1 medium jalapeño pepper

½ bunch cilantro

2 allspice berries

1 teaspoon sea salt, plus more for seasoning

1　Put the tomatillos, onion, garlic, serrano, jalapeño, cilantro, allspice, and salt in a food processor and process until smooth.

2　Pour the sauce into a fine-mesh strainer to strain out most of the liquid.

3　Adjust the seasoning as needed. Transfer the finished salsa into an airtight container and refrigerate or use immediately.

Per 2-tbs serving: Calories: 12; Total fat: <1g; Carbohydrates: 2g; Fiber: 1g; Protein: <1g; Calcium: 4mg; Vitamin D: 0mcg; Vitamin B12: 0mcg; Iron: <1mg; Zinc: <1mg

ROASTED TOMATO SERRANO SALSA

2 pounds plum tomatoes

1 medium white onion, quartered

6 garlic cloves, halved

2 medium serrano peppers, stemmed

2 tablespoons extra-virgin olive oil

1 teaspoon sea salt, plus more for seasoning

1 chipotle pepper in adobo

½ cup white vinegar

½ bunch cilantro

Juice of 2 limes

1 Preheat the oven to broil. Line a baking sheet with parchment paper.

2 In a large bowl, toss together the tomatoes, onion, garlic, serrano peppers, olive oil, and salt until the vegetables are well coated.

3 Spread the tomato mixture on the baking sheet and roast, turning occasionally, until it is very soft and deep golden brown, 10 to 15 minutes. Cool slightly.

4 Working in batches, put the roasted vegetables in a food processor and process until smooth but with a little texture. Transfer to a medium bowl. Add the chipotle, vinegar, cilantro, and lime juice to the last batch and pulse, then transfer the mixture to the bowl and stir to combine.

5 Season with salt and use immediately or store covered in the refrigerator until needed.

Per 2-tbs serving: Calories: 16; Total fat: 1g; Carbohydrates: 2g; Fiber: 1g; Protein: <1g; Calcium: 5mg; Vitamin D: 0mcg; Vitamin B12: 0mcg; Iron: <1mg; Zinc: <1mg

PICO DE GALLO

1 pound plum tomatoes, washed, seeded, and finely diced

1 small red onion, finely chopped

½ bunch cilantro, chopped

1 medium serrano pepper, minced (seeded if desired for a less spicy version)

1 small jalapeño pepper, minced (seeded if desired for a less spicy version)

Juice and zest of 2 limes

1 teaspoon sea salt

1 In a large bowl, stir together the tomatoes, onion, cilantro, serrano, jalapeño, lime juice, lime zest, and salt until well combined.

2 Adjust the seasonings and use immediately or store covered in the refrigerator until needed.

Variation Tip: Add some diced, roasted pineapple to the tomato salsa, or add avocado to the salsa verde. Pico de gallo can be enhanced with diced mango, grilled corn, and black beans.

Per 2-tbs serving: Calories: 4; Total fat: 0g; Carbohydrates: 1g; Fiber: <1g; Protein: <1g; Calcium: 3mg; Vitamin D: 0mcg; Vitamin B12: 0mcg; Iron: <1mg; Zinc: <1mg

HOMEMADE KETCHUP

MAKES **2 cups** //*PREP TIME* **5 minutes** //*COOK TIME* **20 minutes**

Why take the trouble to make homemade ketchup? Because the stuff that's sold in the grocery store is full of sugar and preservatives. Once you taste this homemade version, you'll never go back to store-bought ketchup. Try flavoring your ketchup with ripe stone fruit in the summer or chili powder for a kick of heat.

6 ounces tomato paste

¼ cup honey or
  agave nectar

½ cup white vinegar

¼ cup water

1 teaspoon sugar

¾ teaspoon sea salt

¼ teaspoon onion powder

⅛ teaspoon garlic powder

⅛ teaspoon celery salt

⅛ teaspoon mustard powder

1 whole clove

1 Combine the tomato paste, honey, white vinegar, water, sugar, salt, onion powder, garlic powder, celery salt, mustard powder, and clove in a medium saucepan over medium heat and whisk until smooth.

2 When the mixture comes to a boil, reduce the heat to low and simmer for 20 minutes, stirring often.

3 Remove the sauce from the heat, cover, and allow to cool at room temperature.

4 Chill thoroughly before using it.

Storage: The ketchup will keep for several weeks in an airtight container in the refrigerator.

Ingredient Tip: If you find yourself with some extra ripe tomatoes on hand, puree them until smooth in a blender, strain, and add to the other ingredients in step 1.

Per 2-tbs serving: Calories: 26; Total fat: <1g; Carbohydrates: 7g; Fiber: 1g; Protein: 1g; Calcium: 5mg; Vitamin D: omcg; Vitamin B12: omcg; Iron: <1mg; Zinc: <1mg

FRUIT MUSTARD

DAIRY-FREE, GLUTEN-FREE

MAKES 2 cups //*PREP TIME* 10 minutes, plus 1 hour to infuse //*COOK TIME* 5 minutes

Fruit mustards are great as a spread on sandwiches, as a condiment on a cheese board, and blended into vinaigrettes. This one uses dried figs, but any fruit can be made into a lovely mustard. I like my mustard a little spicy, so I add a chipotle chile, but it's just as wonderful without this extra ingredient.

2½ cups chopped dried
  black Mission figs

1 cup tawny port wine

½ cup yellow mustard seeds

¼ cup champagne vinegar

1 teaspoon sea salt, plus
  more for seasoning

1 Combine the figs and port in a medium bowl and let them stand at room temperature for 1 hour.

2 Toast the mustard seeds in a dry sauté pan or skillet over medium heat until they are fragrant and lightly browned, about 5 minutes.

3 Transfer the fig mixture to a food processor with the toasted mustard seeds, vinegar, and salt, and process until combined. Season with salt as needed and transfer the mustard to a 16-ounce jar and cover tightly.

Storage: The mustard will keep for 2 weeks in the pantry or 4 weeks in the refrigerator.

Ingredient Tip: Dried apricots, cherries, and plums (and combinations) also make great fruit mustards. Use a white dessert wine for lighter mustard.

Per 2-tbs serving: Calories: 109; Total fat: 1g; Carbohydrates: 19g; Fiber: 4g; Protein: 2g; Calcium: 47mg; Vitamin D: 0mcg; Vitamin B12: 0mcg; Iron: 1mg; Zinc: <1mg

AGAVE-LIME VINAIGRETTE

DAIRY-FREE, GLUTEN-FREE

MAKES **2 cups** // *PREP TIME* **10 minutes**

I use this as an all-purpose vinaigrette in my restaurants; it is delicious and enhances anything it touches. It is especially great on salads, but mix it into grains or drizzle it over grilled veggies or avocado slices to serve as light and zesty sides.

Zest of 4 limes

1 cup freshly squeezed lime juice

½ cup extra-virgin olive oil

¼ cup rice vinegar

2 tablespoons agave nectar

1 tablespoon peeled and grated ginger

1 teaspoon sea salt, plus more for seasoning

1 teaspoon freshly ground black pepper, plus more for seasoning

1   Combine the lime zest, lime juice, oil, vinegar, agave, ginger, salt, and pepper in a blender at low speed, then increasing to medium speed until well combined.

2   Season with salt and pepper as needed.

3   Use immediately or place in a 16-ounce glass jar, seal tightly, and refrigerate.

Storage: Store for up to 1 week in the refrigerator.

Ingredient Tip: Substitute or combine other citrus juices such as lemon, orange, or grapefruit for variety.

Per 2-tbs serving: Calories: 73; Total fat: 7g; Carbohydrates: 4g; Fiber: <1g; Protein: <1g; Calcium: 4mg; Vitamin D: 0mcg; Vitamin B12: 0mcg; Iron: <1mg; Zinc: <1mg

APPLE & RED CHILE CHUTNEY

DAIRY-FREE, GLUTEN-FREE

MAKES **1 pint** // *PREP TIME* **10 minutes** // *COOK TIME* **30 minutes**

I have a deep love for the state of New Mexico and its foodways. This chutney is inspired by the blend of cultures there, and I always have a jar in my refrigerator to serve with cheese. In autumn, this is a staple on my vegan cheese board at BKLYNwild.

4 Granny Smith apples, peeled, cored, and diced

4 red Fresno chiles, stemmed, seeded, deveined, and finely diced

1 cup water

½ cup light brown sugar

⅓ cup apple cider vinegar

8 garlic cloves, minced

½ cup toasted pine nuts or pecans

1 tablespoon finely chopped fresh marjoram leaves

1   Put the apples and chiles in a medium, heavy saucepan and add the water, sugar, vinegar, and garlic. Bring to a boil over medium heat, reduce the heat to low, and simmer, stirring occasionally, for about 30 minutes, until the apples are soft and the mixture has thickened.

2   While the chutney is cooking, place a small sauté pan or skillet over medium heat and toast the pine nuts until golden, about 5 minutes.

3   When the chutney has thickened, stir in the pine nuts and marjoram. Allow to cool at room temperature, then transfer to a 16-ounce glass jar with a lid and refrigerate.

Storage: The chutney will keep for up to 1 week in the refrigerator.

Ingredient Tip: Pears in season are a great substitution for the apples in this recipe. If you're lucky enough to have a crab apple tree in your yard, this chutney is a stellar use for the fruit.

Per serving: Calories: 1,149; Total fat: 43g; Carbohydrates: 186g; Fiber: 28g; Protein: 13g; Calcium: 162mg; Vitamin D: 0mcg; Vitamin B12: 0mcg; Iron: 5mg; Zinc: 4mg

VEGAN CAESAR DRESSING

DAIRY-FREE, GLUTEN-FREE

MAKES **1 pint** // *PREP TIME* **10 minutes**

This Caesar dressing is every bit as rich and delicious as a traditional Caesar dressing. Use it in the classic preparation with romaine lettuce or kale, but also consider serving the recipe as the dip for a fabulous veggie platter. If you like green goddess dressing, add pureed avocado and some herbs.

¾ cup non-dairy Greek-style yogurt

½ cup vegan Parmesan cheese

3 tablespoons extra-virgin olive oil

3 tablespoons freshly squeezed lemon juice

2 tablespoons freshly ground black pepper

1½ teaspoons Dijon mustard

½ teaspoon drained capers

Zest of 2 lemons

1 garlic clove

1 teaspoon sea salt

1 Put the yogurt, cheese, oil, lemon juice, pepper, mustard, capers, lemon zest, garlic, and salt in a blender at low speed, then increasing to medium speed until smooth.

2 Adjust the seasonings as needed and use immediately, or place in an airtight container and refrigerate.

Storage: Store in an airtight container for up to 3 days.

Serving Tip: Try this recipe as a tasty sandwich spread or tossed in a summer-themed pasta salad.

Per 2-tbs serving: Calories: 65; Total fat: 5g; Carbohydrates: 4g; Fiber: 1g; Protein: 1g; Calcium: 14mg; Vitamin D: 0mcg; Vitamin B12: 0mcg; Iron: <1mg; Zinc: <1mg

HABANERO HOT SAUCE

DAIRY-FREE, GLUTEN-FREE

MAKES **1 pint** // *PREP TIME* **15 minutes** // *COOK TIME* **10 minutes**

This hot sauce features the beautiful floral heat of habaneros, is packed with veggies, and tastes incredibly fresh. You can whip this up in less than 30 minutes, and this homemade version allows you to control the ingredients. It also makes a beautiful gift for your favorite chilehead.

1 quart water

1 quart white vinegar

4 orange habanero peppers, halved (seeded for a less spicy version)

2 plum tomatoes

2 shallots, halved

2 garlic cloves

2 bay leaves

1 yellow bell pepper, halved

1 large carrot, halved

Sea salt

1 Place the water, vinegar, habanero peppers, tomatoes, shallots, garlic, bay leaves, bell pepper, and carrot in a large, nonreactive stockpot and bring to a boil over medium-high heat. Reduce the heat to low and simmer until the peppers are just tender, about 10 minutes.

2 Strain the ingredients through a fine-mesh strainer over a bowl and reserve the liquid.

3 Place the strained ingredients in a blender at low speed, then increasing to medium speed until smooth, using just enough of the cooking liquid to achieve a sauce texture, about ¼ cup. Then strain the sauce again through the mesh strainer.

4 Season with salt as needed and cool at room temperature.

5 Pour the sauce into a clean glass jar or bottle, seal tightly, and refrigerate.

Storage: The sauce will keep for 1 to 2 weeks in the refrigerator.

Serving Tip: Swirl a bit of this sauce into mayo, mustard, or ketchup to add a little kick to your condiments.

Per 2-tbs serving: Calories: 10; Total fat: <1g; Carbohydrates: 2g; Fiber: 1g; Protein: <1g; Calcium: 5mg; Vitamin D: 0mcg; Vitamin B12: 0mcg; Iron: <1mg; Zinc: <1mg

POMEGRANATE VINAIGRETTE

DAIRY-FREE, GLUTEN-FREE

MAKES **1 pint** *//PREP TIME* **5 minutes**

Try this classic recipe for pomegranate vinaigrette on winter salads and vegetables. The unique tart-sweet taste perks up grain and fruit salads, creating a palate-pleasing meal. When you're craving a simple, flavorful snack, drizzle it over a hard cheese like Parmesan.

1 cup pomegranate arils

½ cup extra-virgin olive oil

¼ cup pure maple syrup

Juice of 1 lemon

1 tablespoon white balsamic vinegar

1 teaspoon Dijon mustard

1 teaspoon sea salt

1 Put the pomegranate arils, oil, maple syrup, lemon juice, vinegar, mustard, and salt in a blender and blend on low speed, gradually increasing to high.

2 Continue blending on high for 30 to 60 seconds, or until the dressing is smooth and all the pomegranate seeds have been blended.

3 This dressing is best used the same day but can be stored in a clean glass jar and refrigerated for later use.

Storage: Store in a covered jar in the refrigerator for up to 2 days.

Serving Tip: This beautifully colored dressing is especially nice on endive or radicchio salad. Reserve some of the seeds to use as a garnish.

Per 2-tbs serving: Calories: 83; Total fat: 7g; Carbohydrates: 6g; Fiber: 1g; Protein: <1g; Calcium: 7mg; Vitamin D: omcg; Vitamin B12: omcg; Iron: <1mg; Zinc: <1mg

HERB VINAIGRETTE

DAIRY-FREE, GLUTEN-FREE

MAKES **1 quart** // *PREP TIME* **10 minutes**

This beautiful, vibrant green vinaigrette is wonderful paired with ripe summer tomatoes or fresh tofu, or used as a topping for a watermelon and feta salad. Toss it with chilled pasta and veggies for a fresh-tasting salad, or whisk it into mashed potatoes instead of butter for a healthier version of this classic side. Don't be surprised by the green-flecked appearance of the potatoes!

2 cups rice vinegar

1 bunch fresh basil, chopped

1 bunch fresh cilantro, chopped

6 garlic cloves, chopped

1 tablespoon honey or agave nectar

1 teaspoon sea salt, plus more for seasoning

2 teaspoons freshly ground black pepper

3 cups extra-virgin olive oil

1 cup avocado oil

1   Put the vinegar, basil, cilantro, garlic, honey, salt, and pepper in a blender, and blend on low speed, then increasing to medium speed until combined.

2   Combine the olive and avocado oils in a large measuring cup. While the blender is running, add the mixture in a thin stream until the dressing is completely emulsified.

3   Adjust the seasonings as needed. Transfer the vinaigrette to a glass jar and refrigerate.

Storage: Store the vinaigrette in an airtight container in the refrigerator for up to 2 days.

Prep Tip: This dressing is best used the same day. To retain the bright green color longer, the herbs may be blanched and cooled completely before blending.

Per 2-tbs serving: Calories: 245; Total fat: 27g; Carbohydrates: 1g; Fiber: <1g; Protein: <1g; Calcium: 5mg; Vitamin D: 0mcg; Vitamin B12: 0mcg; Iron: <1mg; Zinc: <1mg

ORANGE VINAIGRETTE

DAIRY-FREE, GLUTEN-FREE

MAKES **1 cup** // *PREP TIME* **5 minutes**

This zesty citrus vinaigrette is perfect on a simple salad with sliced avocados, and as a marinade for grilling vegetables or tofu. I dress shredded lettuce for tacos with this, and it's lovely drizzled over a grain or legume bowl. For a shortcut, place all the ingredients in a glass jar with a lid, shake vigorously, and pour. Then pop the rest in the refrigerator for later.

Juice of 2 oranges

Juice of 2 lemons

Zest of ½ orange

½ teaspoon lemon zest

½ teaspoon sea salt, plus more for seasoning

¼ teaspoon freshly ground black pepper, plus more for seasoning

½ cup extra-virgin olive oil

1 Pour the orange juice, lemon juice, orange zest, lemon zest, salt, and pepper into a blender. Turn the blender on medium, and while it is running, drizzle in the olive oil until it is used up.

2 Season with salt and pepper and use immediately, or refrigerate in an airtight container.

Storage: Store the vinaigrette in an airtight container for up to 3 days in the refrigerator.

Ingredient Tip: Use blood oranges in season for a gorgeous red-hued dressing, or a combination of oranges and tangerines for a sweeter version.

Per 2-tbs serving: Calories: 133; Total fat: 14g; Carbohydrates: 3g; Fiber: <1g; Protein: <1g; Calcium: 5mg; Vitamin D: 0mcg; Vitamin B12: 0mcg; Iron: <1mg; Zinc: <1mg

THAI-INSPIRED PEANUT SAUCE

DAIRY-FREE, GLUTEN-FREE

MAKES **1 cup** //*PREP TIME* **10 minutes**

This is my favorite all-purpose sauce. If I'm rushed and hungry, a drizzle of this over some brown rice and beans is a satisfying dinner. Use it as a dip for veggies or cold rice noodles, stir-fry fresh veggies with it, or thin it with a little oil and vinegar for salad dressing.

½ cup creamy peanut butter (or any kind of nut butter)

3 tablespoons gluten-free tamari

2 tablespoons maple syrup

1 Thai chile

Juice of 2 limes

1 teaspoon peeled and grated ginger

Water, as needed

Sea salt

1 In a food processor, put the peanut butter, tamari, maple syrup, chile, lime juice, and ginger and pulse to combine. Slowly add water, a tablespoon at a time, until the mixture becomes a thick but pourable sauce.

2 Taste and season with salt. Use immediately or transfer to an airtight container and refrigerate.

Storage: Store in an airtight container in the refrigerator for up to 1 week.

Prep Tip: Adjust the seasonings to reflect your personal taste for heat by adding more or less chile. This can be done with all the ingredients to adjust sweetness, acidity, and saltiness.

Per 2-tbs serving: Calories: 117; Total fat: 8g; Carbohydrates: 8g; Fiber: 1g; Protein: 4g; Calcium: 16mg; Vitamin D: 0mcg; Vitamin B12: 0mcg; Iron: 1mg; Zinc: 1mg

COCONUT CURRY SAUCE

DAIRY-FREE, GLUTEN-FREE

MAKES **2 quarts** //*PREP TIME* **15 minutes** //*COOK TIME* **15 minutes**

Everyone needs an easy, addictive curry recipe in their culinary repertoire, something that can be poured over everything. This sauce will liven up steamed vegetables, cooked lentils, egg salad, or grain dishes. You can simplify this sauce by replacing the spices with a good-quality curry powder blend. Winter squashes and pumpkin are particularly good with this sauce. I like to garnish it with wedges of lime, cilantro sprigs, and some toasted, chopped cashews.

2 tablespoons canola oil

½ medium yellow onion, finely chopped

4 garlic cloves, minced

1-inch piece fresh ginger, peeled and finely grated

1 tablespoon garam masala

2 tablespoons curry powder

2 tablespoons ground cumin

1 teaspoon ground coriander

1 teaspoon paprika (sweet or hot)

½ teaspoon turmeric

1 teaspoon sea salt

1 (14-ounce) can full-fat coconut milk

1 cup vegetable stock

½ cup tomato puree

1   Heat the oil in a medium saucepan or cast iron skillet on medium-high heat. Add the onion, garlic, and ginger and cook until the onion is soft and just turning golden, about 2 minutes.

2   Add the garam masala, curry powder, cumin, coriander, paprika, turmeric, and salt, and stir until fragrant, about 1 minute.

3   Add the coconut milk, stock, and tomato puree. Reduce the heat to medium-low, bring to a simmer, stirring frequently, and allow to simmer for 10 minutes.

4   Adjust the seasonings, then set aside to cool for later use.

Storage: Store the sauce in an airtight container in the refrigerator for up to 1 week.

Cooking Tip: Cook vegetables or lentils right in the curry sauce for an easy 30-minute, one-pot dinner.

Per 1-cup serving: Calories: 141; Total fat: 13g; Carbohydrates: 7g; Fiber: 2g; Protein: 2g; Calcium: 36mg; Vitamin D: 0mcg; Vitamin B12: 0mcg; Iron: 2mg; Zinc: 1mg

Almond Yogurt, Fruit & Muesli Parfait, page 83

CHAPTER FIVE

BREKFAST

Avocado Toast 76

Avocados Rancheros 77

Pumpkin Pancakes with Spiced Crema 80

Spicy Tofu Scramble 81

Power Pancakes 82

Almond Yogurt, Fruit & Muesli Parfait 83

Biscuits & Vegetarian Redeye Gravy 84

Peanut Butter Overnight Oats 86

Açai Breakfast Bowl 87

Spinach Crêpes with Black Bean Sauce 88

Sweet Potato & Colorado Bean Hash 90

Maple Whole-Grain Hot Cereal 91

Power Smoothie 92

Vegan Breakfast Sando 93

Cocoa-Chia Waffles 95

AVOCADO TOAST

DAIRY-FREE

SERVES **1** // *PREP TIME* **10 minutes** // *COOK TIME* **1 minute**

There's a reason why avocado toast is so popular—it's simply delicious. Easy to make and packed with nutrition, this dish is an energy-loaded breakfast, a balanced lunch, or an afternoon snack. This basic avocado toast recipe is versatile, so throw on any additional toppings you choose. I like to add any vegetables I might have in the kitchen, such as shaved radishes, diced tomatoes, or scallions.

1 (6-inch) slice multigrain baguette, about ½-inch thick

Extra-virgin olive oil, for brushing the bread

½ medium Hass avocado, pitted and peeled

1 teaspoon sea salt, plus more for garnish

1 teaspoon freshly ground black pepper

Juice from ½ lime

Pinch red pepper flakes, for garnish

1 Preheat the oven to broil. Lightly brush the bread with olive oil, place it on a baking sheet, and toast to the desired level of doneness, about 30 seconds per side.

2 Meanwhile, place the avocado, salt, pepper, and lime juice in a small bowl and mash with the back of a fork, leaving it a little chunky.

3 Spread the avocado mash on the toast.

4 Sprinkle the toast with red pepper flakes and sea salt and serve immediately.

Serving Tip: Add a fried egg, a sprinkle of cheese, or salsa to kick it up a little.

Per serving: Calories: 265; Total fat: 13g; Carbohydrates: 34g; Fiber: 8g; Protein: 7g; Calcium: 67mg; Vitamin D: 0mcg; Vitamin B12: 0mcg; Iron: 3mg; Zinc: 1mg

AVOCADOS RANCHEROS

GLUTEN-FREE

SERVES **2** // *PREP TIME* **30 minutes** // *COOK TIME* **1 hour 10 minutes**

This great twist on huevos rancheros offers all the crunch, spice, and richness of the traditional dish without the meat. It can easily be modified for vegans by omitting the egg and cheese. If you're a breakfast-for-dinner person, this dish is for you.

FOR THE RANCHERO SAUCE
3 medium tomatoes

1 red bell pepper

1 poblano pepper

1 tablespoon canola oil

½ teaspoon olive oil

1 small onion, diced

3 garlic cloves, chopped

¼ cup tomato paste

1 chipotle pepper in adobo

2 cups vegetable stock

FOR THE REFRIED BLACK BEANS
1 tablespoon canola oil

1 small onion, diced

1 cup cooked or canned black beans, liquid reserved

1 teaspoon sea salt

FOR ASSEMBLY
¼ teaspoon extra-virgin olive oil

4 (6-inch) corn tortillas, toasted or fried until crispy (organic corn tortilla chips are good, too)

4 avocados, peeled, pitted, and halved

2 cups ranchero sauce

1 cup refried black beans

8 large eggs (optional)

4 ounces queso fresco, crumbled (or any kind of soft cheese or non-dairy cheese)

TO MAKE THE RANCHERO SAUCE

1 Preheat the oven to 400°F. Line a baking sheet with parchment paper.

2 In a medium bowl, toss the tomatoes and bell pepper and poblano with the canola oil and place them on the baking sheet.

3 Roast the vegetables in the oven until they are lightly charred and soft, turning several times, for about 40 minutes. Remove from the oven and place them in a medium bowl and cover with plastic wrap. Let them steam for 15 minutes, then seed the peppers and roughly chop the tomatoes and peppers. Set aside.

4 Heat the olive oil in a medium saucepan over medium heat and sauté the onions until lightly browned, about 3 minutes. Add the garlic and continue to cook for 5 minutes, then add the tomato paste and sauté briefly.

5 Add the roasted tomatoes, poblano pepper, chipotle pepper, and vegetable stock, and bring to a simmer for 10 to 15 minutes.

6 Transfer the mixture to a food processor or blender and puree until smooth. Add the roasted red peppers to the finished tomato sauce and set aside.

CONTINUED

TO MAKE THE REFRIED BEANS

7 Heat the oil in a large sauté pan or skillet over medium-high and sauté the onions until translucent, about 3 minutes.

8 Add the black beans and ¼ cup of the bean cooking liquid to the skillet.

9 Use a potato masher to mash the beans in the skillet while you are cooking them, until they are a rough puree. Add more cooking liquid if necessary to keep the beans from getting dry. Season with salt to taste. Remove from the heat and set aside.

TO ASSEMBLE

10 Place a small skillet over medium heat and lightly coat with olive oil. Lightly toast the tortillas until they are lightly crisped but still flexible.

11 Crush the tortillas or chips in a food processor until they are a wet sand texture. Dredge the avocado halves in tortilla meal until they are completely coated.

12 Spoon 3 ounces of ranchero sauce onto a warm plate.

13 Place 1 tortilla-crusted avocado in the center of each plate and spoon a tablespoon of warm refried beans into the avocado half and top with 2 eggs per serving (if using).

14 Pour 2 to 3 ounces of ranchero sauce over the top, sprinkle with crumbled queso fresco, and serve warm.

Ingredient Tip: Any type of beans will work with this recipe, including chickpeas, which are delicious "refried."

Per serving: Calories: 1108; Total fat: 74g; Carbohydrates: 96g; Fiber: 37g; Protein: 30g; Calcium: 510mg; Vitamin D: 2mcg; Vitamin B12: 1mcg; Iron: 6mg; Zinc: 6mg

Power Pancakes, page 82

PUMPKIN PANCAKES *with* SPICED CREMA

SERVES 4 //*PREP TIME* 15 minutes //*COOK TIME* 15 minutes

When autumn rolls around, my restaurant guests start asking for these pancakes, and when pumpkin season is over, they beg me to keep them on the menu! These pancakes are light and fluffy, even though they are made with whole-wheat flour, so no one will suspect that they are healthy as well.

1¼ cups whole-wheat flour

1 tablespoon sugar

2 teaspoons baking powder

1 teaspoon ground cinnamon

¼ teaspoon ground cloves

⅛ teaspoon ground allspice

¾ teaspoon sea salt

1⅓ cups whole milk

¾ cup canned pumpkin puree

4 large eggs

¼ cup unsalted butter, melted

1 teaspoon vanilla extract

¼ cup canola oil or clarified butter, for cooking

¾ cup warm maple syrup, for serving

1   Sift the flour, sugar, baking powder, cinnamon, cloves, allspice, and salt into a large bowl and mix to blend.

2   In a medium bowl, whisk together the milk, pumpkin, eggs, melted butter, and vanilla until well blended.

3   Add the pumpkin mixture to the dry ingredients and whisk until just smooth.

4   Place a large nonstick sauté pan or skillet over medium heat and brush with oil.

5   Pour the batter by ⅓ cup measures into the skillet. Cook until bubbles form on the surface of pancakes and the bottoms are browned, and then flip them over to brown the other side, about 2 minutes per side. Set aside on a plate and cover them loosely with foil to keep warm.

6   Repeat with the remaining batter to make 8 pancakes.

7   Serve with warm maple syrup.

Serving Tip: I like to add caramelized apple slices and toasted pepitas to garnish these beautiful pancakes. Any kind of fruit compote or fresh fruit is a wonderful complement to the dish.

Per serving: Calories: 668; Total fat: 34g; Carbohydrates: 79g; Fiber: 6g; Protein: 14g; Calcium: 344mg; Vitamin D: 2mcg; Vitamin B12: 1mcg; Iron: 3mg; Zinc: 3mg

SPICY TOFU SCRAMBLE

DAIRY-FREE, GLUTEN-FREE

SERVES **4** *//PREP TIME* **20 minutes** *//COOK TIME* **20 minutes**

The key to a good tofu scramble is to press out as much water as possible from the tofu. So once your tofu is drained, press it in a tofu press or under a cast iron skillet to dry it. This spicy tofu scramble can be eaten any time of day, but it is a stellar protein-packed power breakfast that will get you all the way through to lunch. Serve it over avocado toast or as a taco or burrito filling with salsa and cheese.

½ tablespoon extra-virgin olive oil

1 poblano pepper, seeded and diced

1 small jalapeño pepper, seeded and diced

½ medium red onion, diced

3 plum tomatoes, hulled

1 store-bought roasted red bell pepper, chopped (about ½ cup)

1 tablespoon chili powder

1 tablespoon smoked paprika

1 teaspoon sea salt, plus more for seasoning

½ teaspoon ground cumin

¼ teaspoon ground turmeric

16 ounces firm tofu, drained and rinsed

Juice of 1 lime

1   Heat the oil in a large sauté pan or skillet over medium heat. Add the poblano pepper, jalapeño pepper, and red onion, and sauté until softened, 4 to 5 minutes.

2   While the vegetables are sautéing, place the plum tomatoes in a blender and pulse a few times to chop and puree them. Set aside.

3   Add to the sauté pan the roasted red pepper, chili powder, smoked paprika, sea salt, cumin, and

turmeric. Continue to sauté for 1 minute, or until fragrant.

4   Stir in the plum tomato puree, and crumble in the tofu. Simmer for about 10 minutes, until the liquid reduces, stirring occasionally.

5   Stir in the lime juice and continue to simmer, while stirring, for another 1 minute. Remove from the heat.

6   Season with salt as needed and serve immediately.

Storage: This can be stored in an airtight container in the refrigerator for up to 2 days.

Ingredient Tip: If you have easy access to an Indian or gourmet market, Himalayan black salt has a miraculous effect on tofu's flavor, making it taste exactly like scrambled eggs.

Per serving: Calories: 169; Total fat: 9g; Carbohydrates: 10g; Fiber: 4g; Protein: 13g; Calcium: 159mg; Vitamin D: 0mcg; Vitamin B12: 0mcg; Iron: 3mg; Zinc: <1mg

POWER PANCAKES

DAIRY-FREE, GLUTEN-FREE

SERVES 2 //*PREP TIME* 20 minutes //*COOK TIME* 10 minutes

I almost always have a protein smoothie for breakfast, but when I'm craving something heartier, these pancakes are a perfect fit. They are high in protein and satisfy your sweet tooth and, as a bonus, they can be whipped up as quickly as a smoothie. I always add whatever fruit I have around, such as berries, bananas, apples, or peaches. For a luxurious topping, mix together a little Greek yogurt, your favorite berries, and a touch of honey.

2 large eggs, separated

2 scoops vanilla protein powder

1 large very ripe banana

⅛ teaspoon ground cinnamon

¼ teaspoon baking powder

¼ teaspoon sea salt

½ cup sliced banana or berries

1 In a medium stainless steel bowl, beat the egg whites with a hand beater on high for 2 minutes until they form soft peaks. Set aside.

2 In a medium bowl, beat the egg yolks, protein powder, banana, cinnamon, baking powder, and salt with a hand beater until smooth.

3 Gently fold one-third of the egg white mixture into the egg yolk mixture until just combined. Fold another one-third of the egg whites into the mixture and finally the last one-third until all the ingredients are well combined.

4 Heat a medium sauté pan or skillet over low heat. Scoop ¼ cup of the mixture onto the skillet for each of the 4 pancakes and cook until golden brown, flipping once, about 1 minute on each side.

5 Serve warm with fresh fruit.

Storage: Leftover pancakes can be stored in an airtight container in the refrigerator for up to 2 days or in the freezer for up to 1 month.

Make Ahead: You can make a big batch of these in advance, store them in the refrigerator or freezer, and microwave or toast them for breakfast or a quick, healthy snack for kids.

Per serving: Calories: 302; Total fat: 7g; Carbohydrates: 29g; Fiber: 4g; Protein: 32g; Calcium: 191mg; Vitamin D: 1mcg; Vitamin B12: 1mcg; Iron: 1mg; Zinc: 1mg

ALMOND YOGURT, FRUIT & MUESLI PARFAIT

DAIRY-FREE

SERVES 4 //*PREP TIME* 10 minutes, plus 30 minutes to let sit //*COOK TIME* 2 minutes

This classic Swiss-style muesli bears little resemblance to the boxed grocery store cereal. If you've never tried fresh muesli, you will be pleasantly surprised. If you are traveling in Switzerland or Germany, you might find muesli served in the early evening as well as at breakfast. This vegan version is easy to whip up for a healthy morning treat; it can also be made with traditional dairy by the same method.

2 cups rolled oats

½ cup raisins, currants or your favorite dried fruit

1½ cups almond milk

⅓ cup slivered almonds

1¼ cups almond milk yogurt

1 tablespoon honey

4 medium red apples, cored

¼ cup freshly squeezed lemon juice

2 cups berries of your choice

Mint sprigs for garnish

1   Put the oats and raisins in a large bowl. Add the almond milk, stir to combine, and let sit at room temperature for 30 minutes, until the oats have absorbed all the milk.

2   Heat a small sauté pan or skillet over medium heat, add the almonds, and swirl the pan until they turn golden and fragrant, about 2 minutes. Transfer the almonds to a bowl to cool.

3   While the almonds are cooling, add the almond yogurt and honey to the oat mixture. Grate the apples with a box grater into the oats, add the lemon juice, and stir until combined. Set aside.

4   Spoon the muesli into bowls or dessert glasses. Top with the berries and toasted almonds.

5   Garnish with a sprig of mint and serve.

Ingredient Tip: Bananas, coconut milk, and dried mango or pineapple make fun substitutes if you crave tropical muesli.

Per serving: Calories: 531; Total fat: 16g; Carbohydrates: 94g; Fiber: 14g; Protein: 12g; Calcium: 324mg; Vitamin D: 2mcg; Vitamin B12: 0mcg; Iron: 4mg; Zinc: 3mg

BISCUITS & VEGETARIAN REDEYE GRAVY

SERVES **4** //*PREP TIME* **20 minutes** //*COOK TIME* **40 minutes**

Biscuits and sausage gravy is a classic Southern breakfast; this version uses portobello mushrooms instead of sausage and is surprisingly meaty. Top with eggs of any style (if you eat them) for a weekend brunch or satisfying meatless Monday dinner. Any kind of mushroom works here, but firm, flavorful portobellos are a great choice for the desired flavor. Don't forget the hot sauce on the side.

FOR THE GRAVY

3½ tablespoons unsalted butter, divided

1½ cups diced portobello mushrooms

½ teaspoon whole fennel seeds

¼ teaspoon dried thyme

¼ teaspoon red pepper flakes (see Kitchen Notes)

⅓ cup strong black coffee

1½ tablespoons all-purpose flour

2 cups whole milk

Sea salt

Freshly ground black pepper

FOR THE BISCUITS

8 tablespoons (1 stick) unsalted butter

2 cups all-purpose flour

2 teaspoons baking soda

½ teaspoon baking powder

1 teaspoon sugar

¾ teaspoon sea salt

1 cup buttermilk

TO MAKE THE GRAVY

1   Melt 2 tablespoons of butter in a large sauté pan or skillet over medium heat. Add the mushrooms, fennel seeds, thyme, and red pepper flakes, and sauté, stirring frequently, until they are deep golden brown and tender, 5 to 6 minutes. Add the coffee and simmer until almost evaporated, stirring frequently, for 4 to 5 minutes.

2   Remove the mushroom mixture from the heat, transfer to a bowl, and set aside. Melt the remaining 1½ tablespoons of butter in the same skillet and sprinkle in the flour. Cook, stirring constantly, until the flour is combined and turns golden brown, 2 to 3 minutes.

3   Stir in the milk and bring to a simmer over low heat, stirring until the gravy thickens, about 10 minutes.

4   Season with salt and pepper and set aside covered to keep warm.

TO MAKE THE BISCUITS

5   Preheat the oven to 475°F. Line a baking sheet with parchment paper.

6   Melt the butter in a small saucepan over low heat, then cool slightly.

7   In a large bowl, stir together the flour, baking soda, baking powder, sugar, and salt until well combined.

8   Pour the buttermilk into a small bowl. Stir in the melted butter and stir until the mixture begins to clump. Stir the buttermilk mixture into the flour mixture with a spatula and keep scraping the bottom of the bowl until all the flour is worked into the dough.

9   Using a greased ⅓ cup dry measure, scoop the dough and drop it onto the baking sheet, spacing the biscuits about 1½ inches apart. Form them into biscuit shapes, flattening and rounding them with your fingers.

10 Bake the biscuits until golden brown, 10 to 14 minutes. Remove the biscuits from the oven and allow them to cool on the baking sheet for a few minutes.

11 To serve, split the biscuits open, place them on a warm plate, and spoon the warm gravy over them.

Cooking Tip: I used a simple drop biscuit recipe here for simplicity, but if you have a favorite recipe, please use it. This recipe is also great with cornbread.

Per serving: Calories: 657; Total fat: 40g; Carbohydrates: 62g; Fiber: 3g; Protein: 14g; Calcium: 268mg; Vitamin D: 3mcg; Vitamin B12: 1mcg; Iron: 3mg; Zinc: 1mg

PEANUT BUTTER OVERNIGHT OATS

SERVES **2** *//PREP TIME* **15 minutes, plus overnight**

Looking at a busy week and don't know how you will find time for a meal? Look no further for a simple 15-minute, prep-ahead breakfast that is nutrient-dense with protein, as well as filling and delicious. I love peanut butter so much that I could eat this every day, and I use crunchy peanut butter for extra texture. For a special breakfast treat for kids, top the creamy oats with a bit of chopped dark chocolate or chocolate chips.

1½ cups unsweetened vanilla almond milk (or any plant milk)

⅓ cup chia seeds

¼ cup peanut butter

1 tablespoon maple syrup

1 teaspoon vanilla extract

¼ teaspoon sea salt

1 cup old-fashioned oats

1   In a blender, mix the almond milk, chia seeds, peanut butter, maple syrup, vanilla, and salt, and blend until smooth, starting on low speed and gradually increasing to high.

2   Add the oats and pulse to combine, leaving a little texture. Pour the mixture into 2 (8-ounce) glass jars and cover tightly with a lid. Place in the refrigerator overnight and enjoy the next day for breakfast.

Storage: Leftovers can be stored in a clean jar in the refrigerator for 1 day.

Serving Tip: I like to take my oats out of the refrigerator while I'm making my coffee to let it come to a cool room temperature.

Per serving: Calories: 529; Total fat: 29g; Carbohydrates: 54g; Fiber: 15g; Protein: 18g; Calcium: 552mg; Vitamin D: 2mcg; Vitamin B12: 0mcg; Iron: 7mg; Zinc: 4mg

86   WHOLE FOOD VEGETARIAN COOKBOOK

AÇAI BREAKFAST BOWL

GLUTEN-FREE

SERVES **2** // *PREP TIME* **20 minutes, plus 2 to 4 hours to freeze**

Açai, pronounced *ah-sigh-EE*, comes from the açai berry grown on the açai palm tree in South American rainforests. The bulk of its nutrition comes from the seeds, which contain more antioxidants than any other berry. The growing popularity of açai means that its frozen puree is a common product in most grocery stores; if you can, however, make your own at home, because the process is easy and wallet-friendly.

1 banana, sliced

½ cup blueberries

½ cup strawberries

¾ cup milk or juice (dairy, nut, or plant milk or any fruit juice)

½ cup plain yogurt (non-dairy for a vegan version)

200 grams (2 packets) frozen açai puree

Optional toppings like sliced fruits, nuts, seeds, fresh fruit, granola, or coconut

1 Slice the banana and place it on a baking sheet or on a plate lined with parchment paper. Add the blueberries and strawberries. Put the fruit in the freezer until the fruit freezes completely, 2 to 4 hours (store-bought frozen fruit is fine as well).

2 Pour the milk and yogurt into a blender. Add the frozen fruit and açai. Blend on low until smooth, adding additional liquid as needed to move the blades of the blender.

3 Divide the frozen fruit puree into 2 bowls and top with your favorite toppings.

Ingredient Tip: Açai is available in most freezer sections and from online sources. If you can't find it, simply increase the number of berries in the recipe to make up for the difference in volume.

Per serving: Calories: 239; Total fat: 9g; Carbohydrates: 33g; Fiber: 4g; Protein: 7g; Calcium: 209mg; Vitamin D: 1mcg; Vitamin B12: 1mcg; Iron: 1mg; Zinc: 1mg

SPINACH CRÊPES with
BLACK BEAN SAUCE

SERVES **4** //*PREP TIME* **20 minutes** //*COOK TIME* **30 minutes**

Crêpes are surprisingly easy to make, and the spinach in this recipe adds not only flavor and nutrients but also a beautiful bright green color. I love these crêpes served simply with a black bean sauce and a small salad; they are also great stuffed with scrambled eggs or roasted veggies.

FOR THE CRÊPES

2 teaspoons sea salt, divided

8 ounces fresh baby spinach

2 cups all-purpose flour

4 large eggs

1 cup milk

¾ cup cold water

4 tablespoons (½ stick) unsalted butter, melted

1 teaspoon canola oil

FOR THE BLACK BEAN SAUCE

1 tablespoon whole black peppercorns

4 bay leaves

2 tablespoons avocado oil

½ onion, diced

1 teaspoon dried basil

1 teaspoon sea salt

8 ounces canned black beans, drained and rinsed

1 cup water

1 cup crumbled queso fresco

TO MAKE THE CRÊPES

1 Fill a large bowl three-quarters full of ice water and set aside.

2 Bring 4 to 6 quarts of water and 1 teaspoon of salt to a boil in a medium saucepan over high heat. Add the spinach to the boiling water, let cook for 30 seconds, drain, and immediately plunge the spinach into the bowl of ice water. Once cool, drain the spinach thoroughly, roll it into a clean towel, and press to dry the spinach as much as possible.

3 In a large bowl, whisk together the flour and the eggs. Gradually add the milk and water, stirring to combine. Add the remaining 1 teaspoon of salt and the butter and whisk until smooth. Fold in the spinach puree.

4 Lightly oil a griddle or small skillet and place over medium-high heat. Pour or scoop the batter onto the griddle, using about ¼ cup of batter per crêpe. Tilt the pan with a circular motion so that the batter coats the surface evenly.

5 Cook the crêpe for about 2 minutes, until the bottom is light brown. Loosen with a spatula, turn, and cook the other side for 30 seconds.

6 Transfer the crêpe to a plate and cover it while you cook the remaining crêpes.

7   Place a small sauté pan or skillet over medium heat and toast the black peppercorns and bay leaves until fragrant, about 5 minutes.

8   Heat the avocado oil in a large skillet over medium-high heat. Add the onion, peppercorns, bay leaves, dried basil, and salt, and sauté until the onion is golden brown, stirring occasionally, about 3 minutes. Add the black beans and stir to combine. Remove from the heat and cool slightly.

9   Place the black bean mixture in a blender and blend in batches with the water, as needed, until very smooth and velvety.

10 Fold a warm crêpe into quarters and drizzle with the black bean sauce. Sprinkle with the queso fresco and serve warm.

Storage: Crêpes freeze well and can be frozen with layers of parchment paper between them in an airtight container for up to 1 month.

Serving Tip: If desired, stuff the crêpes with scrambled eggs, roasted vegetables, or cheese before adding the sauce.

Per serving: Calories: 703; Total fat: 35g; Carbohydrates: 73g; Fiber: 9g; Protein: 27g; Calcium: 371mg; Vitamin D: 3mcg; Vitamin B12: 1mcg; Iron: 7mg; Zinc: 3mg

SWEET POTATO & COLORADO BEAN HASH

DAIRY-FREE, GLUTEN-FREE

SERVES 4 //*PREP TIME* 20 minutes //*COOK TIME* 25 minutes

This warming hash is a fabulous winter brunch choice. Not only is it delicious with no embellishments, but you can also serve it over avocado toast or stuffed into corn tortillas for breakfast tacos. The recipe is an adaptation of a dish made by my former sous chef Anthony Cotroneo for one of our weekly chef challenges.

2 tablespoons olive oil

1 white onion, diced

1 red bell pepper, diced

1 poblano pepper, diced

1 small jalapeño pepper, thinly sliced

3 garlic cloves, thinly sliced

1 teaspoon ground coriander

1 teaspoon ground cinnamon

1 teaspoon ground cumin

8 ounces canned red kidney beans, plus the cooking liquid

1 cup water

2 large sweet potatoes, peeled and diced into ½-inch cubes

2 plum tomatoes, seeded and diced

1 teaspoon sea salt

1   Heat the oil in a large sauté pan or skillet over high heat and sauté the onion until it begins to soften and becomes golden brown, about 3 minutes. Add the bell pepper, poblano, jalapeño, garlic, coriander, cinnamon, and cumin, and sauté until the peppers are soft.

2   Lower the heat to medium. Add the beans, the bean cooking liquid, and the water, and bring the mixture up to a simmer. Add the sweet potatoes, tomatoes, and salt. Let the hash simmer until the sweet potatoes are fork-tender, about 20 minutes.

3   Adjust the seasonings as needed and serve warm.

Storage: The hash can be made ahead and stored covered in the refrigerator for 2 or 3 days.

Ingredient Tip: If eggs are part of your diet, this dish is amazing topped with a fried or poached egg.

Per serving: Calories: 231; Total fat: 7g; Carbohydrates: 38g; Fiber: 8g; Protein: 6g; Calcium: 89mg; Vitamin D: 0mcg; Vitamin B12: 0mcg; Iron: 3mg; Zinc: 1mg

MAPLE WHOLE-GRAIN HOT CEREAL

DAIRY-FREE

SERVES **4** // *PREP TIME* **15 minutes, plus overnight to soak** // *COOK TIME* **15 minutes**

There's nothing more comforting than a bowl of hot cereal on a cold morning. Instead of the usual oatmeal, try this nutty mixture of whole grains with a touch of maple for a special winter breakfast packed with nutrients. I love hot cereal with some banana slices on top. Feel free to add dried or fresh fruit, nuts, seeds, or shredded coconut. Mix it up and have some fun with it.

¼ cup amaranth grain

¼ cup quinoa

2 tablespoons steel-cut oats

2 tablespoons millet

2 tablespoons flaxseed

3 cups water, divided

1 tablespoon maple syrup

1 teaspoon sea salt

½ teaspoon ground cinnamon

¼ teaspoon ground nutmeg

¼ teaspoon ground cloves

1   Put the amaranth, quinoa, oats, millet, and flaxseed in a medium saucepan, then add 1½ cups of water. Cover the pan and allow the grains to soak at room temperature overnight.

2   In the morning, heat the saucepan with the soaked grains over medium heat. Add the maple syrup, salt, cinnamon, nutmeg, and cloves to the grain mixture, along with the remaining 1½ cups of water.

3   Bring to a simmer, stirring occasionally, and cook until the grains become soft and the mixture thickens.

4   Serve warm.

Ingredient Tip: For this recipe, you can use any of your favorite whole grains as long as the water to grains ratio is 3:1. I use my own favorite mix here, but make it your own and use the same method.

Per serving: Calories: 162; Total fat: 4g; Carbohydrates: 28g; Fiber: 5g; Protein: 6g; Calcium: 50mg; Vitamin D: 0mcg; Vitamin B12: 0mcg; Iron: 2mg; Zinc: 1mg

POWER SMOOTHIE

DAIRY-FREE, GLUTEN-FREE

SERVES 1 // *PREP TIME* 5 minutes

I have run a few marathons, and while the training is grueling, the reward is well worth it. I developed this easy-on-the-stomach smoothie to get me through a long morning run. I still have one of these for breakfast several times a week. The choice of fruits and vegetables is really up to you. This smoothie is lovely as well with berries or mango instead of the pineapple.

1 handful spinach or kale (about 1 cup)

1 frozen banana

1 small cucumber, peeled and diced

½ cup diced frozen pineapple

½ cup coconut water

¼ cup almond milk

¼ cup fruit juice of your choice (I like cherry)

1 tablespoon flax oil

6 to 8 mint leaves (optional)

1 scoop vanilla protein powder

* In a blender, combine the spinach, banana, cucumber, pineapple, coconut water, almond milk, fruit juice, flax oil, mint (if using), and protein powder, and puree until very smooth. Enjoy!

Prep Tip: To save time in the morning, I prep this in advance by portioning the spinach, banana, cucumber, pineapple, and mint in freezer bags and storing them in the freezer. Then I just pull out a bag, throw it into the blender with the liquids and protein powder, and blend.

Per serving: Calories: 525; Total fat: 18g; Carbohydrates: 67g; Fiber: 8g; Protein: 30g; Calcium: 443mg; Vitamin D: 1mcg; Vitamin B12: 0mcg; Iron: 3mg; Zinc: 1mg

VEGAN BREAKFAST SANDO

DAIRY-FREE

SERVES 4 //*PREP TIME* 20 minutes //*COOK TIME* 10 minutes

These flavor-packed vegan breakfast sandwiches feature tofu seasoned with Himalayan black salt. It's my vegan version of a Monte Cristo, a childhood fave that I can't seem to find anywhere anymore. I recommend vegan cheddar in the ingredients, but you can use whatever cheese is your favorite. There are more and more high-quality vegan cheeses available every day.

4 teaspoons extra-virgin olive oil, divided

5 to 10 slices tempeh bacon strips

1 (14-ounce) block firm tofu, drained, rinsed, and cut horizontally into 4 equal flat pieces

½ teaspoon turmeric

Himalayan black salt for seasoning (or any salt you have on hand)

1 teaspoon maple syrup

Freshly ground black pepper

4 slices vegan cheddar cheese

4 English muffins

4 teaspoons strawberry jam

1 avocado, mashed

4 slices tomato

1 In a medium sauté pan or skillet, heat 2 teaspoons of oil over medium-high heat. Add the tempeh bacon strips and sauté until warm, about 4 minutes. Remove the tempeh bacon from the skillet and set aside on a plate covered loosely with aluminum foil to keep warm.

2 Press the tofu gently with paper towels to remove any excess liquid.

3 Heat the remaining 2 teaspoons of oil in a large skillet over high heat. When the oil begins to shimmer, add the tofu, sprinkle the tofu with the turmeric, drizzle the maple syrup, and add a pinch of black salt. Flip the tofu slabs so that they evenly absorb the turmeric powder.

4 Cover the skillet with a lid, reduce the heat to medium, and allow the tofu to cook for 2 minutes. Flip the tofu again, checking for browned edges, and season with pepper.

5 Place the cheese slices on top of the tofu to melt. Set the skillet aside, allowing the tofu to stay warm.

CONTINUED

6 Toast the English muffins and spread the jam on 4 halves and the avocado mash on the other 4 halves.

7 Evenly divide the tofu, tempeh, and tomato on the avocado halves and top with the jam halves.

Ingredient Tip: It is possible to make your own tempeh bacon, but like the vegan cheeses, wholesome vegan meats are now readily available to purchase. Some of the brands I like are Field Roast and Monk's Meats.

Per serving: Calories: 468; Total fat: 24g; Carbohydrates: 43g; Fiber: 8g; Protein: 21g; Calcium: 272mg; Vitamin D: 0mcg; Vitamin B12: <1mcg; Iron: 5mg; Zinc: 1mg

COCOA-CHIA WAFFLES

DAIRY-FREE, GLUTEN-FREE

SERVES **4** *//PREP TIME* **10 minutes** *//COOK TIME* **20 minutes**

Who doesn't like waffles as an indulgent breakfast treat? By using cocoa powder with a coconut flour waffle recipe, you create a gluten-free and guilt-free version that tastes like chocolate cake. Top with Butterless Butter (page 36) and raspberries for an elegant brunch dish.

3 large eggs

⅓ cup coconut milk

¼ cup raw coconut oil

3 tablespoons maple syrup

2 tablespoons chia seeds

⅓ cup coconut flour

¼ cup cocoa powder

½ teaspoon baking soda

½ teaspoon sea salt

1 In a medium bowl, whisk the eggs until combined. Add the coconut milk, oil, maple syrup, and chia seeds. Stir well to combine.

2 Add the coconut flour, cocoa powder, baking soda, and salt, and stir well to combine.

3 Heat a waffle iron according to the manufacturer's instructions.

4 Use a ⅓ cup dry measure to ladle the batter onto the waffle iron and cook until golden and crispy, about 5 minutes. Repeat with the remaining batter to make 4 waffles in total.

Storage: The waffles can be placed in an airtight container and stored in the refrigerator for up to 2 days or in the freezer for up to 1 month.

Serving Tip: I like to top these waffles with some smashed raspberries and a drizzle of honey. They are also wonderful served with ice cream for dessert.

Per serving: Calories: 334; Total fat: 25g; Carbohydrates: 22g; Fiber: 8g; Protein: 8g; Calcium: 82mg; Vitamin D: 1mcg; Vitamin B12: <1mcg; Iron: 2mg; Zinc: 1mg

Beet Hummus Toast, page 116

CHAPTER SIX

SANDWICHES & HANDHELDS

The Better Black Bean Burger   98

Warm Pita with Hummus & Grilled Vegetables   100

PB & J   103

Vegan Ricotta, Peach & Basil Panini   105

Vegan Pulled Pork Sandwiches   106

Tofu Banh Mi   108

Vegan Egg Salad Sando   110

Grilled Mushroom Cheesesteaks   111

The Best BLT   112

Vegan Sloppy Joes   113

Guacamole Grilled Cheese   115

Beet Hummus Toast   116

Plant Meatball Marinara Hero   117

Avocado Milanesa Torta   119

THE BETTER BLACK BEAN BURGER

DAIRY-FREE

MAKES **8 (4-ounce) burgers** *//PREP TIME* **20 minutes** *//COOK TIME* **45 minutes**

There are a ton of meat alternatives out there, including some being served at fast-food chains. But if you are like me, you like to know what you are eating. I've experimented with many recipes for veggie burgers, and this is the one I keep coming back to—it really is better than the rest.

½ cup water

¼ cup red quinoa, rinsed

4 teaspoons extra-virgin olive oil, divided

1 small red onion, finely diced

Sea salt

Freshly ground black pepper

1 cup finely chopped mushrooms

2 cups canned black beans, drained and rinsed

1 cup finely grated raw beets

1 teaspoon ground cumin

½ teaspoon ancho chile powder

¼ teaspoon smoked paprika

½ cup raw walnuts, ground into a meal

1 Into a medium saucepan, pour the water and quinoa and bring to a boil over high heat. Reduce the heat to medium-low and simmer until the water is absorbed and the quinoa is tender, about 20 minutes. Remove from the heat and let sit for 5 minutes, then fluff with a fork. Set aside.

2 Heat 3 teaspoons of olive oil in a large sauté pan or skillet over medium-low heat. Sauté the onion for 5 minutes with a pinch of salt and pepper.

3 Increase the heat to medium and add the mushrooms. Season with another pinch of salt and pepper and cook until the mushrooms and onions are slightly browned and fragrant, about 3 minutes.

4 Remove the skillet from the heat, add the black beans, and mash to a rough paste, leaving a bit of texture.

5 Transfer the mixture to a large bowl and add the quinoa, beets, cumin, ancho chile powder, and paprika, and stir to combine.

6 Fold in the walnut meal a little at a time until the mixture sticks together when pressed. Form the mixture into 8 equal patties.

7 Heat the remaining 1 teaspoon of oil in a large skillet over medium-high heat and cook the patties until golden brown and crisp, 6 to 8 minutes per side.

8 Serve on a whole-grain bun or lettuce wrap with your favorite burger toppings.

Ingredient Tip: If you like a cheeseburger, add a slice of your favorite cheese (or vegan cheese) while cooking the burger on the second side. A gluten-free bun can replace the burger bun for a gluten-free burger.

Per serving: Calories: 208; Total fat: 11g; Carbohydrates: 22g; Fiber: 7g; Protein: 7g; Calcium: 61mg; Vitamin D: 0mcg; Vitamin B12: <1mcg; Iron: 2mg; Zinc: 1mg

WARM PITA *with* HUMMUS & GRILLED VEGETABLES

DAIRY-FREE

SERVES 4 // *PREP TIME* 30 minutes, plus 1½ hours to let rest // *COOK TIME* 15 minutes

Make your own pita at home? Yes. It's straightforward once you get the hang of it, and the warm, light, fluffy puffs of pita are well worth the effort. This is a fun project to share with kids; they will be mesmerized by the puffing of the bread, rewarding their hard work.

FOR THE PITAS

1 cup warm water

2 teaspoons active dry yeast

1 teaspoon sugar

2½ cups whole-wheat flour, divided, plus more for dusting

1 tablespoon extra-virgin olive oil

1½ teaspoons sea salt

FOR THE HUMMUS

1 recipe Mediterranean-Style Hummus (page 38)

FOR THE VINAIGRETTE

2 tablespoons balsamic vinegar

2 tablespoons light agave nectar

2 tablespoons fresh lime juice

6 tablespoons olive oil

Coarse salt

Freshly ground black pepper

FOR THE GRILLED VEGETABLES

3 Japanese eggplants

3 medium zucchini, cut lengthwise into ⅓-inch-thick pieces

2 red bell peppers, seeded

2 fresh ears corn, shucked

1 bunch scallions, white and light green parts only

3 tablespoons extra-virgin olive oil

Sea salt to taste

2 heads butter lettuce, leaves separated, cut into thick strips

½ pint grape tomatoes, quartered

2 avocados, diced

⅓ cup fresh cilantro, roughly chopped

¼ cup fresh basil, roughly torn

1 lime, quartered

TO MAKE THE PITAS

1   In a large bowl, combine the warm water, yeast, and sugar, and stir until dissolved. Stir in ½ cup of flour and let the mixture sit for 15 minutes at room temperature until the mixture bubbles.

2   Add the oil, salt, and the remaining 2 cups of flour and stir with a wooden spoon until dough begins to form. Dust a clean work surface with flour and knead until the dough becomes smooth and stretchy, about 8 minutes, adding more of the flour as needed. The dough should be soft and slightly moist. Place the dough in a large bowl and cover with a clean towel. Leave in a warm place until the dough has doubled in size, about 1 hour.

3 Dust a clean work surface with flour. Punch down the dough and turn it out onto the floured surface. Divide the dough into 8 pieces and roll them into balls. Cover the balls with a towel and let rest for 10 to 15 minutes.

4 Preheat a large cast iron skillet over medium heat. Working one at a time, flatten each ball into an 8-inch round, sprinkling the dough with a little extra flour if it sticks.

5 Place the pita rounds one at a time in the skillet and cook them until they begin to puff, then turn them over and cook for 1 minute more.

6 Cover the cooked pitas with a clean kitchen towel to keep them warm for serving.

TO MAKE THE HUMMUS

7 Make a small slit in the edge of each pita with a paring knife. Stuff the pitas with about 2 ounces of hummus and 4 ounces of grilled vegetables.

TO MAKE THE VINAIGRETTE

8 Whisk the vinegar with the agave nectar and lime juice in a bowl. Slowly whisk in the oil; add salt and pepper to taste. Set aside.

TO MAKE THE GRILLED VEGETABLES

9 Rub the eggplant, zucchini, red pepper, corn, and scallions with oil and sprinkle with salt. Grill the vegetables until browned and cooked through, about 10 minutes. Cut the zucchini and scallions into a medium dice. Cut the corn off the cob.

10 Toss the grilled vegetables with the lettuce, tomatoes, avocado, cilantro, and basil; toss with the vinaigrette; and garnish with lime quarters.

11 Serve immediately.

Ingredient Tip: You can leave out the small amount of sugar if you'd like, but the sugar contributes to the tenderness of the pita. For a lower glycemic index choice, coconut sugar is a good replacement.

Per serving: Calories: 1,390; Total fat: 71g; Carbohydrates: 164g; Fiber: 41g; Protein: 42g; Calcium: 327mg; Vitamin D: 0mcg; Vitamin B12: <1mcg; Iron: 14mg; Zinc: 5mg

PB & J

DAIRY-FREE

MAKES 4 sandwiches //*PREP TIME* 20 minutes, plus 1 hour to steep //*COOK TIME* 25 minutes

Sometimes, nothing is better than a humble peanut butter and jelly sandwich, and if you're a peanut butter addict like I am, that happens pretty often. This is my favorite way to make it, spiced up with a little hot pepper jam. The jam recipe can be used to make any kind of fruit jam.

4 cups halved fresh blackberries (or your favorite berries)

1 cup sugar, divided

4 jalapeño peppers, finely chopped

Juice and zest of 1 lemon

½ package dry pectin

8 thick slices of your favorite bread

Extra-virgin olive oil, for brushing the bread

¼ cup peanut butter

1 In a large bowl, combine the blackberries with ½ cup of sugar and let the mixture steep at room temperature, about 1 hour, stirring occasionally.

2 Transfer the berry mixture to a large saucepan, add the jalapeño peppers, lemon zest, and lemon juice, and place it over medium-high heat. Bring the mixture to a simmer, stirring occasionally, then reduce the heat to low and simmer for 15 minutes. The berries will produce a lot of liquid as they simmer. Once the fruit has softened, the liquid is reduced, and the mixture begins to thicken slightly, remove from the heat and cool slightly. Taste for sweetness and stir in the remaining ½ cup of sugar, or less, as needed.

3 Remove the mixture from the heat. Using an immersion blender or food processor, partially puree the berry mixture, leaving the texture somewhat chunky.

4 Return the berry mixture to a full boil over medium heat and very slowly add the pectin, stirring constantly so that it doesn't clump. Cook, stirring frequently, for about 5 minutes. Remove the jam from the heat and ladle it into clean jars. Let the jars cool for about 20 minutes, at room temperature, then transfer them to the refrigerator uncovered and let them cool completely before covering with lids.

5 Heat a charcoal grill, gas grill, or grill pan to medium-high. Meanwhile, prep the sandwiches by spreading the bread with the peanut butter and the jam, like making a regular PB & J, then brush the outsides of the bread with olive oil.

CONTINUED

6 Place the sandwiches on the grill, cover, and cook for about 2 minutes, until the bread has browned and has grill marks. Turn the sandwiches over, cover the grill, and cook for 1 minute more, until the other side is golden.

7 Transfer the sandwiches to a platter. Let them rest for 5 minutes and serve.

Ingredient Tip: If you find that you have very sweet berries, you may not need as much sugar, so use your taste buds to decide the amount. As with all recipes that contain fresh chile peppers, for a milder result, remove the seeds and the ribs, then rinse and dry the peppers.

Per serving: Calories: 619; Total fat: 13g; Carbohydrates: 119g; Fiber: 19g; Protein: 16g; Calcium: 93mg; Vitamin D: 0mcg; Vitamin B12: 0mcg; Iron: 4mg; Zinc: 3mg

VEGAN RICOTTA, PEACH & BASIL PANINI

DAIRY-FREE

SERVES 3 or 4 //*PREP TIME* 20 minutes //*COOK TIME* 10 minutes

This awesome summer sandwich is one of my favorites. The vegan ricotta is simple to make and can be used for any recipe that includes ricotta cheese. Serve it in the winter with slices of ripe pear and a drizzle of honey—any fruit in season is excellent.

FOR THE TOFU RICOTTA

½ (14-ounce) block extra-firm tofu, rinsed and drained

Juice and zest of 1 lemon

2 teaspoons extra-virgin olive oil

1 garlic clove, minced

½ teaspoon sea salt, plus more for seasoning

¼ teaspoon freshly ground black pepper, plus more for seasoning

2 teaspoons dried basil

FOR THE SANDWICHES

6 or 8 slices of your favorite bread (ciabatta is a great choice)

½ cup sliced ripe peach or frozen and thawed peach slices

½ bunch fresh basil

1 tablespoon agave nectar

2 tablespoons extra-virgin olive oil

TO MAKE THE TOFU RICOTTA

1 Place the tofu in a clean kitchen towel or paper towels and press and squeeze it in a colander to get as much of the liquid out as you can. Then place the tofu, lemon juice, lemon zest, oil, garlic, salt, pepper, and dried basil in a food processor. Pulse for about 1 minute, until the mixture is smooth but still retains some texture. Taste and season with salt and pepper.

TO MAKE THE SANDWICHES

2 Spread about ¼ cup of the tofu ricotta onto one slice of bread per sandwich, then top with the peach slices, basil, a drizzle of agave, and another piece of bread.

3 In a large sauté pan or skillet, heat the oil over medium-high heat. Place a sandwich in the skillet and press down with a spatula as it cooks. When one side is golden brown, about 1 minute, turn the sandwich over and press again until the other side is browned. Repeat with the remaining sandwiches.

4 Serve immediately.

Per serving: Calories: 455; Total fat: 16g; Carbohydrates: 62g; Fiber: 4g; Protein: 16g; Calcium: 121mg; Vitamin D: 0mcg; Vitamin B12: 0mcg; Iron: 5mg; Zinc: <1mg

VEGAN PULLED PORK SANDWICHES

SERVES **6** // *PREP TIME* **30 minutes** // *COOK TIME* **2 hours 15 minutes**

Jackfruit is a vegan's dream food, with a texture that both imitates meat and absorbs flavors quickly. This recipe for vegan pulled pork can even fool a carnivore. I usually buy frozen jackfruit, which reduces prep time, and it is just as delicious as fresh. Coleslaw mix tossed with cider vinegar, a bit of sugar, salt, and a drizzle of olive oil makes a fabulous topping for these sandwiches.

3 cups jackfruit, fresh or frozen

2 tablespoons extra-virgin olive oil

1 medium yellow onion, sliced

3 garlic cloves, minced

2 teaspoons sea salt

1 teaspoon freshly ground black pepper

1 teaspoon ground cumin

1 teaspoon chili powder

1 teaspoon smoked paprika

½ teaspoon cayenne powder

1 teaspoon vegan Worcestershire sauce

1 teaspoon liquid smoke

2 cups vegetable stock

½ cup barbecue sauce

6 vegan buns

Dairy-free coleslaw or greens, for serving

Pickle chips, for serving

1 Cut the jackfruit in half if using fresh. Carefully remove the core of the jackfruit by cutting into it diagonally. Pull each piece of fruit out and remove its seeds and the outer coating. Rinse the fruit thoroughly, then dry.

2 Heat the oil over medium heat in a stockpot or Dutch oven. Sauté the onion and garlic until the onion is softened and translucent, about 3 minutes. Add the jackfruit, salt, pepper, cumin, chili powder, paprika, cayenne, Worcestershire sauce, and liquid smoke. Stir to coat evenly.

3 Add the stock and bring to a simmer. Reduce the heat to low, cover, and simmer until the liquid is mostly reduced and the jackfruit has softened, about 45 minutes. Remove the pot from the heat.

4 Preheat the oven to 350°F. Line a baking sheet with parchment paper.

5 Spread the jackfruit on the baking sheet. Bake for 60 to 75 minutes, or until the jackfruit has dried and is a deeper brown color.

6 Pour the barbecue sauce over the jackfruit and toss to combine, then return to the oven for 15 minutes.

7 Serve the barbecue jackfruit warm on vegan buns with dairy-free coleslaw or lettuce and pickle chips.

Storage: The leftover pulled "pork" jackfruit can be kept in an airtight container in the refrigerator for up to 1 week and in the freezer for up to 6 months.

Ingredient Tips: For a quick sandwich, there are many great bottled barbeque sauces available, or make your own favorite recipe and keep a bottle stored in the refrigerator.

Per serving: Calories: 334; Total fat: 8g; Carbohydrates: 60g; Fiber: 5g; Protein: 8g; Calcium: 112mg; Vitamin D: 0mcg; Vitamin B12: 0mcg; Iron: 3mg; Zinc: 1mg

TOFU BANH MI

DAIRY-FREE

SERVES **2 to 4** //*PREP TIME* **20 minutes, plus 2 hours to chill** //*COOK TIME* **5 minutes**

A mash-up of traditional Vietnamese flavors with French influences makes this amazing sandwich a crowd-pleaser. Typically made with pork and pâté, this delicious vegetarian version is a light and refreshing change. Use a softer roll or baguette for easier eating or all the fillings might squish out on the first bite.

FOR THE TOFU

6 ounces extra-firm tofu

2 bulbs lemongrass, minced

1 garlic clove, minced

1 tablespoon avocado oil

1 tablespoon low-sodium soy sauce

1 teaspoon sesame oil

FOR THE PICKLES

1 cup water

½ cup white vinegar

¼ cup sugar

½ teaspoon sea salt

1 cup julienned daikon

1 cup julienned carrots

FOR THE SPREAD

¼ cup Eggless Mayonnaise (page 37)

1 tablespoon finely chopped cilantro

1 teaspoon low-sodium soy sauce

1 tablespoon avocado oil

FOR THE SANDWICHES

2 (8-inch) soft baguettes or other soft rolls

1 medium cucumber, cut lengthwise into ¼-inch-thick pieces

1 or 2 jalapeño peppers, sliced

Small handful cilantro

TO MAKE THE TOFU

1   Cut the tofu into ¼-inch-thick slices and press them between a clean kitchen towel or paper towels in a colander to get rid of the excess water.

2   In a shallow baking dish, combine the lemongrass, garlic, avocado oil, soy sauce, and sesame oil. Add the tofu and spoon the marinade over it to coat the slices completely. Cover and refrigerate for at least 2 hours.

TO MAKE THE PICKLES

3   In a large bowl, stir together the water, vinegar, sugar, and salt. Add the daikon and carrots and toss to combine. Cover and refrigerate for at least 1 hour. Drain before using.

4 In a small bowl, whisk together the mayonnaise, cilantro, and soy sauce. Set aside.

5 Heat the avocado oil in a large sauté pan or skillet over medium heat. Add the tofu and sauté until brown and crisp on each side, about 4 minutes in total.

6 Slice the baguettes in half lengthwise. Spread the mayonnaise on both halves of each baguette. Pile on the tofu, pickles, cucumber, jalapeño, and cilantro as desired.

7 Serve.

Storage: The leftover cooked tofu will keep in an airtight container in the refrigerator for up to 3 days.

Tip: For the vegetable pickling liquid, the measurements given are flexible; feel free to adjust the sugar, vinegar, and salt to your own taste.

Per serving: Calories: 757; Total fat: 36g; Carbohydrates: 92g; Fiber: 7g; Protein: 20g; Calcium: 219mg; Vitamin D: 0mcg; Vitamin B12: 0mcg; Iron: 4mg; Zinc: 1mg

VEGAN EGG SALAD SANDO

DAIRY-FREE

SERVES **4** *//PREP TIME* **15 minutes**

Vegan egg salad is put together in a snap and is customizable with your favorite add-ins like pickles, herbs, flavored mustard, or curry powder. This sandwich filling is the perfect versatile meal-prep staple. I find this "egg" salad just as delicious as the real thing.

1 (14-ounce) block tofu (silken, soft, or medium-firm, as you prefer)

¼ cup Eggless Mayonnaise (page 37)

1 celery stalk, diced

1 heaping tablespoon mustard

½ teaspoon turmeric

Pinch sea salt

Pinch freshly ground black pepper

2 tablespoons finely chopped chives

8 slices bread, your choice

Leafy greens, for serving (optional)

Red onion, thinly sliced (optional)

Radishes, thinly sliced (optional)

1   Place the tofu in a clean kitchen towel or paper towels over a colander and press gently to remove excess moisture, pressing to crumble gently.

2   In a medium bowl, stir together the mayonnaise, celery, mustard, turmeric, salt, and pepper until combined. Add the tofu and chives and gently fold them into the mayonnaise mixture until well coated.

3   Serve on your favorite bread with leafy greens (if using), red onion (if using), and radish (if using).

Storage: Place the "egg" salad in the refrigerator in an airtight container for up to 5 days.

Ingredient Tips: For a gluten-free sandwich, use your favorite gluten-free bread or make lettuce wraps.

Per serving: Calories: 310; Total fat: 14g; Carbohydrates: 35g; Fiber: 8g; Protein: 15g; Calcium: 138mg; Vitamin D: 0mcg; Vitamin B12: <1mcg; Iron: 4mg; Zinc: 1mg

GRILLED MUSHROOM CHEESESTEAKS

SERVES 4 *//PREP TIME* 15 minutes *//COOK TIME* 35 minutes

Grilled portobello mushrooms create a soul-satisfying twist on the classic Philly cheesesteak. These hefty sandwiches are a marvelous make-ahead meal for a sports viewing or movie party. You can prep the sandwiches the morning of the event, refrigerate, and heat just before serving. You won't miss any of the game or movie.

2 tablespoons extra-virgin olive oil, divided

1 green bell pepper, thinly sliced

1 large onion, thinly sliced

2 large portobello mushrooms, gills removed and thinly sliced (see Tip)

1 tablespoon vegan Worcestershire sauce

Sea salt

Freshly ground black pepper

8 slices provolone or mozzarella cheese (or vegan cheese)

4 ounces sliced hot or sweet pickled banana peppers (optional)

4 sandwich rolls, sliced lengthwise most of the way through, leaving a "hinge"

1 Preheat the oven to 250°F.

2 Heat 1 tablespoon of olive oil in a large sauté pan or skillet over medium-high heat. Add the green pepper and onion and sauté until they soften and turn golden, 8 to 10 minutes. Add the mushrooms and cook for 5 minutes more, or until softened and browned.

3 Add the Worcestershire sauce and increase the heat to high. Cook until the liquid has evaporated, 2 to 3 minutes.

4 Reduce the heat to low and season with salt and pepper. Top the vegetable mixture with the cheese slices. Once the cheese has melted, remove the skillet from the heat.

5 Divide the veggie mixture between the sandwich rolls and garnish with banana peppers, if using. Wrap each cheesesteak tightly with foil and place it on a baking sheet. Bake for 15 minutes. Remove from the oven, unwrap carefully, and serve hot.

Ingredient Tip: The mushroom gills have a tendency to discolor the bread and onions, so I always remove them before cooking. It takes only a second to scoop them out with a spoon.

Per serving: Calories: 399; Total fat: 19g; Carbohydrates: 37g; Fiber: 3g; Protein: 18g; Calcium: 375mg; Vitamin D: <1mcg; Vitamin B12: <1mcg; Iron: 3mg; Zinc: 1mg

THE BEST BLT

DAIRY-FREE

SERVES **4** // *PREP TIME* **15 minutes**

Everyone loves the smoky flavor of bacon, but it's not something we want in our daily diet. Tempeh bacon re-creates this beloved classic sandwich in a more wholesome way. The sandwich is ideal made in the summer when tomatoes are at their best. Try doubling the recipe and serving the sandwiches open-faced as a tasty meatless Monday dinner option.

1 package tempeh bacon

½ cup Eggless Mayonnaise (page 37)

1 garlic clove, minced

8 slices rye bread or your favorite bread

1 ripe avocado, sliced or smashed

2 large tomatoes at room temperature, sliced

1 head romaine lettuce or romaine hearts

Sea salt

Freshly ground black pepper

1 Cook the tempeh bacon according to package instructions. Set aside.

2 In a small bowl, whisk together the mayonnaise and garlic until combined.

3 Lightly toast the bread slices and spread 1 tablespoon of the garlic mayo on each slice of bread.

4 Layer with the avocado, tomato, lettuce, and tempeh bacon.

5 Season with salt and pepper, then top with another slice of bread.

6 Serve.

Ingredient Tip: If eggs are part of your diet, regular mayo is fine for this sandwich. For tempeh bacon, I like Lightlife brand, which is excellent quality and made with all-natural ingredients.

Per serving: Calories: 588; Total fat: 28g; Carbohydrates: 64g; Fiber: 16g; Protein: 23g; Calcium: 190mg; Vitamin D: <1mcg; Vitamin B12: <1mcg; Iron: 6mg; Zinc: 2mg

VEGAN SLOPPY JOES

DAIRY-FREE

SERVES **4** // *PREP TIME* **15 minutes** // *COOK TIME* **35 minutes**

This savory, sweet, spicy sandwich is a terrific plant-forward choice for feeding a family. Sloppy joes were one of my favorite dinners growing up, and this version made with meaty lentils instead of ground beef is the one I love to eat now. It will even win over skeptical meat lovers. Make your own tomato sauce or choose one like Trader Joe's that contains only wholesome ingredients with no chemical preservatives.

2 cups water or Basic Vegetable Stock (page 32)

1 cup lentils, rinsed and picked through for pebbles

2 tablespoons extra-virgin olive oil

1 small yellow onion, minced

2 garlic cloves, minced

1 green bell pepper, diced

Sea salt

Freshly ground black pepper

1 (15-ounce) can tomato sauce

2 tablespoons coconut sugar (see Tip), plus more as needed

2 tablespoons vegan Worcestershire sauce, plus more as needed

2 teaspoons chili powder, plus more as needed

1 teaspoon ground cumin

Pinch smoked paprika

4 gluten-free or whole-wheat hamburger buns

1 Put the water and lentils in a medium saucepan over medium-high heat. Bring to a boil, then reduce the heat to low and simmer uncovered for 18 to 20 minutes, or until just tender. Drain the lentils and rinse them under cold water to stop the cooking process. Set aside.

2 While the lentils are cooking, heat the oil in a large sauté pan or skillet over medium heat. When the oil begins to shimmer, add the onion, garlic, and bell pepper. Season with salt and pepper and stir to combine.

3 Sauté for about 5 minutes, stirring frequently, or until the peppers and onions are tender and golden brown. Add the tomato sauce, coconut sugar, Worcestershire sauce, chili powder, cumin, and paprika. Stir to combine.

4 Once the lentils are cooked, add them to the onion mixture in the skillet and stir to combine. Cook the mixture over medium-low heat until it thickens to the texture you like, stirring occasionally, 5 to 10 minutes.

CONTINUED

5 Taste and add more chile powder, sugar, or Worcestershire to balance flavors, as desired. Toast the buns, then spoon the hot mixture onto them and serve.

Storage: Leftover sloppy joe mixture will keep in a covered container in the refrigerator for up to 5 days or in the freezer for up to 1 month.

Ingredient Tip: I like to use coconut sugar for the recipe because it has a delicious caramel flavor and a lower glycemic index than regular sugar. If you don't have it, light brown sugar or sugar in the raw are suitable substitutes.

Per serving: Calories: 494; Total fat: 13g; Carbohydrates: 83g; Fiber: 14g; Protein: 19g; Calcium: 53mg; Vitamin D: 0mcg; Vitamin B12: 0mcg; Iron: 5mg; Zinc: 2mg

GUACAMOLE GRILLED CHEESE

SERVES **2** *//PREP TIME* **10 minutes** *//COOK TIME* **5 minutes**

This mash-up comes from making a "family meal" at my restaurant, and the staff always loves sandwich day. When there's some guacamole left from lunch service, we griddle up these warm sandwiches and serve them, with baked sweet potato wedges and salad, to a very happy family of staff. This is another recipe that is wide open for customization, like adding slices of tempeh bacon or ripe tomatoes. I once mashed in a bit of leftover sweet potato, and it was delicious!

1 recipe Fresh, Chunky Guacamole (page 41)

4 slices whole-grain bread

4 slices pepper Jack cheese (or vegan cheese)

2 teaspoons unsalted butter (or vegan butter), divided

1. Spoon 2 to 3 ounces of guacamole onto two slices of bread, spread it out evenly, and top with the cheese. Place the other 2 slices of bread on top to form 2 sandwiches.

2. Melt 1 teaspoon of butter in a cast iron skillet or griddle over medium-high heat. Add the sandwiches and grill on one side for about 2 minutes, or until golden and crispy. Add the remaining 1 teaspoon of butter, flip the sandwiches, and grill until golden brown. Serve warm.

Ingredient Tip: Use the same method but substitue corn tortillas for the bread to make a guacamole quesadilla.

Per serving: Calories: 903; Total fat: 61g; Carbohydrates: 79g; Fiber: 30g; Protein: 24g; Calcium: 394mg; Vitamin D: 0mcg; Vitamin B12: <1mcg; Iron: 5mg; Zinc: 4mg

BEET HUMMUS TOAST

DAIRY-FREE

SERVES 4 //*PREP TIME* 15 minutes //*COOK TIME* 45 minutes

Beets are a vegetable that people have strong feelings about—you either love them or you hate them. I land firmly in the love category. This simple, red-hued hummus is a treat served on toast or pita, or as a dip for fresh vegetables.

1 beet, scrubbed, rinsed, and dried

4 tablespoons extra-virgin olive oil, divided

1 (15-ounce) can chickpeas, drained and rinsed, or 1½ cups cooked

2 garlic cloves, smashed

Juice of ½ lemon, plus more as needed

Pinch sea salt

Pinch freshly ground black pepper

8 slices 12-grain bread, toasted

1 avocado, sliced

1 recipe Crispy Cinnamon Chickpeas (page 44)

1 Preheat the oven to 375°F.

2 In a small bowl, rub the beet with 1 tablespoon of oil and wrap in foil. Place in the oven and roast until cooked through, about 45 minutes. Remove from the oven and let cool until you can safely remove the foil. Peel the beet and chop it coarsely.

3 Place the chickpeas, remaining 3 tablespoons of oil, and garlic in a food processor and blend. While the food processor is running, add the lemon juice (plus more as desired, to taste).

4 Add the beet and blend until smooth. Season with salt and pepper.

5 Spread the toast with the beet hummus. Top with the avocado and sprinkle with crispy chickpeas. Serve immediately.

Storage: The beet hummus can be stored in an airtight container in the refrigerator for up to 2 days.

Serving Tip: This recipe makes a particularly beautiful and easy canapé for parties: just top smaller toast triangles or crackers with the beet hummus.

Per serving: Calories: 824; Total fat: 35g; Carbohydrates: 110g; Fiber: 28g; Protein: 25g; Calcium: 181mg; Vitamin D: 0mcg; Vitamin B12: 0mcg; Iron: 6mg; Zinc: 3mg

PLANT MEATBALL MARINARA HERO

SERVES **4** *//PREP TIME* **30 minutes** *//COOK TIME* **1 hour**

These versatile "meatballs" can be made both gluten-free and vegan depending on your preference. They can be served over regular pasta, over a grain mix, or on vegetable ribbons with marinara sauce as an entrée. I like to make a big batch and freeze some for a quick weeknight dinner.

¾ cup dried lentils (or 2 cups cooked or canned)

2 tablespoons extra-virgin olive oil, divided, plus more for greasing and for brushing

1 medium yellow onion, diced

3 garlic cloves, minced, divided

1 cup rolled oats

2 tablespoons tomato paste

1 tablespoon soy sauce or tamari

1½ teaspoons red wine vinegar

1 teaspoon dried oregano

1 teaspoon dried thyme

1 teaspoon dried basil

½ teaspoon red pepper flakes

½ teaspoon liquid smoke (optional, see Tip)

½ teaspoon sea salt, plus more for seasoning

½ teaspoon freshly ground black pepper, plus more for seasoning

1 recipe marinara sauce (page 176)

4 hero or other soft rolls (gluten-free, if desired)

¼ cup grated Parmesan cheese (or vegan cheese)

1   Put the dried lentils in a small saucepan and cover them with cold water by about 2 inches. Place the saucepan on high heat and bring to a boil. Reduce the heat to low and simmer, uncovered, for about 20 minutes, until the lentils are tender.

2   Remove the lentils from the heat and drain. Give the lentils a quick rinse in cold water to stop the cooking process.

3   Heat 1 tablespoon of oil in a medium sauté pan or skillet over medium heat. When the oil begins to shimmer, add the onion and sauté for about 5 minutes, until soft and translucent. Add two-thirds of the garlic

and sauté for about 1 minute more. Remove from the heat.

4   Preheat the oven to 400°F. Lightly oil a baking sheet.

5   Place the oats in a food processor and blend to a powder. Add the cooked lentils, cooked onion and garlic, remaining one-third of garlic, tomato paste, soy sauce, vinegar, oregano, thyme, basil, red pepper flakes, liquid smoke (if using), salt, and pepper in a food processor. Pulse a couple of times just to combine the ingredients and retain texture. Taste the mixture and adjust any of the seasonings as desired.

CONTINUED

6 Roll the mixture into 1-inch balls (about 24 of them) and arrange them on the baking sheet. Lightly brush or spray the balls with the remaining 1 tablespoon of olive oil. Bake for 25 to 30 minutes, until firm and golden brown, flipping them halfway through.

7 While the meatballs are baking, heat the marinara in a medium saucepan over medium heat and bring to a simmer. Reduce the heat to low and keep warm until you are ready to serve the sandwiches.

8 Split the rolls lengthwise leaving a "hinge," fill with 6 meatballs each, top with hot marinara sauce, and sprinkle with Parmesan cheese.

Ingredient Tip: Liquid smoke is made from condensing the smoke vapor into a liquid flavoring. Many people are concerned about whether it is safe or not. It does contain carcinogens in tiny amounts, and while I wouldn't necessarily drink a bottle of it, using it in small quantities for a special recipe is not a concern.

Per serving: Calories: 643; Total fat: 24g; Carbohydrates: 73g; Fiber: 11g; Protein: 24g; Calcium: 212mg; Vitamin D: 0mcg; Vitamin B12: <1mcg; Iron: 6mg; Zinc: 2mg

AVOCADO MILANESA TORTA

SERVES 4 //*PREP TIME* 30 minutes, plus 30 minutes to let sit //*COOK TIME* 20 minutes

This is a vegetarian version of the famous Milanesa torta made in Mexico. It is a wonder of textures and flavors, and one of the most magical things you will ever eat. Typically made with chicken or beef, avocado makes a great plant-forward substitution.

4 ripe avocados, sliced

2 cups panko bread crumbs, seasoned with salt

4 pasilla Oaxaca chiles, stemmed and seeded (or any type of dried chiles or chili powder)

1 cup Eggless Mayonnaise (page 37)

Sea salt

2 tablespoons extra-virgin olive oil

2 cups cooked black beans or 2 (15-ounce) cans, drained and rinsed

Freshly ground black pepper

2 cups canola oil

8 slices tempeh bacon

4 sandwich rolls

4 ounces shredded queso Oaxaca or mozzarella cheese

1 cup shredded romaine lettuce

2 tomatoes, sliced

1 white onion, thinly cut into rings

1   Preheat the oven to 200°F.

2   In a shallow baking dish, dredge the avocado slices in the bread crumbs, pressing gently for the bread crumbs to adhere, and set aside.

3   Toast the chiles in a large sauté pan or skillet over medium-high heat until they become flexible and slightly translucent, about 30 seconds. Put the chiles in a medium bowl and cover by 1 inch with boiling water. Place a plate on top of the chiles to weigh them down and allow them to sit for 30 minutes.

4   Strain the chiles (reserve the soaking liquid) and place them in a food processor along with the mayonnaise. Process at high speed, using a little of the soaking liquid as needed to move the blades. Season with salt.

5   Heat the olive oil in a large skillet over medium heat and add the beans. Warm the beans and mash them with the back of a fork until you have a spreadable texture. Season with salt and pepper.

6   Heat the canola oil in a large skillet to 350°F. Fry the avocados in a single layer in 2 batches until golden brown, turning once, about 6 minutes in total. Repeat until all the avocado slices are fried.

7   Place the avocado on an ovenproof plate and put it in a warm oven.

CONTINUED

8   Place a large skillet over medium-high heat and cook the tempeh bacon until crispy and warm, turning once, about 6 minutes. Place the bacon in the oven on the plate with the avocado.

9   When ready to serve, remove the avocado and bacon from the oven and preheat the oven to broil. Split the sandwich rolls down the center and scoop out excess bread. Place the rolls on a baking sheet and toast under a broiler until golden, about 30 seconds.

10 For each sandwich, spread the top half with the mayonnaise. Spread the bottom half with the warm bean mash. Top the bottom half of the roll with bacon, 2 fried avocado slices, shredded cheese, lettuce, tomato, and onion. Top with the top half of the roll. Serve hot.

Cooking Tip: It is also possible to bake the avocados for this dish: just spread them out on a lightly oiled baking sheet and bake at 400°F until golden and crispy, about 10 minutes.

Per serving: Calories: 2,093; Total fat: 178g; Carbohydrates: 107g; Fiber: 25g; Protein: 35g; Calcium: 394mg; Vitamin D: <1mcg; Vitamin B12: <1mcg; Iron: 7mg; Zinc: 3mg

Heirloom Tomato & Watermelon Salad, page 130

CHAPTER SEVEN

BOWLS, SALADS
& SIDES

Vegan Brussels Sprout Caesar Salad   124

Kale, Frisée & Asparagus Salad with Toasted Pepita Vinaigrette   125

Lentil Salad with Caramelized Shallots & Feta   127

Pear, Arugula & Endive Salad with Candied Walnuts   128

Heirloom Tomato & Watermelon Salad   130

Watercress, Jicama & Orange Salad   131

Fennel, Apple & Celery Salad   132

Black-Eyed Pea & Baby Spinach Salad   133

Grains & Greens Bowl   134

Sweet Potato & Lentil Bowl   135

Vegan Macaroni & Cheese   137

Ancient Grain & Wild Mushroom Pilaf   139

Brussels Sprouts with Chile & Mint   141

Coconut Cauliflower Rice   142

Creamless Creamed Corn   143

Collard Greens with Pickled Apples & Walnuts   144

Gingered Sweet Potato Mash   146

Lemon-Herb Red Quinoa   147

VEGAN BRUSSELS SPROUT CAESAR SALAD

DAIRY-FREE, GLUTEN-FREE

SERVES 2 //*PREP TIME* 5 minutes

This Caesar salad is made heartier and more nutritious by using Brussels sprouts to replace the traditional romaine lettuce. The toasted almonds add a satisfying crunch and keep the salad gluten-free. If you want even more texture, serve the dish with croutons instead. Top this salad with some tofu, seitan, tempeh, or avocado for a protein-packed dinner entrée.

8 ounces Brussels sprouts, shaved on a mandoline, or cored and leaves separated

3 ounces Vegan Caesar Dressing (page 66)

1 small bunch Italian parsley leaves

2 tablespoons toasted almond slices, for serving

2 tablespoons shaved vegan Parmesan cheese, for serving

Freshly ground black pepper

1   In a medium bowl, toss together the Brussels sprouts, dressing, and parsley.

2   Transfer the salad to a serving bowl or plates and sprinkle with the toasted almonds and Parmesan.

3   Season with pepper and serve.

Ingredient Tip: I love the texture and sweet flavor of shaved Brussels sprouts, and many grocery stores sell them already shaved, saving you the work. If you don't have a mandoline, cut off the small core of the Brussels sprouts with a paring knife and separate the leaves.

Per serving: Calories: 236; Total fat: 14g; Carbohydrates: 23g; Fiber: 7g; Protein: 8g; Calcium: 128mg; Vitamin D: 0mcg; Vitamin B12: <1mcg; Iron: 4mg; Zinc: 1mg

KALE, FRISÉE & ASPARAGUS SALAD with TOASTED PEPITA VINAIGRETTE

DAIRY-FREE, GLUTEN-FREE

SERVES 1 //*PREP TIME* 30 minutes //*COOK TIME* 10 minutes

This is a vegetarian take on a classic frisée aux lardons, one of my favorite salads. I use tempeh bacon here and an egg, but if you want to substitute another protein source for the egg, toss in some chickpeas or crumbled farmer cheese.

FOR THE TOASTED PEPITA VINAIGRETTE

1 cup fresh cilantro

1 scallion, both white and green parts

¼ cup extra-virgin olive oil

¼ cup Eggless Mayonnaise (page 37)

¼ cup freshly squeezed lime juice

3 tablespoons store-bought toasted pepitas

1 large garlic clove

1 teaspoon red wine vinegar

½ teaspoon honey

1 teaspoon sea salt, plus more for seasoning

FOR THE SALAD

Sea salt

2 spears jumbo asparagus

2 tablespoons extra-virgin olive oil, divided

½ cup frisée, washed and dried

½ cup shredded kale

1 teaspoon avocado oil

2 ounces tempeh bacon, diced

1 teaspoon freshly ground black pepper

2 ounces toasted pepita vinaigrette

1 large egg (optional)

2 tablespoons store-bought toasted pepitas, for garnish

TO MAKE THE TOASTED PEPITA VINAIGRETTE

1 Put the cilantro, scallion, olive oil, mayonnaise, lime juice, pepitas, garlic, vinegar, honey, and salt in a blender and blend on high for about 30 seconds, until the dressing is smooth and creamy.

2 Adjust the seasoning as necessary and set aside.

TO MAKE THE SALAD

3 Fill a medium saucepan half full with water, then place it over medium-high heat and add a pinch of salt. Bring to a boil and add the asparagus. Cook until crisp-tender, about 2½ minutes. Drain and toss the asparagus in 1 tablespoon of olive oil, place on a plate, and put in the refrigerator to cool.

4 When it is cool, cut the asparagus into thirds and put the pieces in a large bowl. Tear the frisée into bite-size pieces and place them in the bowl along with the kale.

5 Heat the avocado oil in a large, heavy sauté pan or skillet over medium heat. Cook the tempeh bacon,

CONTINUED

stirring occasionally, until golden. While the bacon is cooking, in a small bowl, stir together the remaining 1 tablespoon of olive oil and the pepper.

6 Add the warm bacon to the bowl with the greens and asparagus, then add the vinaigrette and toss to coat thoroughly. Arrange the salad on a serving plate and garnish with pepitas.

7 Fill a small saucepan three-quarters full of water and bring to a simmer over high heat. Reduce the heat to low so that the water simmers gently, and poach the egg (if using) for about 2 minutes. Immediately remove the egg with a slotted spoon and place on top of the salad. Drizzle with the black pepper oil and a sprinkle of sea salt, as desired.

Storage: The dressing will keep in the refrigerator for up to 1 week in an airtight container.

Ingredient Tip: Pepitas are hulled pumpkin seeds. They are high in protein and fiber and can be found in the nut section of the grocery store. Pepitas are great on their own as a snack or sprinkled on pretty much anything.

Per serving: Calories: 646; Total fat: 56g; Carbohydrates: 21g; Fiber: 9g; Protein: 22g; Calcium: 129mg; Vitamin D: 0mcg; Vitamin B12: <1mcg; Iron: 6mg; Zinc: 3mg

LENTIL SALAD with CARAMELIZED SHALLOTS & FETA

GLUTEN-FREE

SERVES 2 //*PREP TIME* 15 minutes //*COOK TIME* 30 minutes

The feta adds a bright punch of flavor to the earthy lentils and sweet shallots in this hearty salad. Serve it with homemade bread and hummus for a comforting weeknight dinner, or as a great side dish or component for a grain bowl. The leftovers are lovely cold over greens as a light lunch.

3 tablespoons extra-virgin olive oil

5 shallots, thinly sliced

2 cups water or vegetable broth

1 cup French (or other dried) lentils

½ cup chopped fresh basil

1 cup crumbled feta, regular or vegan

Sea salt

Freshly ground black pepper

2 cups baby arugula, or other greens

2 ounces Pomegranate Vinaigrette (page 68)

1 In a heavy sauté pan or skillet, heat the olive oil over medium heat until it shimmers, then add the shallots. Reduce the heat to low, cover, and cook for about 15 minutes, or until the shallots are soft and caramelized, stirring occasionally. Set aside to cool.

2 In a medium saucepan, combine the water and lentils and bring to a boil over high heat. Reduce the heat to low and simmer until the lentils are just tender, about 15 minutes. Remove from the heat, rinse the lentils with cool water to stop the cooking process, and transfer to a medium bowl. Let the lentils cool completely.

3 To the lentils, add the basil, feta, and caramelized shallots, and stir well to combine. Season with salt and pepper.

4 In another medium bowl, toss the arugula with the pomegranate vinaigrette.

5 Serve the greens on a plate topped with the lentil mixture. Serve immediately.

Storage: The cooked lentils will keep in an airtight container in the refrigerator for up to 1 week.

Per serving: Calories: 819; Total fat: 37g; Carbohydrates: 87g; Fiber: 16g; Protein: 34g; Calcium: 520mg; Vitamin D: <1mcg; Vitamin B12: 1mcg; Iron: 9mg; Zinc: 3mg

PEAR, ARUGULA & ENDIVE SALAD with CANDIED WALNUTS

DAIRY-FREE, GLUTEN-FREE

SERVES 4 //*PREP TIME* 15 minutes //*COOK TIME* 15 minutes

This colorful winter salad is one of my favorites. Pears are at their absolute best in December, which makes this a superb holiday entertaining dish. Just add some grains or tofu for protein to make it a complete meal. If you don't have time to candy the nuts, plain toasted walnuts (or any kind of nuts) are just as delicious.

FOR THE CANDIED WALNUTS

Nonstick vegetable oil spray

1 cup walnuts

2 tablespoons agave nectar

1 tablespoon coconut sugar

½ teaspoon sea salt

¼ teaspoon freshly ground black pepper

Generous pinch cayenne pepper

FOR THE SALAD

1 tablespoon sherry wine vinegar

1 tablespoon fresh lemon juice

1 tablespoon chopped fresh parsley

1 teaspoon Dijon mustard

3 tablespoons walnut oil or extra-virgin olive oil

2 tablespoons extra-virgin olive oil

Sea salt

Freshly ground black pepper

3 cups arugula, torn into pieces

2 heads red Belgian endive, trimmed, leaves separated

2 firm ripe pears, halved, cored, and thinly sliced lengthwise

TO MAKE THE CANDIED WALNUTS

1 Preheat the oven to 325°F. Spray a baking sheet with nonstick spray.

2 In a medium bowl, combine the walnuts, agave nectar, coconut sugar, salt, pepper, and cayenne pepper. Toss until the walnuts are completely coated. Spread the nut mixture on the prepared baking sheet.

3 Bake until the nuts are a deep golden and the sugar mixture is bubbling, stirring occasionally to break up clumps, about 15 minutes. Cool completely on the baking sheet.

4 Transfer to an airtight container and store at room temperature for up to 5 days.

5   In a medium bowl, whisk together the vinegar, lemon juice, parsley, and mustard until well combined. Add the walnut and olive oils and whisk until well blended. Season with salt and pepper.

6   In a large bowl, toss the arugula with enough dressing to coat it. Arrange the arugula on a plate and top it with endive and pear. Drizzle with more dressing, sprinkle with the candied walnuts, and serve.

Storage: The walnuts can be stored in an airtight container in the pantry for up to 2 weeks.

Ingredient Tip: This salad is particularly good with some crumbled blue cheese, feta, or goat cheese. Cheese also adds some protein, so if you eat dairy, I highly recommend throwing a bit on top.

Per serving: Calories: 459; Total fat: 34g; Carbohydrates: 38g; Fiber: 13g; Protein: 8g; Calcium: 193mg; Vitamin D: 0mcg; Vitamin B12: 0mcg; Iron: 3mg; Zinc: 3mg

HEIRLOOM TOMATO & WATERMELON SALAD

DAIRY-FREE, GLUTEN-FREE

SERVES **2** // *PREP TIME* **15 minutes** // *COOK TIME* **3 minutes**

This absolutely gorgeous and refreshing summer salad is a great light meal. Fortunately, heirloom tomatoes and watermelon peak at the same time, so you use the freshest seasonal ingredients when they are at their best. This salad can also be made with any ripe summer fruit like plums or peaches.

1 tablespoon sesame seeds, toasted, for garnish

1 small bunch wild or regular arugula

2 ounces Agave-Lime Vinaigrette (page 64), plus more as needed

¼ small watermelon, quartered and cut into ½-inch-thick slabs

1 medium heirloom or beefsteak tomato, sliced

2 ounces Dairy-Free Soft Cheese (page 33), or farmer cheese

6 to 8 small basil leaves

½ red onion, sliced and rinsed in ice-cold water

1. In a small sauté pan or skillet over medium heat, toast the sesame seeds, shaking the skillet, for about 3 minutes. Set aside.

2. In a small bowl, toss the arugula and vinaigrette until well combined.

3. Evenly divide the arugula between 2 serving plates.

4. Place the watermelon slabs on top of the arugula and top with a few tomato slices, cheese crumbles, basil leaves, and onion slices.

5. Drizzle with more agave-lime vinaigrette, if desired.

6. Garnish with toasted sesame seeds and serve.

Ingredient Tips: I like to rinse the onion for this salad to mellow its bite. This Mediterranean-style salad is really great with feta cheese if you eat dairy.

Per serving: Calories: 200; Total fat: 6g; Carbohydrates: 31g; Fiber: 5g; Protein: 6g; Calcium: 96mg; Vitamin D: 0mcg; Vitamin B12: <1mcg; Iron: 1mg; Zinc: 1mg

WATERCRESS, JICAMA & ORANGE SALAD

DAIRY-FREE, GLUTEN-FREE

SERVES 2 // *PREP TIME* **15 minutes**

This crunchy, light, and refreshing salad is a Mexican classic. It combines a little kick from peppery, nutrient-dense watercress with the sweetness of juicy oranges. Any peppery green like arugula or mizuna is fine in place of watercress; whatever is freshest is the best choice. Pile this salad on top of a grilled Mexican-spiced slab of tofu for a weeknight fiesta.

2 oranges

1 small jicama, peeled and cut into matchsticks

½ small bunch cilantro leaves

¼ cup Orange Vinaigrette (page 70)

Sea salt

Freshly ground black pepper

1 bunch watercress, thick stems trimmed

½ ounce store-bought toasted pepitas

1 Cut the peel and white pith from the oranges. Over a large bowl to catch the juices, cut the oranges between the membranes to release the segments into the bowl.

2 Add the jicama and cilantro to the bowl and toss to mix. Add the dressing and toss to coat. Season with salt and pepper.

3 Arrange the watercress on a serving platter. Top with the orange salad and pepitas and serve.

Serving Tip: This salad is ripe for customization: use pink grapefruit in place of oranges; add pomegranate seeds, nuts, or feta cheese to make it a light meal in itself.

Per serving: Calories: 304; Total fat: 17g; Carbohydrates: 37g; Fiber: 13g; Protein: 5g; Calcium: 100mg; Vitamin D: 0mcg; Vitamin B12: 0mcg; Iron: 2mg; Zinc: 1mg

FENNEL, APPLE & CELERY SALAD

DAIRY-FREE, GLUTEN-FREE

SERVES **4** // *PREP TIME* **15 minutes**

This crunchy, textured, and brightly colored salad never fails to cheer me up on a gray winter day. I love apples, any kind of apples, but the juicy, sweet-tart McIntosh has always been my favorite. Use your own favorite apples to personalize this salad.

2 McIntosh apples, cored and thinly sliced

2 small fennel bulbs, trimmed, halved vertically, and thinly sliced

2 celery stalks, thinly sliced (reserve the leaves for garnish)

½ cup fresh parsley leaves

¼ cup fresh mint leaves

Pomegranate Vinaigrette (page 68)

Sea salt

Freshly ground black pepper

Extra-virgin olive oil for drizzling (optional)

½ cup walnuts, lightly toasted

1   In a large bowl, toss together the apples, fennel, celery, parsley, and mint. Add the vinaigrette and toss to coat. Season with salt and pepper.

2   Drizzle the salad lightly with oil (if using).

3   Sprinkle with the walnuts and celery leaves and serve immediately.

Make Ahead: If you're prepping ahead, place the apple slices in ice water with a little bit of lemon juice to keep them from browning.

Per serving: Calories: 520; Total fat: 38g; Carbohydrates: 47g; Fiber: 10g; Protein: 5g; Calcium: 129mg; Vitamin D: 0mcg; Vitamin B12: 0mcg; Iron: 2mg; Zinc: 1mg

BLACK-EYED PEA & BABY SPINACH SALAD

DAIRY-FREE, GLUTEN-FREE

SERVES **2** // *PREP TIME* **15 minutes, plus 1 hour to marinate** // *COOK TIME* **20 minutes**

My mother is from the South, so I ate a lot of black-eyed peas growing up, and I still love their earthy sweetness. Serve this for New Year's Day brunch for good luck.

2 ears of corn, shucked

2 tablespoons canola oil, divided

Sea salt

Freshly ground black pepper

2 cups fresh black-eyed peas

2 tablespoons extra-virgin olive oil

Juice of 2 lemons

1 teaspoon balsamic vinegar

1 small red bell pepper, finely diced

1 small red onion, finely diced

½ small bunch cilantro, finely chopped

1 teaspoon ground cumin

1 jalapeño pepper, seeded and minced

6 ounces fresh baby spinach

1 Preheat a grill or heat a grill pan to medium heat. Brush the corn with 1 tablespoon of the canola oil and season with salt and pepper. Lightly brush the grill with the remaining 1 tablespoon of canola oil and grill the corn until it is lightly charred and almost tender, about 5 minutes. Remove from the heat and cool until you can handle the cobs. Over a medium bowl, cut the kernels from the cobs.

2 Fill a medium saucepan three-quarters full with water, add the black-eyed peas, and bring to a boil over medium-high heat. Cook the peas until tender, 10 to 12 minutes. Drain the peas, refresh them under cold water, and pat them dry.

3 In a large bowl, whisk together the olive oil, lemon juice, and balsamic vinegar. Season with salt and pepper.

4 Add the grilled corn, black-eyed peas, bell pepper, onion, cilantro, cumin, and jalapeño and toss well. Cover and refrigerate the salad for at least 1 hour or up to 4 hours to allow the flavors to combine.

5 Just before serving, toss the salad with the spinach.

Per serving: Calories: 521; Total fat: 25g; Carbohydrates: 67g; Fiber: 14g; Protein: 19g; Calcium: 153mg; Vitamin D: 0mcg; Vitamin B12: 0mcg; Iron: 8mg; Zinc: 4mg

GRAINS & GREENS BOWL

DAIRY-FREE, GLUTEN-FREE

SERVES **4** *//PREP TIME* **15 minutes** *//COOK TIME* **35 minutes**

Grain bowls have been an ongoing hot food trend for good reasons: they're easy to put together and are composed of nutrient-dense ingredients. Mix and match different grains, veggies, and sauces for endless versatility. Bowls are a great way to upcycle leftovers.

4 cups water or vegetable broth

½ cup uncooked farro, rinsed

½ cup uncooked lentils

½ tablespoon extra-virgin olive oil

1 cup corn kernels cut off the cob, or frozen and thawed (see Tip)

Sea salt

Freshly ground black pepper

1 cup halved cherry tomatoes

1 cup sliced cucumbers (see Tip)

1 cup sugar snap peas, stringed

1 avocado, peeled, pitted, and sliced

1 small bunch fresh basil leaves

2 tablespoons store-bought toasted sunflower seeds

1 recipe Thai-Inspired Peanut Sauce (page 71)

1. Bring the water to a boil in a medium saucepot over high heat. Add the farro and cook for about 10 minutes. Add the lentils and continue cooking for 20 minutes more, until the farro and lentils are both just tender. Drain and rinse in cold water. Set aside in the strainer to cool completely.

2. Heat the oil in a small skillet over medium-high heat and sauté the corn for 3 minutes. Season the corn with salt and pepper.

3. To serve, arrange the bowls with the farro and lentil mixture on the bottom. Arrange the cherry tomatoes, cucumbers, and sugar snap peas attractively on top, add a few avocado slices, sprinkle with the basil and sunflower seeds, and drizzle with the peanut sauce.

Ingredient Tip: If corn isn't in season, it freezes well and frozen can be substituted for fresh here. To peel or not to peel cucumbers? It's up to you, but keep in mind many of the nutrients and fiber are retained in the skin.

Per serving: Calories: 560; Total fat: 27g; Carbohydrates: 67g; Fiber: 13g; Protein: 22g; Calcium: 81mg; Vitamin D: 0mcg; Vitamin B12: 0mcg; Iron: 5mg; Zinc: 3mg

SWEET POTATO & LENTIL BOWL

DAIRY-FREE, GLUTEN-FREE

SERVES 4 *//PREP TIME* 20 minutes *//COOK TIME* 55 minutes

Sweet potatoes are a powerhouse of nutrition and one of my favorite foods to eat and cook in my restaurant. This Indian-inspired dish can be customized to your taste and is great for meal preppers because it holds up exceptionally well in the refrigerator for a few days.

1 large sweet potato, skin left on, scrubbed, and cut into medium cubes

1 cauliflower head, cut into large florets, stalk diced

1 tablespoon garam masala (see Tip)

3 tablespoons avocado oil, divided

Sea salt

Freshly ground black pepper

2 garlic cloves

8 ounces lentils

1-inch piece fresh ginger, peeled and grated

1 teaspoon whole-grain mustard

Juice of 2 limes, divided

2 medium carrots, grated

½ small red cabbage, shredded

½ small bunch cilantro, chopped

1   Preheat the oven to 375°F.

2   In a large bowl, toss the sweet potato, cauliflower, garam masala, and 1½ tablespoons of oil until well coated. Season with salt and pepper.

3   Place the vegetables and garlic in a large roasting pan, and roast for 30 to 35 minutes, until the vegetables are golden brown and just tender.

4   While the vegetables are roasting, put the lentils in a medium saucepan and cover with about 2 inches of cold water. Bring to a boil over high heat, then reduce the heat to low and simmer for about 20 minutes until the lentils are just tender. Drain and rinse under cool water to stop the cooking process.

5   Remove the garlic cloves from the roasting pan and smash them with the side of a knife. Put the garlic in a large bowl with the remaining 1½ tablespoons of oil, the ginger, the mustard, and half the lime juice. Whisk to combine and add the still slightly warm lentils, then stir and season to taste.

6   In a medium bowl, toss together the carrots, cabbage, cilantro, and remaining half of the lime juice. Season with salt and pepper.

CONTINUED

7 Divide the lentil mixture among 4 bowls. Top each serving with a quarter of the carrot slaw and a quarter of the sweet potato and cauliflower mix. Serve immediately or refrigerate for later use.

Storage: Leftovers can be stored in an airtight container in the refrigerator for up to 4 days.

Ingredient Tip: Garam masala is an Indian spice blend that can contain more than 30 ingredients, and it's a great pantry item for adding an exotic touch to your veggies. If you don't have any on hand, you can mimic the basic flavor by combining 1 part ground cumin and ¼ part ground allspice.

Per serving: Calories: 403; Total fat: 12g; Carbohydrates: 61g; Fiber: 13g; Protein: 19g; Calcium: 113mg; Vitamin D: 0mcg; Vitamin B12: 0mcg; Iron: 5mg; Zinc: 3mg

VEGAN MACARONI & CHEESE

DAIRY-FREE, GLUTEN-FREE

SERVES **2** // *PREP TIME* **30 minutes** // *COOK TIME* **15 minutes**

We all love a little indulgence every now and then, but it doesn't have to be an unhealthy choice. This cheesy, creamy mac and cheese is one of our most popular dishes at BKLYNwild, and I'm happy to share it with you. I like to add broccoli to create a balanced dish, and I love the flavor combo, but if you'd prefer, omit the broccoli altogether. You can also substitute another favorite vegetable such as kale or any kind of legume.

8 ounces whole-grain macaroni (see Tip)

1 head broccoli, cut into small florets

1½ tablespoons avocado oil

1 small yellow onion, chopped

½ teaspoon sea salt, plus more for seasoning

1 small baking potato, peeled and grated

3 garlic cloves, minced

½ teaspoon garlic powder

½ teaspoon onion powder

½ teaspoon dry mustard powder

Pinch red pepper flakes

1 cup water, plus more as needed

⅔ cup raw cashews

¼ cup nutritional yeast

1 tablespoon apple cider vinegar

1 Bring a large stockpot of salted water to boil for the pasta. Cook the pasta until al dente, about 15 minutes. Add the broccoli when 2 to 3 minutes remain. Drain, and place the mixture back in the pot and set aside.

2 While the pasta is cooking, in a medium sauté pan or skillet, heat the oil over medium heat. Add the onion and a pinch of salt and cook, stirring, until the onion is soft and translucent, 3 to 4 minutes.

3 Add the grated potato, garlic, garlic powder, onion powder, mustard powder, salt, and red pepper flakes to the skillet. Stir to combine, and cook, stirring, for 1 minute.

4 Add the water and cashews and stir to combine. Bring the mixture to a simmer. Reduce the heat to low and continue simmering, stirring frequently, until the potatoes are cooked through, about 5 minutes. Remove the skillet from the heat and cool slightly.

CONTINUED

5 Transfer the mixture to a blender, add the nutritional yeast and vinegar, and blend until the mixture is silky smooth, about 2 minutes, scraping down the sides as needed. If the mixture won't blend easily, add a bit of water one tablespoon at a time until you get the desired consistency.

6 Season with salt, then add the sauce to the pasta. Stir over low heat until the pasta is well coated with the cheese sauce and serve immediately.

Storage: Leftovers can be stored in an airtight container in the refrigerator for up to 4 days.

Substitution Tip: For a gluten-free version, use your favorite gluten-free pasta. I've lately become a big fan of cauliflower pasta; it mimics the texture of wheat pasta better than any version of gluten-free pasta that I've tried.

Per serving: Calories: 930; Total fat: 33g; Carbohydrates: 140g; Fiber: 25g; Protein: 39g; Calcium: 220mg; Vitamin D: 0mcg; Vitamin B12: 5mcg; Iron: 11mg; Zinc: 6mg

ANCIENT GRAIN & WILD MUSHROOM PILAF

DAIRY-FREE

SERVES 4 //*PREP TIME* **15 minutes** //*COOK TIME* **1 hour**

This healthy pilaf is a go-to recipe for me; it's great for meal prepping, and it can be used in a grain bowl, in a salad, or as a side dish. This recipe makes a bunch, and I use it throughout the week; it can be cut in half, as needed.

- 1 tablespoon unsalted butter (or dairy-free butter)
- 1 tablespoon avocado oil or extra-virgin olive oil
- 1 small onion, finely chopped
- 1 garlic clove, minced
- 2 cups sliced shiitake mushrooms
- 2 cups sliced cremini mushrooms
- 1 cup pearl barley
- ½ cup soft wheat berries
- ¼ cup millet
- ½ cup wild rice, rinsed
- 3 cups hot vegetable stock
- ¼ cup chopped fresh herbs, such as basil, parsley, thyme, oregano, chives
- 2 tablespoons extra-virgin olive oil
- Sea salt
- Freshly ground black pepper

1   Preheat the oven to 350°F.

2   Melt the butter in a large ovenproof stockpot or Dutch oven with a lid over low heat. Add the oil, onion, and garlic. Cook until the onion is softened and translucent, 5 to 6 minutes. Increase the heat to medium-high and add the shiitake and cremini mushrooms. Cook until soft and golden, about 5 minutes, allowing any liquid to release and evaporate.

3   Add the barley, wheat berries, millet, and wild rice, and stir well, coating them with oil. Cook, stirring often, for 10 to 15 minutes. Stir in the stock and bring to a boil. Cover the pot and put it in the oven. Bake for 30 minutes, or until the grains are soft. Remove from the oven and fold in the chopped herbs.

4   To serve, drizzle with olive oil, season with salt and pepper, and serve hot.

Storage: The pilaf will keep in an airtight container in the refrigerator for 3 or 4 days.

Ingredient Tip: You can use any type of mushrooms. Asparagus or green beans are good options as well. For a gluten-free dish, substitute buckwheat, amaranth, or teff for the barley and wheat berries.

Per serving: Calories: 535; Total fat: 15g; Carbohydrates: 89g; Fiber: 15g; Protein: 15g; Calcium: 45mg; Vitamin D: <1mcg; Vitamin B12: <1mcg; Iron: 3mg; Zinc: 2mg

BRUSSELS SPROUTS *with* CHILE & MINT

DAIRY-FREE, GLUTEN-FREE

SERVES **4** //PREP TIME **10 minutes** //COOK TIME **10 minutes**

I love Brussels sprouts, always have, even as a child. They are best in fall and winter; seek them out at a farmers' market while they are still on the stalk for the absolute best quality. If you think you don't like them, just try them prepared this way, and I believe you will change your mind!

1 tablespoon extra-virgin olive oil

¼ teaspoon red pepper flakes

1½ pounds Brussels sprouts, trimmed and cut lengthwise into ¼-inch-thick pieces

½ teaspoon sea salt, plus more for seasoning

⅓ cup vegetable stock or water

1 teaspoon dried mint

3 or 4 fresh mint sprigs, for garnish

1   Heat the oil with the red pepper flakes in a large sauté pan or skillet over medium-high heat until the oil shimmers. Add the Brussels sprouts and salt, and sauté until crisp-tender, about 5 to 6 minutes.

2   Add the stock and simmer until evaporated and the Brussels sprouts are tender, about 2 minutes.

3   Remove the skillet from the heat and stir in the dried mint. Adjust the seasonings and serve with fresh mint sprigs.

Storage: Leftovers can be stored in an airtight container in the refrigerator for up to 2 days.

Substitution Tip: If you're not a fan of Brussels sprouts, this preparation is also great with green beans, spinach, kale, or any vegetable that you like to eat.

Per serving: Calories: 105; Total fat: 4g; Carbohydrates: 16g; Fiber: 7g; Protein: 6g; Calcium: 76mg; Vitamin D: 0mcg; Vitamin B12: <1mcg; Iron: 3mg; Zinc: 1mg

COCONUT CAULIFLOWER RICE

DAIRY-FREE, GLUTEN-FREE

SERVES 4 //*PREP TIME* **10 minutes** //*COOK TIME* **10 minutes**

This yummy way of preparing cauliflower is ideal for introducing kids to this versatile vegetable, which is a natural carrier for other flavors. I love serving this side with curries because it soaks up the taste of the curry while cooling down the heat at the same time. I like to leave the ginger and cinnamon whole in this recipe and remove them before serving to retain the beautiful white color of the dish.

1 medium cauliflower head, cut into large florets

½ tablespoon coconut oil

¼ cup finely diced white onion

1 inch cinnamon stick, preferably Ceylon

1-inch piece fresh ginger, smashed (see Tip)

1 cup full-fat coconut milk

¼ cup unsweetened coconut flakes

Sea salt

1   Grate the cauliflower in a food processor with the grating attachment, or pulse until the cauliflower resembles rice.

2   Heat the oil in a large sauté pan or skillet over medium-high heat. Add the onion and sauté until tender, about 5 minutes. Add the cinnamon stick and ginger and stir with a wooden spoon until fragrant, about 30 seconds.

3   Add the cauliflower rice and coconut milk, stirring to combine. Sauté the cauliflower rice for 5 to 6 minutes, until the coconut milk is absorbed, and stir in the coconut flakes.

4   Remove the cinnamon stick and ginger and season with salt before serving.

Storage: Leftovers can be stored in an airtight container in the refrigerator for up to 2 days.

Prep Tip: Ginger can be smashed with the back of a knife to release the oils and flavor without peeling. I use this technique often when I just want to flavor a dish with ginger; it also saves time.

Per serving: Calories: 193; Total fat: 16g; Carbohydrates: 13g; Fiber: 5g; Protein: 4g; Calcium: 45mg; Vitamin D: 0mcg; Vitamin B12: 0mcg; Iron: 1mg; Zinc: 1mg

CREAMLESS CREAMED CORN

DAIRY-FREE, GLUTEN-FREE

SERVES **4** //*PREP TIME* **15 minutes** //*COOK TIME* **20 minutes**

This dairy-free version of creamed corn is rich and delicious, with the pureed corn mimicking the cream. Add some roasted peppers and cilantro for a Southwestern touch. Creamed corn is a classic barbecue side dish, so try this vegan version with the Barbecue Tofu Kebabs (page 218).

4 ears corn, shucked and kernels removed, divided

1 cup corn stock or vegetable stock (see Tip)

Sea salt

2 tablespoons non-dairy butter

1 small yellow onion, finely diced

2 garlic cloves, minced

Freshly ground black pepper

1 Put half the corn and the stock in a food processor with a pinch of salt. Process until mostly smooth, retaining a bit of the texture.

2 Melt the butter in a large sauté pan or skillet over medium heat. Add the onion and sauté until soft and translucent, about 3 minutes. Add the garlic and cook 1 minute more.

Add the remaining half of the corn and warm gently, about 4 minutes.

3 Add the pureed corn mixture to the skillet, reduce the heat to low, and cook for about 10 minutes, stirring occasionally.

4 Season with salt and pepper and serve.

Storage: Leftovers can be stored in an airtight container in the refrigerator for up to 4 days.

Cooking Tip: Simmer the cobs from the corn for 10 minutes to make a quick corn stock or to enhance your veggie stock.

Per serving: Calories: 162; Total fat: 7g; Carbohydrates: 25g; Fiber: 3g; Protein: 4g; Calcium: 10mg; Vitamin D: 0mcg; Vitamin B12: 0mcg; Iron: 1mg; Zinc: 1mg

COLLARD GREENS with PICKLED APPLES & WALNUTS

DAIRY-FREE, GLUTEN-FREE

SERVES 4 // *PREP TIME* **20 minutes, plus 1 hour to chill** // *COOK TIME* **5 minutes**

This Southern-inspired, hearty, and beautiful fall dish is great for holiday entertaining and can be served warm or cold. Kale, chard, and spinach also work well, so use your favorite dark leafy greens. Dice up a bit of crisp tempeh bacon and sprinkle it over the top for an unexpected burst of flavor.

2 red apples

1 cup water

½ cup cider vinegar

½ cup sugar

1½ teaspoons sea salt, divided

1 teaspoon pickling spice (see Tip)

¼ cup extra-virgin olive oil

½ cup walnut halves

1 bunch collard greens (about 1 pound)

Freshly ground black pepper

1 Quarter and core the apples, then cut each quarter lengthwise into ⅛-inch-thick slices.

2 In a medium saucepan, bring the water, vinegar, sugar, 1 teaspoon of salt, and pickling spice to a boil over medium-high heat, stirring until the sugar is dissolved. Add the apples and return to a boil. Remove from the heat, transfer the apples to a bowl, and cool slightly. Chill, uncovered, in the refrigerator until cold, about 1 hour.

3 Heat the oil in a small sauté pan or skillet over medium heat. Toast the walnuts, stirring occasionally, until golden, then let the nuts cool in the oil. Transfer the nuts to a cutting board with a slotted spoon, reserving the oil, and coarsely chop them.

4 Halve each collard leaf lengthwise with a paring knife, cutting out and

discarding the tough rib. Stack the leaves and cut them crosswise into ¼-inch-wide strips. Transfer them to a large bowl.

5 Add the nuts and the oil from the skillet to the collards and toss with the remaining ½ teaspoon of salt. Season with pepper. Add the apple slices, discarding the pickling liquid and spices, and toss again. Serve.

Storage: Leftovers can be stored in an airtight container in the refrigerator for up to 2 days.

Ingredient Tip: Pickling spice can be purchased premixed at the grocery store, or you can mix your own blend. I make mine from a mixture of black peppercorns, mustard seeds, coriander seeds, allspice berries, bay leaves, and red pepper flakes.

Per serving: Calories: 385; Total fat: 23g; Carbohydrates: 46g; Fiber: 7g; Protein: 6g; Calcium: 286mg; Vitamin D: omcg; Vitamin B12: omcg; Iron: 1mg; Zinc: <1mg

GINGERED SWEET POTATO MASH

DAIRY-FREE, GLUTEN-FREE

SERVES **4** // *PREP TIME* **15 minutes** // *COOK TIME* **1 hour**

If you've been reading this book, you know by now how much I love sweet potatoes, not only for their nutrients but for their lovely, earthy flavor. This is a tropical version I learned to make from my grandmother, who is from St. Maarten.

2 large sweet potatoes

Extra-virgin olive oil, for drizzling

Sea salt

Freshly ground black pepper

1 tablespoon coconut oil

2 tablespoons peeled and grated fresh ginger

1 cup coconut milk (see Tip)

1 teaspoon honey

Chopped cilantro for garnish

1   Preheat the oven to 350°F.

2   Place the potatoes on a baking sheet, drizzle them with olive oil, and season with salt and pepper.

3   Bake the potatoes for 45 minutes to 1 hour, until tender and a knife is easily inserted to the center. When the potatoes have finished baking, remove them from the oven and allow them to cool enough to handle.

4   Cut the potatoes lengthwise. Scoop out the cooked insides using a spoon and transfer to a bowl.

5   Melt the coconut oil in a large saucepan over medium heat and add the ginger. Sauté for a couple of seconds and add the potato flesh, stirring to combine. Add the coconut milk, then mash everything together until smooth.

6   Add the honey and season with salt and pepper.

7   Serve topped with cilantro.

Storage: The sweet potato mash will keep in an airtight container in the refrigerator for 3 or 4 days.

Ingredient Tip: You can use either light or full-fat coconut milk in this recipe. I like the full-fat for the richer flavor, but it's up to you, depending on your taste and dietary needs.

Per serving: Calories: 228; Total fat: 14g; Carbohydrates: 25g; Fiber: 4g; Protein: 3g; Calcium: 33mg; Vitamin D: 0mcg; Vitamin B12: 0mcg; Iron: 1mg; Zinc: 1mg

LEMON-HERB RED QUINOA

DAIRY-FREE

SERVES **4** *//PREP TIME* **10 minutes** *//COOK TIME* **30 minutes**

Another favorite bowl component, quinoa is an ancient Peruvian grain that is packed with protein. It can replace pasta or rice in your favorite recipes. Serve this warm with a protein for dinner or take it along with you cold as the perfect picnic salad. I love this dish in the spring when fresh asparagus rolls around, but it's equally good with green beans, snap peas, or any vegetable you choose.

½ cup pine nuts

1 teaspoon ground cumin

4½ cups water

2 cups red quinoa, rinsed

½ cup very finely chopped asparagus

2 tablespoons extra-virgin olive oil

Juice and zest of 1 lemon

Sea salt

Freshly ground black pepper

1 small red onion, finely chopped, for garnish

½ small bunch fresh basil, chopped, for garnish

1 teaspoon chopped fresh thyme, for garnish

1 Place a small sauté pan or skillet over medium heat and toast the pine nuts until golden, about 3 minutes. Transfer to a bowl to cool and place the skillet back on the heat. Toast the cumin until fragrant, about 1 minute. Remove from the heat and set aside.

2 Put the water and quinoa in a large saucepan over medium-high heat and bring to a boil.

3 Reduce the heat to medium-low, cover, and simmer until the water is absorbed and the quinoa is tender, about 20 minutes. Transfer the quinoa to a large bowl and add the asparagus, stirring to combine. Cover and let sit for 5 minutes, then fluff with a fork.

4 Add the oil, cumin, and lemon juice to the quinoa. Season with salt and pepper.

5 Add the pine nuts, lemon zest, onion, basil, and thyme to the warm quinoa just before serving.

Storage: The quinoa will keep in an airtight container in the refrigerator for up to 3 days. Do not add the garnishes until you are ready to reheat and serve.

Per serving: Calories: 522; Total fat: 21g; Carbohydrates: 69g; Fiber: 11g; Protein: 15g; Calcium: 61mg; Vitamin D: 0mcg; Vitamin B12: 0mcg; Iron: 5mg; Zinc: 1mg

Pistou Soup, page 165

SOUPS & STEWS

*Butternut Squash–Apple Soup
with Chile Yogurt & Pepitas*   150

Cabbage Soup with Apples & Thyme   152

Carrot, Ginger & Jalapeño Soup   153

Charred-Tomato Gazpacho   155

Green Grape Gazpacho   157

Corn Chowder   158

White Bean & Pasta Soup   159

Butternut Squash & Lentil Chili   160

*Chickpea Soup with Black Kale, Harissa
& Spiced Yogurt*   161

Greek Gigante Bean & Tomato Stew   164

Pistou Soup   165

Mediterranean Tomato & Eggplant Stew   167

Garden Vegetable & Quinoa Soup   169

Veggie Hot Pot   170

Moroccan Mushroom Stew   172

BUTTERNUT SQUASH–APPLE SOUP with CHILE YOGURT & PEPITAS

DAIRY-FREE, GLUTEN-FREE

SERVES **4 to 6** // *PREP TIME* **30 minutes** // *COOK TIME* **1 hour 5 minutes**

A customer favorite at my restaurant, this vitamin-packed soup is as nutritious as it is beautiful and delicious. The sweetness of the apples, the earthiness of the squash, and the aroma of the fresh sage make it autumn in a bowl. It is hearty enough to make a meal with a salad and some bread, and you can also heat up a cup of the leftovers for breakfast.

1 medium (2-pound) butternut squash

Pinch allspice

1 tablespoon avocado oil

1 small yellow onion, chopped roughly

1 leek, white part only, washed, halved lengthwise, and sliced

2 Granny Smith apples, peeled, cored, and diced

1 teaspoon fresh sage, chopped

4 cups vegetable stock

1½ cups apple cider

Sea salt

Freshly ground black pepper

1 cup non-dairy yogurt

1 tablespoon chili powder

Store-bought toasted pepitas, for garnish

1. Preheat the oven to 375°F. Cut the squash in half lengthwise. Place it cut-side down on a baking sheet and sprinkle with the allspice. Roast it in the oven for about 1 hour, or until the squash is very soft. When it is done, remove it from the oven and cool slightly.

2. While the squash is roasting, heat the oil in a medium saucepan over medium heat. When the oil begins to shimmer, add the onion, leek, apples, and sage. Reduce the heat to low, cover, and simmer for 8 to 10 minutes, or until tender.

3. Add the vegetable stock and apple cider. Bring to a simmer and continue to cook for about 15 minutes.

4. When the squash is cool enough to handle, scoop out the seeds and discard, then scoop out the pulp. Add the pulp to the vegetable stock mixture and simmer for 5 minutes. Remove from the heat and carefully puree the soup in small batches in a blender until very smooth. Strain through a fine sieve into another medium saucepan.

5. When you're ready to serve, reheat the soup over medium heat until it just reaches a simmer. Season with salt and pepper.

6 In a small bowl, whisk together the yogurt and chili powder until well blended.

7 Ladle the soup into bowls and garnish with the chili yogurt and toasted pepitas.

Storage: The soup will keep well in an airtight container in the refrigerator for 1 week or in the freezer for 1 month.

Variation Tip: Pumpkin is also lovely instead of butternut squash. Look for small pie pumpkins in the fall or purchase frozen, cubed pumpkin.

Per serving: Calories: 319; Total fat: 10g; Carbohydrates: 58g; Fiber: 11g; Protein: 6g; Calcium: 197mg; Vitamin D: 1mcg; Vitamin B12: 0mcg; Iron: 3mg; Zinc: 1mg

CABBAGE SOUP with APPLES & THYME

DAIRY-FREE, GLUTEN-FREE

SERVES **4 to 6** //*PREP TIME* **10 minutes** //*COOK TIME* **40 minutes**

Cabbage is a fabulous vegetable to work with and eat; it's nutritious, filling, and low in calories. This warming fall soup is perfect for a blustery day. I use Golden Delicious apples in this soup for their honeyed flavor, which is a perfect partner for the peppery-sweet cabbage.

2 tablespoons avocado oil, divided

1 medium head green cabbage, cored and thinly sliced

1 medium yellow onion, chopped

4 sprigs fresh thyme

3 cups vegetable stock

Sea salt

Freshly ground black pepper

4 large Golden Delicious apples, peeled, cored, and cut into ½-inch cubes, for garnish

Chopped fresh thyme leaves, for garnish

1   Heat 1 tablespoon of oil in a large stockpot over medium-high heat. Add the cabbage and onion and sauté until the vegetables are wilted and browned, stirring occasionally, about 15 minutes.

2   Add the thyme sprigs and sauté for 1 minute more. Add the stock and bring to a boil. Reduce the heat to medium-low and simmer for about 5 minutes. Season with salt and pepper and keep warm.

3   Heat the remaining 1 tablespoon of oil in a large sauté pan or skillet over medium-high heat. Add the apples and sauté until brown and tender, stirring occasionally, about 12 minutes. Season with salt and pepper.

4   Remove the thyme sprigs from the soup. Ladle the soup into bowls, garnish with the apples and thyme, and serve immediately.

Storage: The soup can be stored in an airtight container in the refrigerator for 3 or 4 days.

Make Ahead: If you're making the soup ahead, do not sauté the apples until ready to serve. After reheating the soup, garnish with the apples and thyme and serve hot.

Per serving: Calories: 245; Total fat: 7g; Carbohydrates: 46g; Fiber: 9g; Protein: 4g; Calcium: 118mg; Vitamin D: 0mcg; Vitamin B12: 0mcg; Iron: 2mg; Zinc: 1mg

CARROT, GINGER & JALAPEÑO SOUP

DAIRY-FREE, GLUTEN-FREE

SERVES **4 to 6** // *PREP TIME* **15 minutes** // *COOK TIME* **20 minutes**

The jalapeños add extra zing to the sweet and spicy magic that is carrot-ginger soup. Pair with a quick grain bowl or salad for a healthy and hearty weeknight dinner. This soup is great hot or chilled and can be made year-round with simple, easy-to-obtain pantry ingredients.

1 tablespoon avocado oil

1 celery stalk, chopped coarsely

1 small yellow onion, chopped coarsely

1 or 2 jalapeño peppers, seeds and ribs removed, chopped roughly

Sea salt

2 pounds carrots, peeled and chopped coarsely

3-inch piece fresh ginger, peeled and grated

Juice and zest of 1 orange

4 cups vegetable stock or water

Freshly ground black pepper

Chopped cilantro or parsley, for garnish

1   Heat the oil in a deep saucepan over medium heat. Sauté the celery, onion, jalapeño, and a pinch of salt until softened and translucent, about 4 minutes. Add the carrots and continue to cook until soft, about 5 minutes.

2   Add the ginger, orange juice, and stock, and bring to a boil. Reduce the heat to low and simmer until the carrots are very tender, about 8 minutes. Remove the soup from the heat and cool slightly.

3   Puree the soup carefully in small batches in a blender until it is smooth. Pass it through a fine-mesh sieve if desired for extra silky texture.

4   Season with salt and pepper. Rewarm the soup and garnish with the orange zest and cilantro.

Storage: The soup can be stored in an airtight container in the refrigerator for 4 or 5 days.

Serving Tip: Add a dollop of yogurt to add a bit of protein for a complete meal, and sweeten it with honey.

Per serving: Calories: 159; Total fat: 4g; Carbohydrates: 29g; Fiber: 7g; Protein: 3g; Calcium: 86mg; Vitamin D: 0mcg; Vitamin B12: 0mcg; Iron: 1mg; Zinc: 1mg

CHARRED-TOMATO GAZPACHO

DAIRY-FREE

SERVES 4 to 6 //PREP TIME 30 minutes, plus 2 hours to chill //COOK TIME 15 minutes

The little char on the tomatoes in this classic Spanish gazpacho adds a subtle smokiness to the sweetness of the ripe produce. This stunning soup is cooling on a hot summer night and is ideal for pouring into a chilled thermos to take along for a light lunch.

3½ pounds tomatoes
(3 large or 6 medium)

1 medium red bell pepper

1 red onion, unpeeled,
quartered lengthwise

8 tablespoons extra-virgin
olive oil, divided, plus
more for drizzling

Sea salt

Freshly ground black pepper

3 slices country-style bread
(gluten-free, if desired)

3 garlic cloves, divided

1 cucumber, peeled, halved,
seeded, and diced

3 tablespoons
sherry vinegar

2 teaspoons chopped fresh
marjoram

¾ teaspoon smoked paprika

½ teaspoon ground cumin

¼ teaspoon cayenne pepper

¾ cup tomato juice,
low-sodium canned or
fresh (see Tip) (optional)

3 scallions, both white
and green parts, cut into
thin strips

1   Heat a grill or grill pan over medium-high heat. Place the tomatoes, pepper, and onion on a baking sheet, brush with 3 tablespoons of oil, and season with salt and pepper. Grill the vegetables until the skins are charred, turning frequently, 8 to 10 minutes. Return to the baking sheet.

2   Brush both sides of the bread slices with 2 tablespoons of oil. Grill the bread until toasted, about 1½ minutes per side. Cut 1 garlic clove in half and rub it over the toasted sides of the bread. Cut the bread into small cubes and reserve them in a small bowl.

3   Remove the tomato cores, seed and core the pepper, and chop it coarsely. Peel the onion. Working in small batches, place the tomatoes, pepper, onion, and cucumber in a food processor and blend until a puree forms. Transfer the mixture to a large

CONTINUED

bowl. Repeat until all the vegetables are used up. Mince the remaining 2 garlic cloves and stir them in.

4 In a small bowl, stir together the remaining 3 tablespoons of oil, the sherry vinegar, marjoram, paprika, cumin, and cayenne. Add the mixture to the soup. Thin the soup, if desired, with tomato juice. Season with salt and pepper and chill for at least 2 hours, until very cold.

5 Ladle the gazpacho into chilled bowls and serve topped with the croutons, a drizzle of olive oil, and scallions.

Storage: The soup will keep well in an airtight container in the refrigerator for up to 4 days.

Prep Tip: The tomatoes, pepper, and onion can be charred under a broiler; just be sure to turn them frequently so they brown evenly. To make fresh tomato juice, just puree fresh, ripe whole tomatoes in a blender and strain—you'll never go back to canned again.

Per serving: Calories: 431; Total fat: 29g; Carbohydrates: 39g; Fiber: 8g; Protein: 8g; Calcium: 113mg; Vitamin D: 0mcg; Vitamin B12: 0mcg; Iron: 3mg; Zinc: 1mg

GREEN GRAPE GAZPACHO

DAIRY-FREE, GLUTEN-FREE

SERVES **4 to 6** *//PREP TIME* **15 minutes, plus 3 hours freezing time**

On a sultry August day, there's nothing more refreshing than this bright green, light, chilled soup. A customer favorite at my restaurant, this elegant soup is easy to make ahead and marvelous for entertaining. I bring it back every year to our menu in the hottest summer months with the frozen grape garnish as a special touch. You might want to freeze extra for a refreshing snack.

1 cup halved green and red grapes

1 small cucumber, seeded and finely diced, divided

1 Granny Smith apple, peeled, cored, and finely diced, divided

4 medium tomatillos, finely diced, divided

1 pound seedless green grapes (about 3 cups)

½ cup chopped walnuts

1 cup plain yogurt or non-dairy yogurt

1 cup white grape juice

1 teaspoon rice wine vinegar

1 jalapeño pepper, seeded and chopped roughly

1 serrano pepper, seeded and chopped roughly

10 large mint leaves, divided

Sea salt

1   Put the halved green and red grapes in an airtight container and place in the freezer until frozen, about 3 hours.

2   Put half the cucumber, half the apple, and half the tomatillos into a blender. Add the seedless grapes, walnuts, yogurt, grape juice, vinegar, jalapeño, serrano, and 6 mint leaves. Blend until smooth and transfer to a medium bowl. Stir in the remaining halves of the cucumber, apple, and tomatillo. Season with salt. Chill the soup for 2 hours in the refrigerator before serving. Adjust the seasonings.

3   Ladle the soup into chilled bowls and serve garnished with red and green frozen grape halves and the remaining 4 mint leaves.

Ingredient Tip: Think beyond grapes if you like gazpacho. Other summer fruits like peaches, melons, cherries, and watermelon make great gazpacho, too.

Per serving: Calories: 315; Total fat: 12g; Carbohydrates: 52g; Fiber: 5g; Protein: 7g; Calcium: 121mg; Vitamin D: 0mcg; Vitamin B12: <1mcg; Iron: 1mg; Zinc: 1mg

CORN CHOWDER

DAIRY-FREE, GLUTEN-FREE

SERVES **4 to 6** //*PREP TIME* **15 minutes** //*COOK TIME* **35 minutes**

My father used to drive us directly to the cornfield in Boulder, Colorado, to buy the best sweet corn from a farmer for a few dollars a bag. I highly recommend making this soup with late-summer corn, which has a beautiful balance of sweet and savory flavors.

6 ears corn

4 cups water

2 tablespoons extra-virgin olive oil

1 medium onion, finely diced

2 garlic cloves, minced

2 medium red potatoes, finely diced

Sea salt

Freshly ground black pepper

1 cup almond milk or regular milk

¼ cup Fresh, Chunky Guacamole (page 41), for garnish

Paprika, for garnish

1   Shuck the corn and use a paring knife to strip the kernels into a large bowl. Put the cobs in a stockpot with the water and bring to a boil over high heat. Reduce the heat to low, cover, and simmer for 10 minutes.

2   While the corncobs are simmering, heat the oil in a large saucepan over medium-high heat. When the oil shimmers, add the onion, garlic, and potatoes and season with salt and pepper. Cook, stirring occasionally, until the onion softens, about 5 minutes.

3   After the corncobs have cooked for at least 10 minutes, strain the liquid into the onion and potato mixture. Bring the soup to a boil, reduce the heat to low, and simmer until the potatoes are tender, about 10 minutes. Add the corn kernels and almond milk and heat through, about 10 minutes.

4   Ladle half the soup mixture into a blender or food processor and puree until smooth, then return it to the soup pot.

5   Taste and season with salt and pepper, as desired. Garnish each serving with 1 tablespoon of the guacamole and some paprika and serve.

Cooking Tip: If dairy is part of your diet, use regular milk in place of the almond milk. For a more brothy soup, skip step 4 and just simmer the soup mixture for 10 minutes or so until the flavors combine.

Per serving: Calories: 324; Total fat: 11g; Carbohydrates: 56g; Fiber: 7g; Protein: 8g; Calcium: 139mg; Vitamin D: 1mcg; Vitamin B12: 0mcg; Iron: 2mg; Zinc: 1mg

WHITE BEAN & PASTA SOUP

DAIRY-FREE

SERVES **4 to 6** *//PREP TIME* **15 minutes** *//COOK TIME* **50 minutes**

This simple winter soup is delicious, soul-satisfying, fast, and inexpensive to prepare. When fresh cranberry beans are in season in fall, grab a bunch at your farmers' market for this dish. Pair it with a hearty salad of winter greens or a sandwich to create a balanced, filling meal.

2 tablespoons extra-virgin olive oil, plus more for garnish

1 medium yellow onion, diced

1 medium carrot, diced

1 celery stalk, diced

3 cups water or vegetable stock

2 cups canned low-sodium white beans with canning liquid

2 cups canned tomatoes, undrained

1 cup short dry pasta of your choice

Sea salt

Freshly ground black pepper

2 scallions, both white and pale green parts, sliced

Chopped parsley, rosemary, thyme, or other herbs, for garnish

1   Heat the oil in a large stockpot over medium heat. Add the onion, carrot, and celery. Sauté until the vegetables are soft, about 12 minutes.

2   Add the water, beans with the canning liquid, and tomatoes with juice, and bring to a simmer. Reduce the heat to medium-low and simmer for 25 minutes to blend flavors, stirring occasionally.

3   Increase the heat to medium-high, stir in the pasta, and bring to a boil. Cook until the pasta is al dente, about 10 minutes, adding more water if the soup is too thick. Season with salt and pepper.

4   Ladle the soup into bowls and garnish with scallions, herbs, and olive oil, and serve.

Storage: The soup will keep well in an airtight container in the refrigerator for 3 or 4 days.

Prep Tip: You can make this a gluten-free dish by substituting a gluten-free pasta for the wheat pasta.

Per serving: Calories: 354; Total fat: 8g; Carbohydrates: 59g; Fiber: 13g; Protein: 13g; Calcium: 133mg; Vitamin D: 0mcg; Vitamin B12: 0mcg; Iron: 5mg; Zinc: 2mg

BUTTERNUT SQUASH & LENTIL CHILI

DAIRY-FREE, GLUTEN-FREE

SERVES 4 //*PREP TIME* **15 minutes** //*COOK TIME* **35 minutes**

You won't miss the meat in this wholesome, filling chili, which is wonderful because you will whip it up again and again. Luckily, it is a speedy and warming weeknight meal made with simple pantry ingredients.

2 tablespoons extra-virgin olive oil

1 medium onion, diced

1 large yellow bell pepper, diced

4 garlic cloves, minced

2 cups lentils, rinsed

1 tablespoon chili powder

2 teaspoons ground cumin

2 teaspoons dried oregano

1 (32-ounce) can diced Italian tomatoes

1 bay leaf

7 cups vegetable stock

1 medium (2-pound) butternut squash, peeled, seeded, and cut into 1-inch cubes

2 cups low-sodium canned red kidney beans

Sea salt

Freshly ground black pepper

1   Heat the oil in a large heavy stockpot or Dutch oven over medium heat. Add the onion and bell pepper. Cook for 5 to 6 minutes, or just until the vegetables begin to soften. Stir in the garlic and cook for 30 seconds, or until fragrant.

2   Add the lentils, chili powder, cumin, and oregano, and sauté for about 1 minute.

3   Add the tomatoes, bay leaf, and stock, and bring to a boil, then reduce the heat to low and simmer, partially covered, for 10 to 15 minutes. The lentils should be soft around the edges but firm to the bite.

4   Add the butternut squash and continue to simmer for about 10 minutes, until the squash is just tender.

5   Stir in the beans and cook until just heated through, 2 to 3 minutes. Season with salt and pepper.

6   Discard the bay leaf and serve with your favorite chili topping (see Tip).

Storage: The chili will keep in an airtight container in the refrigerator for 4 or 5 days or in the freezer for 6 months.

Serving Tips: Topping options include sliced scallions, chopped red onion, pickled jalapeños, shredded cheese (or plant-based cheese), tortilla strips, or plain Greek yogurt (or non-dairy yogurt).

Per serving: Calories: 662; Total fat: 9g; Carbohydrates: 114g; Fiber: 23g; Protein: 34g; Calcium: 246mg; Vitamin D: 0mcg; Vitamin B12: 0mcg; Iron: 10mg; Zinc: 4mg

CHICKPEA SOUP with BLACK KALE, HARISSA & SPICED YOGURT

GLUTEN-FREE

SERVES 4 //*PREP TIME* 1 hour //*COOK TIME* 1 hour 20 minutes

Don't be intimidated by the ingredients list in this recipe. Most of the ingredients are common pantry spices and herbs. The layered earthy, spicy, and cool flavors of this Moroccan-style stew are well worth the effort to create this dish. Serve it with homemade pita bread (page 100) if you'd like to complete the Middle Eastern theme.

FOR THE CHICKPEAS

1 pound dried chickpeas

1 yellow onion, quartered

1 carrot, peeled and quartered

2 garlic cloves, smashed

1 bay leaf

4 fresh thyme sprigs

Sea salt

FOR THE SPICED YOGURT

¼ teaspoon coriander seeds

¼ teaspoon cumin seeds

1 cup Greek yogurt (or non-dairy yogurt)

2 tablespoons chopped fresh cilantro

1 tablespoon chopped fresh mint

2 tablespoons extra-virgin olive oil

2 teaspoons white wine vinegar

Juice of ½ lemon

Sea salt

FOR THE SOUP BASE

1 teaspoon coriander seeds

1 teaspoon fennel seeds

½ teaspoon cumin seeds

¼ cup extra-virgin olive oil

3 carrots, peeled and cut into half-moons

1 yellow onion, chopped coarsely

3 garlic cloves, minced

Freshly ground black pepper

1 teaspoon smoked paprika

¼ teaspoon ground turmeric

3 fresh thyme sprigs

1 bay leaf

2 tablespoons tomato paste

1 cup dry white wine

4 cups vegetable stock

1 bunch black kale (or regular kale), stemmed and cut into 2-inch strips

1 teaspoon red wine vinegar

⅓ cup spiced yogurt

¼ cup harissa or hot sauce, for garnish

TO MAKE THE CHICKPEAS

1 In a large stockpot over medium-high heat, combine the chickpeas, onion, carrot, garlic, bay leaf, and thyme. Add enough water to cover the ingredients by about 2 inches. Season with salt and bring to a boil, then reduce the heat to low and simmer until the chickpeas are tender but still hold their shape, about 45 minutes.

CONTINUED

2 Discard the bay leaf and cool the chickpeas in the cooking liquid. When cool, drain and discard the liquid. Set the chickpeas aside.

TO MAKE THE SPICED YOGURT

3 In a small dry sauté pan or skillet over medium heat, toast the coriander seeds and cumin seeds until just fragrant and beginning to brown, about 3 minutes. Remove from the heat and let cool, then grind to a powder in a spice grinder or with a mortar and pestle.

4 In a food processor, combine the yogurt, ground coriander and cumin, cilantro, and mint. Process until the herbs are broken down and the yogurt is tinted green, about 5 seconds. Add the oil, vinegar, and lemon juice, and pulse just until incorporated. Taste and season with salt.

TO MAKE THE SOUP BASE

5 In a small dry skillet over medium heat, toast the coriander seeds, fennel seeds, and cumin seeds until fragrant, about 3 minutes. Remove from the heat and let cool. With a spice grinder, or mortar and pestle, grind the seeds to a powder. You may skip this step and use ground spices, but give them a quick toast.

6 Heat the oil in a large stockpot over medium-high heat until it shimmers. Add the carrots, onion, and garlic, and season with salt and pepper. Cook until the vegetables begin to soften and brown slightly, about 5 minutes.

7 Add the ground spice mixture, paprika, turmeric, thyme, and bay leaf, and cook until fragrant, about 3 minutes. Stir in the tomato paste, scraping the bottom of the pot frequently so that it does not burn, and cook until fragrant and beginning to brown, about 5 minutes.

8 Add the wine, bring to a boil, and cook until reduced by more than half, about 3 minutes. Discard the bay leaf, add the stock, and return to a simmer for 5 minutes.

9 Transfer 1 cup of the soup base and 2 cups of the cooked chickpeas to a blender and puree until smooth. Return the pureed mixture to the soup pot with the soup base. Add the remaining cooked chickpeas and stir. Remove the soup from the heat and let stand at room temperature for about 20 minutes.

10 To serve, place the soup on medium-low heat, add the kale, and cook until softened, 5 to 10 minutes. Adjust the seasoning and add the vinegar. Serve with a dollop of the spiced yogurt and a drizzle of harissa.

Storage: The stew and yogurt will both keep well in separate airtight containers in the refrigerator for 3 or 4 days.

Substitution Tip: If you cannot find harissa, substitute a chile paste such as *sambal oelek* or one of your favorites.

Per serving: Calories: 790; Total fat: 31g; Carbohydrates: 95g; Fiber: 25g; Protein: 33g; Calcium: 332mg; Vitamin D: 0mcg; Vitamin B12: <1mcg; Iron: 18mg; Zinc: 1mg

GREEK GIGANTE BEAN
& TOMATO STEW

DAIRY-FREE

SERVES 6 // *PREP TIME* 10 minutes, plus overnight to soak // *COOK TIME* 2½ hours

Gigante beans are what they sound like: giant white beans that are sweet, creamy, and tender. My favorite way to prepare them is in this rustic Greek-style tomato stew served with some crusty peasant bread. This is a good one for the slow cooker, and a method is in the Tip.

1 pound dry gigante beans

2 tablespoons extra-virgin olive oil, plus more for drizzling

2 medium yellow onions, peeled and diced

4 garlic cloves, smashed

1 (32-ounce) can diced Italian tomatoes

2 cups vegetable stock or water

2 bay leaves

1 teaspoon sea salt

1 teaspoon sugar

1 teaspoon dried oregano

½ teaspoon dried thyme

½ teaspoon anise seed

¼ teaspoon red pepper flakes

Crusty bread and black pepper, for serving

1 Put the beans in a medium bowl and cover them with about 3 inches of water. Let soak at room temperature overnight. Drain and set aside.

2 Heat the oil in a large heavy stockpot over medium heat until it shimmers, then add the onions and garlic and sauté until the onions are softened and translucent, about 5 minutes. Add the tomatoes and sauté for 2 minutes more to combine flavors.

3 Add the beans, stock, bay leaves, salt, sugar, oregano, thyme, anise seed, and red pepper flakes and bring to a boil. Reduce the heat to low and simmer until the beans are just tender, 2 to 2½ hours. Adjust the seasonings and remove the bay leaf. Serve hot with crusty bread, a grind of black pepper, and a drizzle of olive oil.

Storage: The stew will keep in an airtight container in the refrigerator for 4 or 5 days.

Cooking Tip: Place all the ingredients in a slow cooker. Cook for 8 to 10 hours on low. If you can't find gigante beans in your local market, large lima beans or white beans make a suitable substitution.

Per serving: Calories: 356; Total fat: 5g; Carbohydrates: 61g; Fiber: 18g; Protein: 17g; Calcium: 203mg; Vitamin D: 0mcg; Vitamin B12: 0mcg; Iron: 14mg; Zinc: <1mg

PISTOU SOUP

SERVES **4** // *PREP TIME* **20 minutes, plus overnight to soak** // *COOK TIME* **1 hour**

In the Provence region of France, they make this bright green, flavorful version of minestrone in every home kitchen and restaurant. It's packed with nutritious vegetables and is delicious and easy to make year-round with items you probably already have in your pantry.

FOR THE SOUP

1¼ cups dry white beans

4 quarts vegetable stock or water

1 teaspoon sea salt, divided

1 bay leaf

2 tablespoons extra-virgin olive oil

1 yellow onion, peeled and diced

1 red bell pepper, diced

2 carrots, diced

1 teaspoon dried thyme

1 small yellow squash, diced

4 tomatoes, diced

4 small zucchini, thinly sliced

4 small red potatoes, quartered

½ pound fresh green beans, stemmed and cut into 1-inch pieces

1 cup small pasta (mini shells or macaroni)

½ teaspoon freshly ground black pepper

1 cup packed chopped Swiss chard

FOR THE PISTOU

2 cups fresh basil leaves, packed

½ cup plus 2 tablespoons extra-virgin olive oil

4 garlic cloves

4 ounces Parmesan cheese, grated

TO MAKE THE SOUP

1   Put the beans in a medium bowl and cover them with about 3 inches of water. Let them soak at room temperature overnight.

2   Drain the beans and put them in a large stockpot with the stock, ½ teaspoon of salt, and the bay leaf. Bring to a boil over high heat, reduce the heat to low, cover, and simmer until the beans are al dente, about 45 minutes.

3   While the beans cook, heat the oil in a large sauté pan or skillet over medium-high heat and sauté the onion, bell pepper, carrots, and the remaining ½ teaspoon of salt until the vegetables are softened and translucent, about 5 minutes. Add the thyme and the squash and cook until the squash begins to soften, about 5 minutes more.

4   When the beans are done cooking, add the onion and squash mixture to the cooked beans and water. Add the tomatoes, zucchini, potatoes, green beans, pasta, and pepper. Cook until the pasta is al dente, about 15 minutes. Stir in the chard and remove from the heat. Remove the bay leaf.

CONTINUED

TO MAKE THE PISTOU

5 Put the basil, oil, and garlic in a food processor or blender and process until smooth. Spoon the mixture into a bowl and fold in the cheese.

6 Ladle the soup into soup bowls and garnish each with a large spoonful of the pistou.

Storage: The stew will keep in an airtight container in the refrigerator for 1 week or the freezer for up to 1 month.

Make Ahead: The soup can be made ahead, but do not make the bright green pistou until just before serving.

Per serving: Calories: 1,012; Total fat: 50g; Carbohydrates: 110g; Fiber: 19g; Protein: 33g; Calcium: 495mg; Vitamin D: <1mcg; Vitamin B12: <1mcg; Iron: 11mg; Zinc: 3mg

MEDITERRANEAN TOMATO & EGGPLANT STEW

GLUTEN-FREE

SERVES **4** // *PREP TIME* **20 minutes** // *COOK TIME* **30 minutes**

This lush, healthy stew is summer in a bowl but can be made any time of year with San Marzano tomatoes. Stirring in the creamy ricotta (or tofu) cheese as a garnish just adds to the luxurious presentation of the stew. Serve it over Mediterranean-Style Hummus (page 38).

4 tablespoons extra-virgin olive oil, divided, plus more as needed and for garnish

1 medium (1-pound) eggplant, diced (see Tip)

1 teaspoon sea salt, plus more as needed

2 medium yellow onions, diced

2 medium fennel bulbs, diced

6 garlic cloves, minced

3 cups vegetable stock

1 (28-ounce) can crushed San Marzano tomatoes

2 teaspoons freshly ground black pepper

2 teaspoons whole dried fennel seeds

1½ teaspoons dried oregano

1 teaspoon fresh thyme leaves

½ teaspoon red pepper flakes

1 (28-ounce) can whole peeled San Marzano tomatoes

¼ cup ricotta cheese, for sprinkling

½ small bunch fresh basil leaves, torn into pieces for garnish

1 Heat 2 tablespoons of oil in a medium stockpot or Dutch oven over medium heat. Add the eggplant and a pinch of sea salt and sauté for 5 minutes, stirring frequently, until tender, adding a little more oil as needed.

2 To the pot add the remaining 2 tablespoons of oil, the onions, and fennel and cook for 5 to 6 minutes, stirring, until the onions are softened and translucent. Add the garlic and cook for 1 minute, stirring.

3 Add the stock, crushed tomatoes, 1 teaspoon of salt, pepper, fennel seeds, oregano, thyme, and red pepper flakes, stirring to combine.

CONTINUED

4 Put the whole tomatoes, including the liquid, into a food processor and pulse until the tomatoes are coarsely chopped. Add the tomatoes and the liquid to the pot. Bring to a boil over medium-high heat, then reduce the heat to low, and simmer for 15 minutes, stirring occasionally.

5 Taste and adjust the seasoning as needed. Serve hot in large bowls topped with the ricotta cheese, fresh basil, and a drizzle of olive oil.

Storage: The stew will keep in an airtight container in the refrigerator for 1 week or the freezer for up to 1 month.

Ingredient Tip: To dice the eggplant, cut in half lengthwise, cut into slices, and then dice. When buying your tomatoes, read the label carefully to ensure that you are purchasing a quality tomato without anything added. I like the Muir Glen brand from California.

Per serving: Calories: 359; Total fat: 16g; Carbohydrates: 50g; Fiber: 14g; Protein: 10g; Calcium: 253mg; Vitamin D: 0mcg; Vitamin B12: <1mcg; Iron: 6mg; Zinc: 1mg

GARDEN VEGETABLE & QUINOA SOUP

DAIRY-FREE

SERVES **4** // *PREP TIME* **15 minutes** // *COOK TIME* **35 minutes**

This herb- and spice-infused soup is a great option for weekend meal preppers. It is a balanced meal in a bowl with vitamins and fiber from the veggies and protein from the beans and quinoa. This recipe is versatile, so throw in whatever veggies you have around, including the produce drawer stragglers that are leftovers from other meals.

1 tablespoon extra-virgin olive oil

1 medium yellow onion, diced

Sea salt

4 garlic cloves, minced

3 carrots, cut into rounds

3 celery stalks, sliced

2 cups low-sodium canned kidney beans

2 cups diced tomatoes

1 cup quinoa, rinsed

2 teaspoons freshly ground black pepper, plus more for seasoning

1 teaspoon dried oregano

½ teaspoon dried basil

½ teaspoon smoked paprika

4 cups vegetable stock

2 cups water

4 ounces fresh baby spinach

1   Heat the oil in a large stockpot over medium heat, add the onion, and sauté with a pinch of salt until soft and transparent, about 5 minutes. Add the garlic and sauté for 1 minute more.

2   Add the carrots and celery and continue to sauté until they just begin to soften, about 5 minutes.

3   Add the kidney beans, diced tomatoes, quinoa, pepper, oregano, basil, and paprika, stirring to combine.

4   Add the stock and water, cover, and increase the heat to medium-high. Bring the mixture to a boil, reduce the heat to low, and simmer for 25 minutes, or until the quinoa is tender and translucent.

5   Add the spinach and continue to simmer for 1 minute, until heated through.

6   Taste and adjust the seasoning, if necessary. Serve hot.

Storage: The soup can be kept in an airtight container in the refrigerator for up to 1 week or frozen for up to 2 months.

Substitution Tip: Other grains such as barley or wheat berries are nice choices instead of the quinoa.

Per serving: Calories: 386; Total fat: 7g; Carbohydrates: 65g; Fiber: 12g; Protein: 16g; Calcium: 151mg; Vitamin D: 0mcg; Vitamin B12: 0mcg; Iron: 5mg; Zinc: 2mg

VEGGIE HOT POT

SERVES 4 //*PREP TIME* 20 minutes //*COOK TIME* 20 minutes

This dish is deceptively simple, so the spicy-hot, complex flavors will be a lovely surprise. This is a country-style Japanese variation that you won't find in a restaurant, and it's easy and inexpensive to prepare. Feel free to mix and match your veggies with what you like and what you have on hand.

5 cups vegetable stock

2-inch piece fresh peeled ginger, smashed

2 garlic cloves, smashed

2 teaspoons avocado oil

4 ounces shiitake mushrooms, stemmed, wiped clean, and sliced

½ teaspoon red pepper flakes

1 small bok choy, cut into ½-inch pieces, stems and greens separated

4 ounces soba noodles

1 (14-ounce) block firm tofu, drained, patted dry, and cut into ½-inch cubes

2 large carrots, grated

2 tablespoons rice vinegar

2 teaspoons low-sodium soy sauce

1 teaspoon toasted sesame oil

2 scallions, white and light green parts, sliced, for garnish

1   In a large heavy stockpot or Dutch oven, heat the stock, ginger, and garlic over medium-low heat and bring to a simmer. Increase the heat to medium-high and simmer, covered, for 15 minutes. Remove the ginger and garlic with a slotted spoon and discard.

2   While the stock is simmering, heat the avocado oil in a large sauté pan or skillet over medium-high heat. Add the mushrooms and red pepper flakes and sauté until the mushrooms are tender and golden, about 5 minutes. Add the bok choy stems and sauté until tender, about 4 minutes.

3   Add the mushroom mixture to the broth. Add the noodles, reduce the heat to medium-low, and simmer for 3 minutes. Add the bok choy greens and tofu and simmer until heated through, about 2 minutes. Stir in the carrots, vinegar, soy sauce, and sesame oil.

4   Serve hot, garnished with the scallions.

Storage: The soup can be kept in an airtight container in the refrigerator for up to 4 days.

Serving Tip: Hot pot is a family style dish typically served with a boiling hot pot of broth in the center of the table. Family or friends dip their vegetables and noodles in the pot to cook, then scoop them out with some of the broth. You can re-create this traditional style of serving using this recipe; just place the broth in a fondue pot in the center of the table and surround it with an assortment of raw vegetables, tofu, and noodles.

Per serving: Calories: 305; Total fat: 10g; Carbohydrates: 38g; Fiber: 5g; Protein: 19g; Calcium: 366mg; Vitamin D: <1mcg; Vitamin B12: 0mcg; Iron: 5mg; Zinc: 1mg

MOROCCAN MUSHROOM STEW

GLUTEN-FREE

SERVES 2 //*PREP TIME* **30 minutes** //*COOK TIME* **35 minutes**

This filling Moroccan dish is packed full of vitamins and vegetables and can be ready in less than an hour. This is what comfort food is all about. Mushrooms are one of the healthiest things you can eat, and I've included my preferred blend of types in the recipe. This stew doesn't have to be limited to mushrooms; pearl onions, baby potatoes, or carrots are great additions and a good use for leftover veggies.

6 tablespoons extra-virgin olive oil, divided

2 pounds mixed mushrooms (such as cremini, oyster, chanterelle, and shiitake), chopped, divided

½ pound shallots, finely diced, divided

1 tablespoon tomato paste

2 teaspoons chopped fresh thyme leaves

2 teaspoons ground cumin

1 teaspoon ground coriander

1 teaspoon ground cinnamon

½ teaspoon ground allspice

5 cups vegetable stock or water, plus more if needed

1 teaspoon sea salt, plus more for seasoning

1 teaspoon freshly ground black pepper, plus more for seasoning

5 ounces fresh baby spinach

Juice of 2 limes

2 tablespoons plain yogurt, for garnish

2 teaspoons harissa, for garnish

Chopped parsley for sprinkling

Crusty bread, couscous, or pasta, for serving

1 Pour 3 tablespoons of oil in a large stockpot over medium-high heat. Add half the mushrooms and half the shallots and cook, stirring occasionally, until most of the liquid has evaporated and the mushrooms are well browned, 10 to 12 minutes. Transfer the mushroom mixture to a medium bowl and repeat this cooking process with the remaining 3 tablespoons of oil, remaining half of mushrooms, and remaining half of shallots. Leave this batch of mushrooms in the pot.

2 Return the first batch of mushrooms to the pot and add the tomato paste, thyme, cumin, coriander, cinnamon, and allspice and cook for about 1 minute, until fragrant.

3 Stir in the stock, salt, and pepper. Bring the mixture to a boil over medium-high heat, reduce the heat to low, and simmer for 20 minutes. Add the spinach and let cook until just wilted, about 1 minute.

4 Transfer the mixture to a food processor in batches and process to a coarse stew, then transfer to a large saucepan. Repeat until all the mixture is processed. Add the lime juice and thin with more stock, if needed.

5 Taste and adjust the seasoning.

6 Serve topped with yogurt, harissa, and parsley.

7 Serve with crusty bread, or over couscous or pasta.

Storage: The stew can be stored in an airtight container in the refrigerator for up to 1 week or up to 1 month in the freezer.

Variation Tip: This is also lovely served with rice or spooned over Mediterranean-Style Hummus (page 38).

Per serving: Calories: 671; Total fat: 44g; Carbohydrates: 62g; Fiber: 14g; Protein: 20g; Calcium: 251mg; Vitamin D: 2mcg; Vitamin B12: <1mcg; Iron: 13mg; Zinc: 5mg

Whole Roasted Cauliflower in Herb Salsa Verde, page 208

CHAPTER NINE

DINNER MAINS

Veggie Meatballs with Tomato Ragout   176
Vegan Spinach & Tofu Enchiladas   178
Spaghetti with Braised Kale, Chile & Lemon   180
Vegan Green Risotto with Broccoli   182
Pumpkin & Cashew Curry   184
Calabacitas Tacos   186
Cabbage & Veggie Lasagna   187
Salt & Pepper Tofu   188
Vegetable Shepherd's Pie   189
Turkish Eggplant Casserole   191
Carrot Falafel with Zuccanoush   193
Butternut Squash, Black Bean & Grain Chili   195
Moroccan Veggie Tagine with Couscous   196
Jerk Tofu Steaks   198
Green Tea Soba Noodles with Sesame Dipping Sauce   200
Riced Cauliflower & Chickpea Pilaf   202
Caribbean Chard, Sweet Potato & Spicy Peanut Jumble   204
Cauliflower Crust Pizza   205
Vegan Pad Thai   206
Whole Roasted Cauliflower in Herb Salsa Verde   208
Spicy Vegan Sweet Potato Maki with Coconut Rice   210
Zucchini Rolls with Spaghetti Squash & Quinoa   212
Buffalo Cauliflower Steaks   214
Provençal Vegetable Tian   216
Barbecue Tofu Kebabs   218

VEGGIE MEATBALLS *with* TOMATO RAGOUT

SERVES 2 *//PREP TIME* 30 minutes, plus 2 hours to overnight to chill
COOK TIME 1 hour 30 minutes

These addictive wild mushroom meatballs are superb served on a hero or over grains and, of course, with spaghetti. Make mini meatballs for the perfect party starter.

FOR THE MARINARA

2 tablespoons extra-virgin olive oil

1 medium yellow onion, finely diced

1 teaspoon sea salt

2 large garlic cloves

1 (28-ounce) can San Marzano crushed tomatoes

2 or 3 fresh basil leaves

Pinch red pepper flakes

FOR THE MEATBALLS AND RAGOUT

1 tablespoon extra-virgin olive oil

1 pound fresh mushrooms (white, cremini, shiitake, portobello), finely chopped

1 teaspoon sea salt

1 tablespoon unsalted butter or non-dairy butter

1 small yellow onion, finely diced

4 garlic cloves, minced

½ cup quick oats

4 tablespoons grated Parmesan cheese, divided

½ cup bread crumbs

½ small bunch Italian parsley, chopped

2 large eggs, divided, or flax eggs

Pinch cayenne pepper

Pinch dried oregano

½ teaspoon freshly ground black pepper

3 cups marinara sauce

Chopped fresh parsley, for garnish

TO MAKE THE MARINARA

1   In a medium, heavy-bottomed saucepan, heat the oil over medium heat. Add the onion and salt and sauté until translucent, about 5 minutes. Add the garlic and sauté for 1 minute more.

2   Increase the heat to medium-high and add the tomatoes, basil leaves, and red pepper flakes. Bring the sauce to a simmer, lower the heat to low, and simmer for about 45 minutes. Smash the garlic cloves against the side of the pot with a fork and stir the smashed garlic into the sauce. For a smoother sauce, blend with an immersion blender or stand blender.

3   Adjust the seasoning and use right away, or store, covered, in the refrigerator for up to 1 week or in the freezer for up to 6 months.

4 Heat the oil in a large sauté pan or skillet over medium-high heat. Add the mushrooms and sauté for 1 minute to sear and release the liquid. Add a pinch of salt and the butter, reduce the heat to medium, and sauté the mushrooms until golden brown, about 5 minutes.

5 Add the onion and sauté until translucent, about 5 minutes. Add the garlic and sauté until fragrant, about 1 minute. Transfer the mixture to a large bowl.

6 Add the oats to the mushroom mixture and stir until combined. Add 3 tablespoons of Parmesan cheese, bread crumbs, parsley, 1 egg, cayenne, oregano, salt, and pepper. Mix together with a fork until crumbly. Stir in the remaining 1 egg. Cover the mixture and refrigerate for at least 2 hours or overnight.

7 Preheat the oven to 450°F. Line a baking sheet with parchment paper.

8 Form the mixture into small meatballs using a 1-ounce scoop. Roll the meatballs lightly between your hands until smooth and arrange them on the baking sheet.

9 Bake until the meatballs are golden brown, 12 to 15 minutes.

10 While the meatballs are baking, heat the marinara sauce to a simmer in a large saucepan over medium-high heat. Reduce the heat to low and add the meatballs. Simmer until the meatballs are heated through, about 1 hour. Transfer the sauce and meatballs to a serving bowl and garnish with the remaining 1 tablespoon of Parmesan cheese and some parsley.

Storage: The meatballs and sauce can be kept in an airtight container in the refrigerator for up to 1 week or in the freezer for up to 3 months.

Make Ahead: The longer you refrigerate the meatball mixture, the better the texture and flavor. The meatballs can be prepared up through step 6 and refrigerated or frozen until ready to serve. Just reheat, garnish, and serve hot. I like to freeze these in individual portions and thaw as needed.

Per serving: Calories: 741; Total fat: 40g; Carbohydrates: 70g; Fiber: 12g; Protein: 29g; Calcium: 350mg; Vitamin D: 2mcg; Vitamin B12: 1mcg; Iron: 8mg; Zinc: 4mg

VEGAN SPINACH & TOFU ENCHILADAS

DAIRY-FREE, GLUTEN-FREE

SERVES 4 to 6 //*PREP TIME* 30 minutes, plus 30 minutes to rehydrate //*COOK TIME* 1 hour

Traditional gooey, cheesy enchiladas are not known for their health benefits. However, this version made with homemade sauce, tofu, and avocados is just as rich, and you won't miss the cheese. Divide them into individual portions, freeze, and reheat later for convenient, quick meals.

FOR THE ENCHILADA SAUCE

4 garlic cloves

6 large dried guajillo chiles, or other dried chile

1 teaspoon dried oregano

1 teaspoon whole black peppercorns

1 teaspoon cumin seeds

2 cups vegetable stock, divided

1 tablespoon avocado or canola oil

Sea salt

Freshly ground black pepper

FOR THE SPINACH AND TOFU

1 tablespoon extra-virgin olive oil

2 garlic cloves, minced

1 (14-ounce) block firm tofu, rinsed, drained, and excess water pressed out

1 (9-ounce) bag fresh baby spinach

FOR THE ENCHILADAS

12 (6-inch) blue or white corn tortillas

2 avocados, peeled, pitted, and sliced

2 radishes, julienned

½ head lettuce, shredded

½ cup non-dairy yogurt

TO MAKE THE ENCHILADA SAUCE

1 In a large cast iron skillet over medium heat roast the garlic, turning occasionally, until blackened and soft, about 15 minutes. Remove from the skillet and roughly chop.

2 While the garlic is roasting, break the stems off the chiles and remove the seeds. Toast the chiles in the skillet just until they begin to soften. Transfer the chiles to a bowl, cover with hot water, and rehydrate for 30 minutes. Drain and set aside.

3 Put the oregano, peppercorns, and cumin in a blender and pulse to grind. Add the drained chiles, roasted garlic, and 1 cup of stock. Process to a smooth puree, scraping the sides as needed.

4 Ladle the puree into a fine-mesh strainer over a medium bowl, pressing it through with the bottom of the ladle. Taste and season with salt.

5 Heat the oil in a medium saucepan over medium-high heat. When the oil shimmers, carefully add the

puree all at once. Cook, stirring constantly, as the puree sears, reduces, and darkens, about 10 minutes. Stir in the remaining 1 cup of stock and bring to a simmer, stirring occasionally, about 30 minutes. Season with salt and pepper as needed.

TO MAKE THE SPINACH AND TOFU

6 Heat the oil in a medium sauté pan or skillet on medium heat until the oil shimmers. Add the garlic and sauté for 1 minute, until translucent. Add the tofu and sauté until golden, about 7 minutes. Add the spinach and sauté quickly until wilted, about 1 minute.

TO MAKE THE ENCHILADAS

7 Warm the tortillas in the microwave for 30 seconds.

8 Dip 1 tortilla in the sauce, then add a spoonful of the spinach filling to the tortilla and spread it out evenly. Add a few slices of avocado. Cover the filling with another tortilla and more sauce. Repeat with the remaining tortillas, spinach filling, avocado slices, and sauce, creating stacked enchiladas.

9 Serve garnished with the radishes, lettuce, and yogurt.

Storage: The sauce can be stored in an airtight container in the refrigerator for up to 1 week or in the freezer for 6 months.

Prep Tip: It's fine to use a purchased enchilada sauce to save time; just be sure to check the label for chemicals and preservatives.

Per serving: Calories: 538; Total fat: 29g; Carbohydrates: 56g; Fiber: 16g; Protein: 21g; Calcium: 333mg; Vitamin D: <1mcg; Vitamin B12: 0mcg; Iron: 7mg; Zinc: 2mg

SPAGHETTI with BRAISED KALE, CHILE & LEMON

SERVES 2 //*PREP TIME* **15 minutes** //*COOK TIME* **30 minutes**

I usually get home from the restaurant late in the evening, and this is my favorite quick after-work dinner. It can be made year-round with ingredients you likely have on hand. Any hearty greens like Swiss chard or spinach are excellent in this recipe.

1 bunch kale, center ribs and stems removed, and cut crosswise into ½-inch slices

3 tablespoons extra-virgin olive oil, divided

1 medium yellow onion, finely diced

6 large garlic cloves, thinly sliced

Sea salt

1 teaspoon red pepper flakes, plus more for seasoning

½ pound whole-wheat spaghetti

Juice and zest of 1 lemon

Freshly ground black pepper

1 tablespoon grated Parmesan cheese

1   Rinse the kale thoroughly under cold water and drain, then transfer it to a bowl.

2   Heat 2 tablespoons of oil in a heavy, large saucepan over medium heat. Add the onion and cook until soft and translucent, stirring occasionally, about 5 minutes. Add the garlic, a pinch of salt, and the red pepper flakes. Sauté until the onion is golden brown, about 5 minutes.

3   Add the kale and remaining 1 tablespoon of oil and stir until wilted, about 3 minutes. Cover and reduce the heat to low. Continue cooking until the kale is very tender, stirring occasionally and adding water as needed, about 15 minutes.

4   While the kale is cooking, pour water into a medium stockpot until it is three-quarters full, and bring it to a boil over high heat. Cook the spaghetti until al dente, stirring occasionally. Drain, and reserve ¼ cup of the pasta water.

5 Add the spaghetti to the kale mix-ture. Add the lemon juice and 2 tablespoons of pasta water; stir to combine, adding more pasta water as needed. Season with salt, pepper, and red pepper flakes.

6 Garnish with the lemon zest and Parmesan cheese and serve.

Storage: The sauce can be stored in an airtight container in the refrigerator for up to 2 days.

Ingredient Tip: This recipe is great for customization and for using up any leftover veggies; just toss them in with the pasta to heat, and serve. You can also add tofu or fresh beans to get a bit of protein in the mix.

Per serving: Calories: 639; Total fat: 23g; Carbohydrates: 97g; Fiber: 11g; Protein: 20g; Calcium: 183mg; Vitamin D: 0mcg; Vitamin B12: <1mcg; Iron: 5mg; Zinc: 3mg

VEGAN GREEN RISOTTO with BROCCOLI

NON-DAIRY, GLUTEN-FREE

SERVES 2 //*PREP TIME* 30 minutes //*COOK TIME* 40 minutes

Risotto is one of my favorite comfort foods, and this pretty green version is packed with nutrients. The elegant presentation and the vibrant color are ideal for entertaining. Serve the risotto on its own, with a protein such as tofu folded right in, or as a filling side dish.

FOR THE PESTO

6 cups water

2 tablespoons sea salt

1 large stalk broccoli, cut into florets

3 tablespoons pine nuts

2 tablespoons walnuts

1 cup extra-virgin olive oil

½ small bunch Italian parsley

½ small bunch fresh basil

3 tablespoons vegan Parmesan cheese

1 teaspoon white miso paste

2 garlic cloves

Juice and zest of 1 lemon

Sea salt

Freshly ground black pepper

FOR THE RISOTTO

1 teaspoon extra-virgin olive oil

1 large stalk broccoli, cut into florets

Sea salt

Freshly ground black pepper

5 tablespoons Butterless Butter (page 36)

3 shallots, finely chopped

1 garlic clove, minced

1¼ cups arborio rice

1 cup dry white wine

2 cups vegetable stock

Zest of 1 lemon

Vegan Parmesan cheese, for garnish (optional)

TO MAKE THE PESTO

1   In a large stockpot, bring the water and salt to a boil over high heat. Add the broccoli and cook for about 3 minutes, or until it's bright green and crisp-tender. Strain and rinse under cold water. Roughly chop the florets.

2   Place a small sauté pan or skillet over medium-high heat and toast the pine nuts and walnuts, stirring occasionally, until golden, about 3 minutes.

3   Put the oil, broccoli, parsley, basil, pine nuts, walnuts, Parmesan, miso, garlic, lemon juice, and lemon zest in a food processor and process

until the mixture is smooth but still slightly textured. Season with salt and pepper.

TO MAKE THE RISOTTO

4   Heat the oil in a medium sauté pan or skillet over medium-high heat. Add the broccoli florets with a sprinkle of salt and pepper and sear until golden brown, about 3 minutes. Set aside.

5   Melt the butter in a large saucepan over medium heat. Add the shallots, garlic, and a pinch of salt, and sauté until the vegetables are soft, about 5 minutes.

6   Add the rice and stir over low heat until the rice is translucent, about 5 minutes.

7   Deglaze the rice mixture with the wine and let it simmer until the wine is reduced completely and absorbed into the rice, about 2 minutes.

8   Add the stock in ¼-cup measures and let it slowly simmer, stirring constantly until the stock is almost completely absorbed before adding more. The rice mixture should have a "wet sand" texture before each addition of stock. Continue the process until all the broth is incorporated and the rice is al dente, about 20 minutes.

9   Once the risotto is done, remove it from the heat and stir in ¼ cup of the pesto.

10 Place the risotto in a large, shallow serving dish and spoon the sautéed broccoli florets on top. Garnish with the lemon zest and a bit of vegan Parmesan (if using).

Storage: The risotto can be stored in an airtight container in the refrigerator for up to 1 week.

Cooking Tip: Continuous stirring to release the starch in the rice is key to a creamy risotto. It is a dish that needs attention to get the perfect texture.

Per serving: Calories: 966; Total fat: 39g; Carbohydrates: 121g; Fiber: 10g; Protein: 16g; Calcium: 145mg; Vitamin D: <1mcg; Vitamin B12: <1mcg; Iron: 3mg; Zinc: 1mg

PUMPKIN & CASHEW CURRY

DAIRY-FREE

SERVES 4 //*PREP TIME* **20 minutes** //*COOK TIME* **25 minutes**

This easy, creamy curry tastes a lot more complicated than it really is; don't tell anyone that you weren't sweating over a hot stove for hours. Serve over Coconut Cauliflower Rice (page 142) rather than the ancient grain and wild mushroom pilaf if you prefer.

2 tablespoons avocado or canola oil, divided

4½ cups (¾-inch) cubes sugar pumpkin

½ teaspoon black mustard seeds

8 curry leaves or the zest of 1 lime

2 small red onions, halved and cut into ½-inch-thick slices

2 garlic cloves, minced

1-inch piece fresh ginger, peeled and grated

3 dried chiles de arbol (dried Thai chiles)

¾ cup unsalted roasted cashews, chopped roughly

1 teaspoon ground turmeric

½ teaspoon ground cumin

1½ cups coconut milk

1 cup unsweetened coconut cream (see Tip)

½ cup coarsely chopped cilantro, plus more for garnish

1 tablespoon freshly squeezed lime juice

2 cups Ancient Grain & Wild Mushroom Pilaf (page 139), for serving

Lime wedges, for garnish

1 Heat 1 tablespoon of oil in a large saucepan over medium heat. Add the pumpkin and cook until golden, stirring occasionally, for 8 to 10 minutes. Transfer to a large bowl.

2 Heat the remaining 1 tablespoon of oil, mustard seeds, and curry leaves in the saucepan and cook until the seeds pop, about 30 seconds. Add the onions, garlic, and ginger. Sauté until the onions are golden, about 4 minutes.

3 Add the chiles, cashews, turmeric, and cumin, and sauté for 1 minute. Add the coconut milk and coconut cream and increase the heat to medium-high. Simmer until thickened, about 2 minutes.

4 Return the pumpkin to the sauce-pan and reduce the heat to medium. Simmer until the pumpkin is tender, about 5 minutes. Stir in ½ cup of cilantro and the lime juice.

5 Spoon the curry over the warm ancient grains and garnish with additional cilantro and lime wedges.

Storage: The curry can be stored in an airtight container in the refrigerator for up to 1 week or frozen for up to 3 months.

Ingredient Tip: Don't confuse coconut cream with the sweet cream of coconut used for baking or cocktails; coconut cream is a richer version of coconut milk that is made from pressed coconut.

Per serving: Calories: 777; Total fat: 58g; Carbohydrates: 62g; Fiber: 11g; Protein: 14g; Calcium: 121mg; Vitamin D: 0mcg; Vitamin B12: <1mcg; Iron: 6mg; Zinc: 3mg

CALABACITAS TACOS

DAIRY-FREE, GLUTEN-FREE

SERVES **4 to 6** // *PREP TIME* **15 minutes** // *COOK TIME* **15 minutes**

My cousin Colleen McGovern has been hooked on plant-based eating for six years now. She is famous among her friends for her tacos, so of course I had to have one of her recipes. I've been known to make a taco or two in my career (I've even written a book completely dedicated to them), so I know a good taco when I eat one! For a fun taco party, place the calabacitas in a bowl surrounded by your favorite toppings and set out warm tortillas in a basket and let everyone make their own.

1 tablespoon extra-virgin olive oil

1 large onion, chopped

Sea salt

3 garlic cloves, minced

4 zucchini, diced

4 yellow pattypans, sliced

1 small head cauliflower, broken up into florets

2 poblano peppers, roasted, peeled, seeded, and diced

1 cup corn kernels

1 cup sodium-free canned pinto beans

1 teaspoon Habanero Hot Sauce (page 67)

12 (4-inch) corn tortillas

2 cups Creamy Chipotle Salsa (see Tip)

6 ounces crumbled queso fresco (or vegan queso fresco), for garnish

2 avocados, sliced, for garnish

Lime wedges, for garnish

1   Heat the oil in a large sauté pan or skillet over medium-high heat. Add the onion and a pinch of salt and cook, stirring, until translucent, for about 5 minutes. Add the garlic and cook for 1 minute more.

2   Add the zucchini, pattypans, cauliflower florets, and poblano pepper, then cover and cook, stirring frequently, until crisp-tender. Stir in the corn, pinto beans, and hot sauce, and heat through. Adjust the seasoning.

3   Warm the tortillas on a griddle or nonstick pan. Place a couple of tablespoons of the filling in the warm tortillas, drizzle with the creamy chipotle salsa, and garnish with the queso fresco, avocado, and lime.

Storage: The sauce can be stored in an airtight container in the refrigerator for up to 3 days.

Ingredient Tip: For the Creamy Chipotle Salsa, combine 1 cup each of Eggless Mayonnaise (page 37) and non-dairy yogurt with 1 or 2 pieces of chipotle in adobo, 1 teaspoon of adobo sauce from the chipotles, and the juice of 1 lime in a food processor, and process until smooth.

Per serving: Calories: 862; Total fat: 60g; Carbohydrates: 64g; Fiber: 18g; Protein: 24g; Calcium: 425mg; Vitamin D: 2mcg; Vitamin B12: 1mcg; Iron: 3mg; Zinc: 3mg

CABBAGE & VEGGIE LASAGNA

SERVES 4 //*PREP TIME* 20 minutes //*COOK TIME* 50 minutes

Lasagna is perpetually a top contender for the best comfort food. Using cabbage to replace the pasta makes a lighter version that is plant-forward. This dish is great for weekend meal preppers; just cover and refrigerate until you're ready to serve.

Nonstick cooking spray

1 tablespoon extra-virgin olive oil

1 recipe Veggie Meatballs (page 176)

1 small bunch kale, large ribs removed and cut crosswise into strips

2 cups ricotta cheese

2 large eggs or flax eggs

¼ cup grated Parmesan, plus more for serving

1 teaspoon freshly ground black pepper

½ teaspoon red pepper flakes

1 recipe marinara sauce (page 176)

1 large green cabbage, leaves separated

4 cups shredded mozzarella or vegan mozzarella, plus more for garnish

1 Preheat the oven to 350°F. Lightly grease a 9-by-13-inch baking dish with cooking spray.

2 Heat the oil in a large sauté pan or skillet over medium heat and crumble in the veggie meatballs. Cook until browned, about 20 minutes, and set aside.

3 In a large bowl, stir together the kale, ricotta, eggs, Parmesan, pepper, and red pepper flakes until well combined.

4 Spread a layer of sauce, about ½ cup, over the entire bottom of the baking dish. Layer one-third of the cabbage leaves, half the ricotta mixture, half the veggie meatballs, another ½ cup of sauce, and one-third of the mozzarella cheese. Repeat the layering one more time and finish with a layer of one-third of cabbage and one-third of mozzarella cheese.

5 Bake for 30 minutes, or until the cheese is starting to brown and bubble.

6 Remove from the oven and allow to cool for 10 minutes before slicing.

7 Garnish with additional Parmesan cheese.

Cooking Tip: If desired, you can add sautéed veggies to this recipe instead of the meatballs. Don't skip the resting step for at least 10 minutes before slicing. This allows the cabbage leaves to soften and the sauce to tighten up, and will hold up better.

Per serving: Calories: 981; Total fat: 56g; Carbohydrates: 61g; Fiber: 15g; Protein: 64g; Calcium: 1360mg; Vitamin D: 1mcg; Vitamin B12: 1mcg; Iron: 5mg; Zinc: 2mg

SALT & PEPPER TOFU

DAIRY-FREE, GLUTEN-FREE

SERVES 2 //*PREP TIME* **10 minutes** //*COOK TIME* **10 minutes**

Crunchy on the outside and creamy on the inside, salt and pepper tofu is a Szechuan classic. It's ready in about 20 minutes, and served with a salad, it's the perfect weeknight dinner. It's also great for topping a veggie stir-fry, or served with veggie noodles or scrambled eggs.

12 ounces firm silken tofu, rinsed and drained

5 tablespoons cornstarch

2 teaspoons sea salt

1 teaspoon freshly ground black pepper, plus more for seasoning

Canola oil, for frying

2 Fresno chile peppers, seeded and thinly sliced

2 scallions, both white and green parts, thinly sliced

1 Place the tofu in a clean kitchen towel or paper towels and press and squeeze it in a colander to get as much of the liquid out as you can. Cut into 1-inch cubes.

2 In a small bowl, stir together the cornstarch, salt, and pepper until well blended.

3 Heat 1 inch of oil in a large sauté pan or skillet over medium heat to 350°F, or until bubbles form when you dip a wooden spoon in the oil.

4 Working in small batches, carefully coat the tofu cubes in a very thin layer of the cornstarch mixture, dusting off any excess. Fry the tofu, turning as needed until all sides are a pale golden brown, about 10 minutes.

5 Remove the tofu from the oil with a slotted spoon and let it drain on paper towels.

6 Serve immediately, garnished with the chile peppers, scallions, and a sprinkle of black pepper.

Serving Tip: I like to make a simple chili sauce to dip the hot tofu bites in; it's made from a bit of minced garlic, soy sauce, rice vinegar, and chili oil.

Per serving: Calories: 185; Total fat: 5g; Carbohydrates: 24g; Fiber: 1g; Protein: 13g; Calcium: 60mg; Vitamin D: 0mcg; Vitamin B12: 0mcg; Iron: 2mg; Zinc: <1mg

VEGETABLE SHEPHERD'S PIE

DAIRY-FREE, GLUTEN-FREE

SERVES 4 //*PREP TIME* **30 minutes** //*COOK TIME* **1 hour**

Shepherd's pie is winter comfort food at its finest. Originally developed to use up leftover meat and mashed potatoes, this veggie take on the British classic can come to the rescue when you're trying to figure out what to do with plain frozen vegetables or lone veggies in the refrigerator.

FOR THE SWEET POTATOES

3 large sweet potatoes, scrubbed, peeled, and chopped roughly into big chunks

2 tablespoons Butterless Butter (page 36)

1 teaspoon maple syrup

¼ teaspoon sea salt

Freshly ground black pepper

FOR THE FILLING

1 tablespoon avocado oil

1 medium yellow onion, finely diced

2 garlic cloves, minced

Pinch sea salt

Pinch freshly ground black pepper

1½ cups dried lentils, rinsed

4 cups vegetable stock

2 teaspoon chopped fresh thyme

1 (16-ounce) bag frozen veggies (of your choice, or leftover veggies)

TO MAKE THE SWEET POTATOES

1 Put the sweet potatoes in a large stockpot and fill with water until they're covered by 1 inch. Bring to a boil over high heat, reduce the heat to medium-high, and simmer for about 15 minutes, or until tender. Drain and transfer the potatoes to a large bowl.

2 Use a fork to mash the potatoes until smooth. Add the butter, maple syrup, and salt, stirring to combine. Season with pepper and set aside.

TO MAKE THE FILLING

3 Preheat the oven to 425°F and lightly oil a 9-by-13-inch baking dish.

4 Heat the oil in a large stockpot over medium heat. When the oil begins to shimmer, add the onion, garlic, salt, and pepper and sauté until the onions are lightly browned and caramelized, 6 to 8 minutes.

5 Stir in the lentils, stock, and thyme. Bring to a low boil, reduce the heat to low, and simmer until the lentils are al dente, about 20 minutes. In the last 10 minutes of cooking the lentils, add the frozen veggies, stir, and finish cooking. Taste and adjust the seasoning as needed.

6 Spoon the lentil mixture into the prepared baking dish and top with

CONTINUED

the mashed sweet potatoes. Smooth down the sweet potatoes with a spoon or fork and season with a little salt and pepper.

7   Bake for 20 minutes, until the potatoes have lightly browned on top and the lentils are bubbling.

8   Let cool briefly before serving to allow the lentils to tighten up a bit.

Storage: The shepherd's pie can be stored in the refrigerator, covered, for up to 4 or 5 days or in the freezer for up to 1 month.

Ingredient Tip: A traditional shepherd's pie is made with mashed russet potatoes, and you can do the same if you'd prefer. Cauliflower mash is also a lovely option.

Per serving: Calories: 570; Total fat: 9g; Carbohydrates: 99g; Fiber: 17g; Protein: 24g; Calcium: 115mg; Vitamin D: 0mcg; Vitamin B12: <1mcg; Iron: 7mg; Zinc: 3mg

TURKISH EGGPLANT CASSEROLE

DAIRY-FREE, GLUTEN-FREE

SERVES 4 //*PREP TIME* 20 minutes, plus 20 minutes to salt eggplant

COOK TIME 50 minutes

I love the super-healthy and fresh food in Turkey. This aromatic Turkish eggplant recipe is a perfect fit for weeknight dinners or weekend meal preppers. It's an excellent make-ahead dish because the flavors continue to blend as the casserole sits over time.

2 medium eggplants (about 1¾ pounds total), cut lengthwise into ¼-inch-thick slices

Sea salt

2 tablespoons extra-virgin olive oil

1 small yellow onion, diced

2 garlic cloves, minced

1 teaspoon ground cumin

1 teaspoon finely chopped fresh thyme

½ teaspoon red pepper flakes

¼ teaspoon ground cinnamon

Freshly ground black pepper

1 (15-ounce) can diced San Marzano tomatoes, undrained

2 tablespoons finely chopped fresh parsley, divided

1 Preheat the oven to 350°F.

2 Lightly salt the eggplant slices, place them in a colander, and allow them to stand for 20 minutes to release the liquid. Pat the slices dry and set aside.

3 Heat the oil in a large cast iron skillet over medium-high heat. Crisp the eggplant until golden brown on both sides, about 3 minutes per side. Remove the eggplant from the skillet and transfer it to a baking sheet.

4 Reduce the heat to medium, add the onion to the same skillet, and sauté until soft, about 5 minutes. Add the garlic, cumin, thyme, red pepper flakes, cinnamon, a pinch of salt, and a pinch of pepper. Cook for 1 minute more, until fragrant. Pour in the tomatoes and simmer until thickened slightly, about 5 minutes. Remove the sauce from the heat and stir in 1 tablespoon of parsley.

5 Spoon 1½ cups of the sauce from the skillet into a bowl, leaving a thin layer in the skillet. Arrange a layer of eggplant over the sauce in the skillet. Spoon another layer of sauce over the eggplant, and repeat layering with the remaining eggplant and sauce.

CONTINUED

6 Cover the skillet, transfer it to the oven, and bake for about 30 minutes, until the eggplant has softened and the sauce has thickened. Let the casserole rest for 10 minutes before serving. Garnish with the remaining 1 tablespoon of parsley and serve warm or at room temperature.

Storage: This casserole can be made ahead of time and refrigerated for up to 1 week covered or frozen for up to 3 months.

Variation Tip: This Turkish version of eggplant casserole leaves out the cheese, but if you prefer the cheesy Italian version, add some mozzarella (or vegan cheese) in between the layers and as a topping.

Per serving: Calories: 148; Total fat: 7g; Carbohydrates: 20g; Fiber: 8g; Protein: 3g; Calcium: 71mg; Vitamin D: 0mcg; Vitamin B12: 0mcg; Iron: 1mg; Zinc: <1mg

CARROT FALAFEL *with* ZUCCANOUSH

DAIRY-FREE

SERVES 2 //*PREP TIME* 30 minutes, plus overnight to soak //*COOK TIME* 35 minutes

Restaurant falafel are generally fried, which creates a delicious and crispy patty. Although it is flavorful, deep-frying is not a healthy cooking process. So, in pursuit of a lighter falafel recipe for my sister, Holly, the falafel queen, I tried cooking these on a baking sheet in the oven with a bit of olive oil. They came out brown and crispy on the outside and tender on the inside without the extra oil of deep-frying.

FOR THE ZUCCANOUSH
1 tablespoon pine nuts

3 (1-pound) zucchini, sliced lengthwise

3 tablespoons extra-virgin olive oil, divided

Sea salt

¼ cup tahini

½ small bunch mint leaves

1 garlic clove

Juice and zest of 1 lemon

FOR THE CARROT FALAFEL
1 cup dried chickpeas

2 tablespoons avocado oil, divided

3 small carrots, shredded

1 small onion, finely diced

3 garlic cloves, minced

1 small bunch Italian parsley, chopped

2 tablespoons tahini

½ teaspoon ground cumin

½ teaspoon ground coriander

Sea salt

Freshly ground black pepper

1 plum tomato, sliced, for serving

1 small cucumber, sliced, for serving

1 avocado, sliced, for serving

½ small red onion, sliced, for serving

4 homemade pitas (page 100), or store-bought, for serving

¼ cup hot sauce, for serving

TO MAKE THE ZUCCANOUSH

1 In a small sauté pan or skillet over medium-high heat, toast the pine nuts, swirling the skillet, until golden, about 3 minutes. Remove from the heat and set aside.

2 Heat a grill or grill pan to medium heat.

3 In a medium bowl, toss the zucchini with 1½ tablespoons of oil and a pinch salt. Then grill the zucchini until softened and charred on all sides, about 10 minutes.

4 Transfer the zucchini to a blender along with the tahini, mint, garlic, and lemon juice, and pulse to combine. With the motor running on low speed, drizzle in the remaining 1½ tablespoons of oil and puree until mostly smooth. Transfer to a serving bowl and top with the lemon zest and pine nuts.

5 Set aside.

CONTINUED

TO MAKE THE CARROT FALAFEL

6 The night before, place the chickpeas in a large bowl and cover by about 3 inches with water. Set aside at room temperature to soak overnight or up to 24 hours.

7 Preheat the oven to 375°F and lightly oil a baking sheet with 1 tablespoon of the oil.

8 Drain the chickpeas and transfer to a food processor with the remaining 1 tablespoon of oil, the carrots, onion, garlic, parsley, tahini, cumin, and coriander, and pulse until you get a crumbly batter; do not overprocess. Season with salt and pepper.

9 Using a 1-ounce scoop, portion out balls of the batter and form them into small patties. Place them on the baking sheet and repeat until all the batter is used up.

10 Bake in the oven for about 20 minutes, or until golden brown, flipping them halfway through.

11 Serve the falafel with the zuccanoush, the plum tomato, cucumber, avocado, onion, pitas, and hot sauce.

Storage: Store leftover falafel in the refrigerator in an airtight container for 3 or 4 days or in the freezer for up to 3 months.

Ingredient Tip: It is important to use the dried, soaked chickpeas; canned chickpeas contain a high water content and will affect the consistency of your falafel, making them soggy.

Per serving: Calories: 1,631; Total fat: 82g; Carbohydrates: 195g; Fiber: 42g; Protein: 55g; Calcium: 632mg; Vitamin D: 0mcg; Vitamin B12: 0mcg; Iron: 21mg; Zinc: 7mg

BUTTERNUT SQUASH, BLACK BEAN & GRAIN CHILI

SERVES **4** //*PREP TIME* **15 minutes** //*COOK TIME* **30 minutes**

The smoky, sweet, and spicy flavors blend beautifully in this nutrient-dense, plant-friendly chili. Serve with a green salad for a weeknight dinner and heat up the leftovers for lunch. It's also excellent as a filling for tacos or as a topping for a warm grain bowl or baked sweet potatoes.

1 tablespoon extra-virgin olive oil

1 medium butternut squash, peeled and cut into ½-inch cubes

2 medium yellow onions, finely diced

1 jalapeño pepper, seeded and minced

Sea salt

4 garlic cloves, minced

2 tablespoons chili powder

2 teaspoons ground cumin

½ teaspoon dried oregano

1 chipotle pepper in adobo, minced

¼ teaspoon smoked paprika

2 cups vegetable stock

1 (15-ounce) can finely diced San Marzano tomatoes

2 cups low-sodium canned black beans

½ cup quick-cooking barley

Freshly ground black pepper

2 scallions, both white and green parts, sliced

½ red onion, diced

½ cup shredded cheese or vegan cheese

¼ cup pickled jalapeño pepper slices

½ cup plain Greek yogurt or dairy-free yogurt, for serving

1   Heat the oil in a large, heavy saucepan over medium heat. Add the butternut squash, onions, and jalapeño with a pinch of sea salt. Sauté until the onion has softened, about 5 minutes. Add the garlic and cook for 1 minute more. Stir in the chili powder, cumin, oregano, chipotle, and paprika, and cook until fragrant, about 30 seconds.

2   Add the stock, tomatoes, beans, and barley, and reduce the heat to low. Cover and simmer until the butternut squash is tender and the barley is cooked through, about 20 minutes. Season with salt and pepper.

3   Serve hot, topped with the scallions, red onion, cheese, pickled jalapeño, and yogurt.

Storage: The chili will keep in an airtight container in the refrigerator for up to 1 week or frozen for up to 6 months.

Make Ahead: This is a fast and easy chili to make ahead when weekend meal prepping. You can substitute wild rice or amaranth for the barley to make a gluten-free dish.

Per serving: Calories: 458; Total fat: 11g; Carbohydrates: 74g; Fiber: 20g; Protein: 20g; Calcium: 339mg; Vitamin D: 0mcg; Vitamin B12: <1mcg; Iron: 5mg; Zinc: 2mg

MOROCCAN VEGGIE
TAGINE *with* COUSCOUS

DAIRY-FREE

SERVES 4 //*PREP TIME* 20 minutes //*COOK TIME* 40 minutes

This exotic veggie tagine can be made in under an hour. It's wonderful for entertaining because everything can be made ahead and simply warmed up for serving. You won't miss a moment with your guests. The vegetables should be the freshest available and in season, but which ones is up to you.

FOR THE TAGINE

¼ cup extra-virgin olive oil, plus more to drizzle

2 medium yellow onions, finely diced

6 garlic cloves, minced

2 medium carrots, finely diced

4 small red potatoes, cut into ¼-inch pieces

1 large sweet potato, peeled and diced

Sea salt

1 tablespoon harissa

1 teaspoon ground coriander

1 teaspoon ground cinnamon

½ teaspoon ground turmeric

1 quart vegetable stock

1 (15-ounce) can San Marzano whole peeled tomatoes

½ cup chopped dried apricots

2 cups low-sodium canned chickpeas

Juice of 1 lemon

½ small bunch Italian parsley leaves

FOR THE COUSCOUS

2 tablespoons pine nuts

2 cups vegetable stock or water

1 tablespoon extra-virgin olive oil

½ teaspoon sea salt

1½ cups couscous

2 tablespoons golden raisins

½ teaspoon ground cinnamon

½ cup chopped Italian parsley, for garnish

TO MAKE THE TAGINE

1   Heat the oil in a large, heavy pot or Dutch oven over medium-high heat until it shimmers. Add the onions and sauté for 5 minutes, until soft and translucent. Add the garlic, carrots, potatoes, and sweet potato, stirring to combine. Season with salt and stir in the harissa, coriander, cinnamon, and turmeric.

2   Reduce the heat to medium and continue to cook for 5 minutes, stirring occasionally.

3   Add the stock, tomatoes, and apricots. Season with a pinch of salt and continue to cook for 10 minutes. Reduce the heat to low, cover, and simmer for 20 minutes more, or until the veggies are al dente.

4 Stir in the chickpeas and cook for 5 minutes more. Stir in the lemon juice and parsley. Taste and adjust the seasoning. Transfer the mixture to serving bowls and top each with a drizzle of olive oil. Serve hot with the couscous.

TO MAKE THE COUSCOUS

5 Place a small sauté pan or skillet over medium-high heat and toast the pine nuts, swirling the skillet, until golden, about 3 minutes. Remove from the heat and set aside.

6 In a medium saucepan over medium-high, bring the stock, oil, and salt to a boil. Stir in the couscous, raisins, cinnamon, and pine nuts, and remove from the heat.

7 Cover and let the couscous steam for 5 minutes. Fluff with a fork and stir in the parsley. Serve.

Storage: The couscous will keep in an airtight container in the refrigerator for up to 1 week or frozen for up to 3 months.

Cooking Tip: Couscous freezes well and is excellent for having on hand to serve with leftover veggies.

Per serving: Calories: 854; Total fat: 23g; Carbohydrates: 143g; Fiber: 19g; Protein: 22g; Calcium: 190mg; Vitamin D: 0mcg; Vitamin B12: 0mcg; Iron: 7mg; Zinc: 2mg

JERK TOFU STEAKS

DAIRY-FREE, GLUTEN-FREE

SERVES 4 //*PREP TIME* 20 minutes, plus 2 hours to marinate //*COOK TIME* 10 minutes

There is a large Jamaican population in my neighborhood, and I am lucky enough to have access to some of the best jerk outside Kingston. Tofu is a common choice of protein. You can re-create these smoky and sweet tofu steaks at home, and they will make anyone a tofu believer. They make a great component for a grain bowl or salad, or serve them with a hearty side for dinner like Coconut Cauliflower Rice (page 142). For a milder version, use seeded jalapeño or Fresno chiles.

1 pound extra-firm tofu, drained and rinsed

1 small red onion, chopped roughly

6 garlic cloves

2 habanero peppers, seeded and minced

2 tablespoons peeled and grated fresh ginger

Juice and zest of 2 limes

3 tablespoons maple syrup

2 tablespoons gluten-free soy sauce

3 tablespoons extra-virgin olive oil, divided

1 teaspoon chopped fresh thyme

2 teaspoons ground allspice

½ teaspoon cayenne pepper

½ teaspoon ground nutmeg

½ teaspoon ground cinnamon

Sea salt

2 cups Gingered Sweet Potato Mash (page 146)

1 Slice the tofu into thick slabs, then lay the slices on several layers of paper towels or on a clean kitchen towel. Cover with paper towels and place a plate holding something heavy on top, for 15 minutes. This will remove the extra moisture, resulting in a crisper texture and better absorption of the marinade.

2 In a blender or food processor, put the onion, garlic, habanero peppers, ginger, lime juice, lime zest, maple syrup, soy sauce, 2 tablespoons of oil, thyme, allspice, cayenne, nutmeg, and cinnamon, and blend to create a smooth paste.

3 Place the pressed tofu slices in a 9-by-13-inch baking dish, spoon the marinade over them, turning the tofu to coat, then cover and set aside at room temperature for at least 2 hours, flipping halfway through.

4 Heat the remaining 1 tablespoon of oil in a heavy sauté pan or skillet over medium-high heat. When the oil shimmers, add the tofu slices in a single layer and season with salt. Sauté until crispy and golden, about 5 minutes on each side.

5 Serve with gingered sweet potato mash or rice.

Storage: The tofu will keep in an airtight container in the refrigerator for up to 1 week.

Make Ahead: Prep the marinade and tofu the day before serving and refrigerate the marinated tofu overnight.

Per serving: Calories: 364; Total fat: 17g; Carbohydrates: 41g; Fiber: 5g; Protein: 15g; Calcium: 248mg; Vitamin D: 0mcg; Vitamin B12: 0mcg; Iron: 3mg; Zinc: 1mg

GREEN TEA SOBA NOODLES *with* SESAME DIPPING SAUCE

SERVES **4** // *PREP TIME* **15 minutes** // *COOK TIME* **10 minutes**

DAIRY-FREE

This elegant dish makes a lovely light lunch and is easy to prep ahead and take along. I love it with a crunchy salad. Thin buckwheat soba noodles contain fewer calories than traditional wheat pasta and can be served cold or warm.

FOR THE DIPPING SAUCE

1 small cucumber, finely grated

Juice and zest of 2 limes

3 tablespoons Japanese chili paste or other chili paste (see Tip)

1 tablespoon peeled and finely grated fresh ginger

1 tablespoon soy sauce or tamari

2 teaspoons toasted sesame oil

1½ teaspoons sugar

FOR THE NOODLES

2 teaspoons sesame seeds

1 teaspoon sea salt

1 (7-ounce) package green tea soba noodles

½ medium cucumber, cut into matchsticks

½ teaspoon toasted sesame oil

½ small bunch basil leaves, for serving

TO MAKE THE DIPPING SAUCE

1 Place the cucumber in a clean kitchen towel and squeeze gently to remove the excess water.

2 In a small bowl, whisk together the cucumber, lime juice, lime zest, chili paste, ginger, soy sauce, oil, and sugar until well blended.

3 Set aside.

TO MAKE THE NOODLES

4 In a small sauté pan or skillet over medium-high heat toast the sesame seeds, swirling the skillet, until the seeds are golden, about 3 minutes. Remove from the heat and set aside.

5   Fill a large saucepan three-quarters full of water, add the salt, and bring to a boil over high heat. Add the noodles and cook, stirring occasionally, until they are al dente, about 5 minutes. Drain and immediately rinse the noodles with cold water to stop the cooking process.

6   Put the noodles in a large bowl and toss with the cucumber, sesame seeds, and sesame oil. Let rest for 5 minutes to allow flavors to combine.

7   Put the noodles in serving bowls and garnish with the basil leaves. Serve with the dipping sauce on the side.

Storage: Leftover noodles can be tossed in a little oil and will keep in an airtight container in the refrigerator for up to 4 days.

Ingredient Tip: Japanese chili paste can be bought at Asian markets or online. You can also make it at home. Toast some dried chiles of your preference, rehydrate them in hot water, and drain and puree them into a paste in a food processor or blender. While the blender is running, drizzle in a little bit of avocado oil in a thin stream. You can also add garlic, soy sauce, rice vinegar, and salt to your taste.

Per serving: Calories: 272; Total fat: 7g; Carbohydrates: 48g; Fiber: 2g; Protein: 9g; Calcium: 37mg; Vitamin D: 0mcg; Vitamin B12: 0mcg; Iron: 2mg; Zinc: 1mg

RICED CAULIFLOWER
& CHICKPEA PILAF

DAIRY-FREE, GLUTEN-FREE

SERVES 2 //*PREP TIME* 15 minutes //*COOK TIME* 15 minutes

This dish is a meatless, one-pot meal with veggies, protein, and tons of flavor. It also makes a great meal-prep dish and bowl component. I often substitute a head of broccoli for the cauliflower in this dish or even use a combination of the two.

1 tablespoon extra-virgin olive oil

2 teaspoons cumin seeds

1 medium yellow onion, finely diced

Sea salt

2 garlic cloves, minced

1 head cauliflower, finely chopped (see Tip)

1 teaspoon ground turmeric

1 teaspoon ground cumin

½ teaspoon red pepper flakes

Freshly ground black pepper

2 cups low-sodium canned chickpeas

½ small bunch Italian parsley, chopped, for garnish

1   Heat the oil in a large sauté pan or skillet over medium heat. Toast the cumin seeds until fragrant, about 30 seconds. Add the onion and a pinch of salt and sauté until soft and translucent, about 5 minutes. Add the garlic and sauté for 1 minute more.

2   Add the cauliflower rice, turmeric, cumin, and red pepper flakes to the skillet and season with salt and pepper. Cook, stirring constantly, for 2 minutes, then add the chickpeas and toss until heated through, about 5 minutes.

3   Taste and adjust the seasoning.

4   Garnish with the parsley and serve warm.

Storage: This will keep well in the refrigerator in an airtight container for up to 1 week and frozen for up to 6 months.

Ingredient Tip: You can also pulse cauliflower florets in the food processor until they look like rice. Trader Joe's and Whole Foods stock both fresh and frozen riced cauliflower.

Per serving: Calories: 391; Total fat: 13g; Carbohydrates: 58g; Fiber: 18g; Protein: 18g; Calcium: 186mg; Vitamin D: 0mcg; Vitamin B12: 0mcg; Iron: 6mg; Zinc: 2mg

CARIBBEAN CHARD, SWEET POTATO & SPICY PEANUT JUMBLE

DAIRY-FREE, GLUTEN-FREE

SERVES **4** *//PREP TIME* **20 minutes** *//COOK TIME* **30 minutes**

This comforting and nutritious vegan stew is based on the Caribbean via West Africa jumble called *maafe*. Traditionally, this is eaten family style with guests, directly from the platter, to demonstrate hospitality and unity. My version is not completely authentic, but it is 100 percent delicious, and I welcome you to enjoy it in a way that is authentic to your home. Serve it over rice or a grain pilaf for a hearty meal complete with protein.

2 tablespoons extra-virgin olive oil

1 small yellow onion, diced

1 jalapeño pepper, stemmed and minced

2 garlic cloves, minced

3 large white sweet potatoes (or yams), peeled and cubed

1 (14-ounce) can diced San Marzano tomatoes

1 (14-ounce) can light, unsweetened coconut milk

2 cups water

1 teaspoon sea salt

1 teaspoon curry powder

½ teaspoon turmeric

¾ cup chopped roasted peanuts

¼ cup creamy peanut butter

1 head Swiss chard, ribs removed, cut crosswise into ½-inch pieces

½ small bunch cilantro, chopped, for serving

Lime wedges, for serving

1 Heat the oil in a large stockpot over medium heat. Add the onion and jalapeño and sauté until soft and fragrant, about 5 minutes. Add the garlic and cook for 1 minute more.

2 Add the sweet potatoes and stir for 1 to 2 minutes. Add the tomatoes, coconut milk, water, salt, curry, turmeric, and ½ cup of peanuts. Simmer until the sweet potatoes are tender but still a little firm.

3 Add the peanut butter and chard. Simmer until the mixture thickens, about 15 minutes. Taste and adjust seasoning.

4 Serve hot, garnished with the remaining ¼ cup of peanuts and cilantro and with lime wedges on the side.

Storage: This will keep in an airtight container in the refrigerator for about 1 week and in the freezer for up to 6 months.

Per serving: Calories: 741; Total fat: 35g; Carbohydrates: 97g; Fiber: 51g; Protein: 19g; Calcium: 194mg; Vitamin D: 0mcg; Vitamin B12: 0mcg; Iron: 7mg; Zinc: 2mg

CAULIFLOWER CRUST PIZZA

GLUTEN-FREE

SERVES **4** *//PREP TIME* **15 minutes** *//COOK TIME* **30 minutes**

This gluten-free pizza crust made from cauliflower is so yummy that I make them four at a time and freeze them so I can have a healthy pizza anytime. Top with a simple marinara sauce (page 176), vegan or regular mozzarella, and your favorite veggie pizza toppings. You have a guilt-free pizza that will please your family and friends, vegetarian or not.

1 head cauliflower, stalk removed and cut into florets

½ cup shredded mozzarella or vegan mozzarella

¼ cup grated Parmesan or vegan Parmesan

2 large eggs, lightly beaten, or flax eggs

1 teaspoon nutritional yeast

1 teaspoon sea salt

½ teaspoon dried oregano

¼ teaspoon garlic powder

Your favorite sauce and toppings

1 Preheat the oven to 400°F. Line a baking sheet with parchment paper.

2 Put the cauliflower florets in a food processor and pulse until they are a fine meal. Steam the cauliflower meal in a steamer basket and strain. Spread the steamed cauliflower out on a clean kitchen towel or paper towels to absorb excess moisture. Let cool completely.

3 In a large bowl, combine the cauliflower with the mozzarella, Parmesan, eggs, nutritional yeast, salt, oregano, and garlic powder until a dough forms.

4 Transfer the dough to the center of the baking sheet and spread out into a circular or rectangular pizza crust shape. Bake for 20 minutes.

5 Remove from the oven and spread with your favorite sauce and toppings. Return to the oven and bake for 10 minutes more. Serve hot.

Storage: The crust will keep in an airtight container in the refrigerator for up to 1 week or in the freezer for up to 6 months.

Make Ahead: The recipe can easily be doubled or multiplied and frozen after step 4. When you're ready to serve, pull the crust out of the freezer, place on a baking sheet, and bake in the oven at 400°F for 10 minutes, then top and bake as in step 5.

Per serving: Calories: 145; Total fat: 8g; Carbohydrates: 9g; Fiber: 3g; Protein: 12g; Calcium: 202mg; Vitamin D: 1mcg; Vitamin B12: 1mcg; Iron: 1mg; Zinc: 1mg

VEGAN PAD THAI

DAIRY-FREE, GLUTEN-FREE

SERVES 2 // *PREP TIME* 15 minutes // *COOK TIME* 20 minutes

I've been making tofu pad thai for years, and it remains one of my go-to dishes. It's made with fresh, healthy, inexpensive ingredients, and takes less than 30 minutes to throw together. This pad thai recipe offers protein in the form of tofu (or eggs) and peanuts, and because it's made with rice noodles, it is also gluten-free. The enoki mushrooms add some earthy flavor and create a more nutritious dish.

1 (7-ounce) package rice noodles

1 teaspoon sea salt

½ (14-ounce) block extra-firm tofu, rinsed and drained

2 tablespoons avocado oil

4 ounces enoki mushrooms

1 bunch garlic chives, thinly sliced (see Tip)

1 garlic clove, minced

1 Thai chile (or jalapeño), thinly sliced

2 tablespoons gluten-free soy sauce

1 tablespoon coconut sugar (or maple syrup or agave nectar)

Juice of 1 lime

¼ cup vegetable stock

1 cup bean sprouts

1 scallion, both white and green parts, thinly sliced

1 tablespoon chopped roasted peanuts, for serving

1 tablespoon chopped cilantro, for serving

Lime wedges, for serving

1   Fill a medium saucepan three-quarters full of water and bring to a boil over high heat. Add the noodles and salt and boil until just tender but still a bit under-cooked, 3 to 5 minutes. Rinse the noodles quickly under cold water to stop the cooking process. Drain and set aside.

2   Place the tofu in between paper towels and press to release any excess water. Dice the tofu into ½-inch cubes or crumble it gently.

3   Heat the oil in a large sauté pan or skillet over medium-high heat, add the tofu, and cook, stirring occasion-ally, for about 5 minutes on each side, until golden. Transfer the tofu to a plate with a slotted spoon and set aside.

4   Reduce the heat to medium and in the same skillet put the noodles, mushrooms, chives, garlic, Thai chile, soy sauce, coconut sugar, and lime juice, and toss to combine.

5   Slowly add the vegetable stock to the skillet, 1 tablespoon at a time,

and continue to cook for 3 to 4 minutes. Reduce the heat to low and add the reserved tofu, the bean sprouts, and the scallion and toss to combine.

6   Transfer to serving bowls, top each bowl with chopped peanuts, cilantro, and a lime wedge, and serve hot.

Storage: The pad thai will keep for 1 or 2 days in the refrigerator in an airtight container but is best served immediately.

Ingredient Tip: Garlic chives are a pretty herb with small white flowers on the tips. They have a chive-like appearance and strong garlic flavor, which give them their name. You may substitute regular chives and increase the garlic if this herb is unavailable.

Per serving: Calories: 705; Total fat: 22g; Carbohydrates: 104g; Fiber: 7g; Protein: 23g; Calcium: 221mg; Vitamin D: <1mcg; Vitamin B12: 0mcg; Iron: 5mg; Zinc: 2mg

WHOLE ROASTED CAULIFLOWER
IN HERB SALSA VERDE

DAIRY-FREE, GLUTEN-FREE

SERVES 4 //*PREP TIME* 20 minutes //*COOK TIME* 40 minutes

Cauliflower was not on my favorite-vegetable list as a kid, but now, knowing so many flavorful and interesting ways of preparing it, I'm all in. This dish is a showstopper for entertaining and is ready in less than an hour. Experiment with different sauces for serving; you really can't go wrong with anything because cauliflower is an excellent flavor absorber. For the herbs in this recipe, use any you'd like; my choices are just a blueprint. You can even bundle together any loose sprigs that you have in the refrigerator.

3 teaspoons sea salt, divided, plus more for seasoning

2 whole heads cauliflower, green outer leaves removed

½ teaspoon freshly ground black pepper, plus more for seasoning

Zest of 1 orange

1 cup baby arugula leaves

¼ bunch parsley leaves, chopped roughly

Juice of 1 lemon

2 tablespoons white balsamic vinegar

1 shallot

1 serrano pepper, seeded

1 garlic clove

2 teaspoons roughly chopped marjoram leaves

2 teaspoons roughly chopped basil leaves

¼ cup extra-virgin olive oil

2 cups Lemon-Herb Red Quinoa (page 147), for serving

1 Preheat the oven to 450°F. Line a baking sheet with parchment paper.

2 Fill a large stockpot three-quarters full of water and bring to a boil over high heat. Add 2 teaspoons of salt and the whole heads of cauliflower and cook in the boiling water for 5 minutes. Carefully remove the cauliflower from the pot, transfer to a colander, drain, and rinse quickly with cold water to stop the cooking process. Set aside to dry.

3 Season the cauliflower all over with the remaining 1 teaspoon of salt and the pepper. Transfer the cauliflower to the baking sheet and roast for 5 minutes. Reduce the heat to 375°F and continue to roast for 30 minutes. Remove the cauliflower from the oven.

4 While the cauliflower is roasting, put the orange zest, arugula, parsley, lemon juice, vinegar, shallot, serrano pepper, garlic, marjoram, and basil in a food processor or blender and puree. With the motor running, drizzle in the olive oil. Season with salt and pepper.

5 Serve the cauliflower drizzled with the sauce and the lemon-herb red quinoa.

Storage: Leftovers can be kept in the refrigerator in an airtight container for up to 3 days.

Make Ahead: This dish is also beautiful with the cauliflower sliced into thick steaks crosswise, the slices shingled onto a serving platter, and the salsa verde drizzled down the center. Like most sauces, the salsa verde improves with age and can be made a day ahead. The cauliflower can also be blanched and refrigerated until ready to serve.

Per serving: Calories: 352; Total fat: 18g; Carbohydrates: 43g; Fiber: 10g; Protein: 10g; Calcium: 98mg; Vitamin D: 0mcg; Vitamin B12: <1mcg; Iron: 3mg; Zinc: 1mg

SPICY VEGAN SWEET POTATO MAKI with COCONUT RICE

DAIRY-FREE

SERVES **2** // *PREP TIME* **30 minutes** // *COOK TIME* **30 minutes**

Making your own sushi may sound intimidating, but it's fun and easy once you get the hang of it. Once the technique is familiar, you can begin to experiment with all sorts of different wraps and fillings. It's also a great project for kids. There are tons of videos online that demonstrate the correct method for making sushi.

FOR THE SWEET POTATO FILLING

1 tablespoon canola oil

1 tablespoon maple syrup

2 teaspoons sea salt

1 teaspoon sesame oil

½ teaspoon red pepper flakes

1 large (1-pound) sweet potato, peeled and cut into batons

FOR THE RICE

1 cup sushi rice

1 cup water

⅓ cup coconut milk

1½ tablespoons rice vinegar

2 teaspoons sea salt

FOR THE MAKI

3 sheets nori

2 tablespoons unsweetened coconut flakes

1 ripe avocado, sliced

2 scallions, both white and green parts, halved and sliced lengthwise

1 teaspoon sesame seeds, for garnish

1 teaspoon wasabi, for serving

1 tablespoon pickled ginger, for serving

2 tablespoons soy sauce, for serving

TO MAKE THE SWEET POTATO FILLING

1 Preheat the oven to 375°F. Line a baking sheet with parchment paper.

2 In a small bowl, combine the canola oil, maple syrup, salt, sesame oil, and red pepper flakes. Add the sweet potatoes to the bowl and toss to coat.

3 Arrange the sweet potatoes on the baking sheet and roast for about 15 minutes, or until just tender.

TO MAKE THE RICE

4 While the sweet potatoes are roasting, place the rice in a fine-mesh sieve and rinse under cold water for about 2 minutes. In a medium saucepan, put the rice, water, coconut milk, vinegar, and salt and heat over high heat. Bring to a boil, reduce the heat to low, cover, and simmer until the liquid is absorbed, 10 to 15 minutes.

5   Remove from the heat and allow the rice to sit, covered, for 10 minutes.

TO MAKE THE MAKI

6   Place a bamboo sushi mat on a clean work surface and put a small dish of water nearby for wetting your hands. If you do not have a sushi mat, use a clean kitchen towel covered with plastic wrap.

7   Place one of the nori sheets on the bamboo mat. Dampen your hands and cover the nori with a thin layer of rice (about one-third) and sprinkle the rice with one-third of the coconut. Arrange one-third of the sweet potatoes in a single line along the width of the nori, about 1 inch away from the edge of the mat. Arrange one-third of the avocado slices and a few scallion slices next to the sweet potatoes.

8   Take the bamboo mat and tightly roll it over the fillings. Tuck the end of the nori in and continue rolling, using the mat to press the roll tight. Dip a finger in the water bowl and run it over the edge of the roll to seal. Once completely rolled, slice into 8 pieces with a very sharp knife. Repeat using the remaining nori sheets and filling.

9   Sprinkle the maki with the sesame seeds and serve with the wasabi, pickled ginger, and soy sauce.

Make Ahead: Sushi by nature should be eaten right away, but you could roll these the night before and cut them in the morning to take for lunch.

Per serving: Calories: 947; Total fat: 32g; Carbohydrates: 153g; Fiber: 19g; Protein: 16g; Calcium: 121mg; Vitamin D: 0mcg; Vitamin B12: 0mcg; Iron: 4mg; Zinc: 2mg

ZUCCHINI ROLLS *with* SPAGHETTI SQUASH & QUINOA

DAIRY-FREE

SERVES 2 // *PREP TIME* **40 minutes** // *COOK TIME* **1 hour 20 minutes**

These fun zucchini rolls mimic sushi maki rolls and are an ideal take-along lunch. Bamboo sushi mats can be purchased inexpensively online and at Asian markets. It's fun to alternate slices of zucchini with yellow summer squash for a beautiful striped effect. Serve these alongside the Spicy Vegan Sweet Potato Maki with Coconut Rice (page 210) for a sushi dinner party.

⅔ cup water

⅓ cup quinoa

1 medium spaghetti squash

1 teaspoon avocado oil

Sea salt

Freshly ground black pepper

2 medium zucchini, cut lengthwise into very thin strips

1 medium carrot, peeled and grated

1 avocado, peeled, pitted, and sliced

1 small bunch fresh mint leaves, chopped

¼ cup Eggless Mayonnaise (page 37)

1 piece chipotle pepper in adobo, minced

Juice and zest of 1 lime

2 tablespoons soy sauce, for serving

1 tablespoon pickled ginger, for serving

1 teaspoon wasabi, for serving

1. Put the water and quinoa in a medium saucepan and bring to a boil over high heat. Reduce the heat to medium-low and simmer until the water is absorbed and the quinoa is tender, about 20 minutes. Remove from the heat and let sit for 5 minutes, then fluff with a fork.

2. Preheat the oven to 400°F.

3. Brush the whole spaghetti squash with the oil and season with salt and pepper. Place the squash in a 9-by-9-inch baking dish.

4. Roast the squash until tender and a knife inserts into the flesh easily, about 1 hour. Remove from the oven and allow to cool slightly. Once cool, cut the squash in half lengthwise, scoop out the seeds and discard them, then scoop out the stringy, spaghetti-like flesh and lay it out on a plate. Cool completely in the refrigerator.

5. Wrap a bamboo sushi mat in plastic wrap.

6 On the bamboo mat, lay out half the zucchini slices so they slightly overlap each other lengthwise, continuing until the zucchini reaches both ends of the mat.

7 Spread ½ cup of quinoa on top of the zucchini and press into an even layer, covering the zucchini horizontally about halfway.

8 Arrange half the spaghetti squash, grated carrots, avocado slices, and mint into a long even strip on top of the quinoa at the bottom of the mat.

9 Roll tightly while gently pressing until you have a nice even roll.

Repeat with the remaining zucchini and fillings until done.

10 Wrap the rolls in plastic wrap and refrigerate for 15 minutes to firm them up before slicing.

11 In a small bowl, whisk together the mayonnaise, chipotle pepper, lime juice, and lime zest until well blended.

12 Remove the rolls from the refrigerator and slice each into 8 even pieces with a very sharp knife.

13 Serve with the soy sauce, pickled ginger, wasabi, and chile mayonnaise.

Ingredient Tip: These are best served immediately but can be made and refrigerated for a few hours before serving. The zucchini roll method is a technique you can use to make any combination of maki rolls. This works well with cucumbers, too.

Per serving: Calories: 487; Total fat: 31g; Carbohydrates: 49g; Fiber: 13g; Protein: 11g; Calcium: 129mg; Vitamin D: <1mcg; Vitamin B12: <1mcg; Iron: 3mg; Zinc: 3mg

BUFFALO CAULIFLOWER STEAKS

DAIRY-FREE, GLUTEN-FREE

SERVES 4 //*PREP TIME* 15 minutes //*COOK TIME* 15 minutes

Buffalo seasoning and cauliflower is a magical combination. Serve these sweet and spicy steaks over a fresh salad or break them up into florets and serve them as you would wings for a party. You will not miss the chicken wings at all.

FOR THE BUFFALO SEASONING

1 tablespoon garlic powder

2 teaspoons smoked paprika

1½ teaspoons powdered mustard

1 teaspoon chili powder

1 teaspoon sea salt

½ teaspoon cayenne pepper

¼ teaspoon onion powder

FOR THE CAULIFLOWER

2 heads cauliflower

3 tablespoons hot sauce (I like the original buffalo sauce, Frank's RedHot)

3 tablespoons maple syrup or agave nectar

2 tablespoons extra-virgin olive oil

½ cup Vegan Caesar Dressing (page 66)

¼ cup vegan blue cheese crumbles

TO MAKE THE BUFFALO SEASONING

1 In a small bowl, whisk together the garlic powder, paprika, mustard, chili powder, salt, cayenne, and onion powder.

2 Set aside.

TO MAKE THE CAULIFLOWER

3 Remove the leaves from the bottom of the cauliflower. Cut each head in half right down the middle, then cut into 1½-inch-thick steaks.

4 In a small bowl, whisk together the hot sauce and maple syrup.

5 Preheat a grill or grill pan to medium-high and brush the cauliflower steaks with the oil. Sprinkle the buffalo seasoning on each side of the steaks.

6 Place the steaks directly over the flames with the lid closed and grill for 12 to 14 minutes. Flip them about halfway through, or until lightly charred and crisp-tender when a knife is inserted. When the cauliflower is ready, transfer it to a baking sheet and brush generously on each side with the maple syrup mixture.

7 Return the cauliflower to the grill over direct heat for 1 minute per side. Remove the cauliflower from the grill and place on a serving platter.

8 Drizzle the steaks the Caesar dressing and top with vegan blue cheese crumbles and serve.

Storage: Leftovers can be kept in the refrigerator in an airtight container for up to 3 days.

Ingredient Tip: Make a large batch of the buffalo seasoning to keep in the pantry to sprinkle over vegetables, baked potatoes, or popcorn. If your diet includes dairy, a side of good-quality blue cheese dressing is the classic dip for buffalo "wings."

Per serving: Calories: 351; Total fat: 21g; Carbohydrates: 38g; Fiber: 8g; Protein: 9g; Calcium: 117mg; Vitamin D: 0mcg; Vitamin B12: <1mcg; Iron: 2mg; Zinc: 1mg

PROVENÇAL VEGETABLE TIAN

SERVES **4 to 6** //PREP TIME **45 minutes** //COOK TIME **1 hour 30 minutes**

This classic Provençal gratin is a casserole of summery, simple vegetables and olive oil. The tian is both delicious and spectacular in its presentation. Pair this dish with a crisp salad and a glass of ice-cold rosé, and transport yourself to Provence. The leftovers are wonderful topped with a poached egg for breakfast or served cold with a salad.

2 large red bell peppers

7 tablespoons extra-virgin olive oil, divided, plus more for greasing the baking dish

1 large yellow onion medium, diced

1 teaspoon sea salt, plus more for seasoning

½ teaspoon freshly ground black pepper, plus more for seasoning

2 garlic cloves, minced

2 large Japanese eggplants (or 2 small eggplants), cut crosswise into ¼-inch-thick slices

1 medium zucchini, cut crosswise into ¼-inch-thick slices

1 yellow squash, cut crosswise into ¼-inch-thick slices

4 plum tomatoes, cut into ¼-inch-thick slices

2 tablespoons fresh thyme leaves

2 tablespoons capers, rinsed

2 tablespoons panko bread crumbs

1 tablespoon grated Parmesan cheese or vegan cheese

1 Preheat the oven to 450°F.

2 Place the red peppers on a baking sheet, drizzle with 1 tablespoon of oil, and bake for about 30 minutes, until the skins are charred, turning as needed.

3 Remove the peppers from the oven and immediately place them in a plastic freezer bag, seal, and let sit for 15 minutes to steam. Remove the skin with a clean kitchen towel, then halve, stem, seed, and cut the flesh into ½-inch strips. Set aside.

4 Lower the oven heat to 375°F. Brush a 12-inch round baking dish or tart pan with oil. Set aside.

5 Heat 2 tablespoons of oil in a large sauté pan or skillet over medium-high heat. Add the onion and season with salt and pepper. Cook until translucent and softened, about 5 minutes. Add the garlic and cook for 1 minute. Spread the onion mixture in the bottom of the pre-pared baking dish.

6   In a large bowl, toss the eggplant, zucchini, yellow squash, and tomatoes with 2 tablespoons of oil, 1 teaspoon of sea salt, ½ teaspoon of pepper, and half the thyme leaves.

7   Arrange the vegetables in the baking dish in an overlapping shingle pattern, alternating the eggplant, zucchini, yellow squash, tomatoes, and roasted red pepper. Drizzle the remaining 2 tablespoons of oil over the vegetables. Sprinkle with the remaining half of the thyme leaves and the capers.

8   Cover the dish tightly with aluminum foil and bake for 30 minutes.

9   Remove the foil and sprinkle evenly with the bread crumbs and Parmesan cheese. Return to the oven and bake uncovered for 20 minutes more, until lightly browned. Serve warm.

Storage: Leftovers can be kept in the refrigerator in an airtight container for up to 2 days.

Make Ahead: The tian can be prepared up to step 7 and refrigerated, covered, until ready to bake. Make sure to let the baking dish sit out to reach room temperature before placing in the oven to bake.

Per serving: Calories: 354; Total fat: 25g; Carbohydrates: 29g; Fiber: 9g; Protein: 6g; Calcium: 58mg; Vitamin D: 0mcg; Vitamin B12: <1mcg; Iron: 2mg; Zinc: 1mg

BARBECUE TOFU KEBABS

DAIRY-FREE, GLUTEN-FREE

SERVES 4 //*PREP TIME* 30 minutes, plus overnight to marinate //*COOK TIME* 25 minutes

Yes, you can have a vegan barbecue with all the fixings. These tofu skewers are a favorite in my family because they are sweet, spicy, and tangy. Your family and friends will love them, too. Serve with the classic barbecue side Creamless Creamed Corn (page 143) and Blackberry Lemonade (page 222) for a real party.

2 (14-ounce) blocks extra-firm tofu, rinsed and drained

4 cups barbecue sauce, divided

4 ounces small red or yellow creamer potatoes (or other potato, cut into 1-inch chunks)

¼ cup extra-virgin olive oil

Juice of 1 lemon

2 garlic cloves, minced

2 teaspoons sea salt

1 teaspoon smoked paprika

2 medium Japanese eggplants, cut into 1-inch chunks

1 medium green bell pepper, cut into 1-inch squares

1 large red bell pepper, cut into 1-inch squares

1 large red onion, cut into eighths

1 pint red or yellow cherry tomatoes

Extra-virgin olive oil, for brushing the grill

2 cups Creamless Creamed Corn (page 143), for serving

1   Put the tofu on a plate or baking sheet lined with paper towels or a clean kitchen towel. Cover with paper towels and then put another plate on top with something heavy to press the excess moisture out of the tofu. Let the tofu sit for about 30 minutes. Drain any excess liquid, pat the tofu dry, and cut it into 1-inch cubes.

2   Pour 2 cups of barbecue sauce into a large plastic freezer bag and add the tofu, shaking gently to coat. Press out most of the air, seal, and refrigerate overnight.

3   Remove the tofu from the refrigerator and bring to room temperature.

4   Put the potatoes in a small saucepan and add enough water to cover them by about 1 inch. Bring to a boil over high heat, reduce the heat to low, and simmer until just tender, about 15 minutes. Cool and cut the potatoes in half.

5   Preheat a grill or grill pan to medium-high heat.

6   In a large bowl, whisk together the oil, lemon juice, garlic, salt, and paprika. Add the cooked potatoes, the eggplants, green and red bell peppers, onion, and tomatoes, and toss gently until evenly coated.

7   Thread the tofu and vegetables evenly onto 4 (12-inch) metal skewers (or pre-soaked bamboo skewers), alternating vegetables and tofu. Set aside.

8   In a small saucepan, bring the remaining 2 cups of barbecue sauce to a boil over high heat, stirring frequently. Reduce the heat to low and continue cooking for about 1 minute. Transfer the sauce to a medium bowl.

9   Brush the grill grates (or grill pan) with olive oil. Place the kebabs on the grill over direct heat, brushing with the barbecue sauce and turning frequently, until the tofu is lightly charred and the vegetables are tender, about 10 minutes.

10 Serve with the barbecue sauce and with the creamless creamed corn on the side.

Storage: Leftovers can be kept in the refrigerator in an airtight container for up to 3 days.

Make Ahead: The skewers, as well as the creamed corn, can be made in advance, the morning of serving or the night before. Then all you have to do is grill the kebabs and heat the corn, and you are ready for dinner.

Per serving: Calories: 1,042; Total fat: 30g; Carbohydrates: 165g; Fiber: 16g; Protein: 31g; Calcium: 465mg; Vitamin D: 0mcg; Vitamin B12: 0mcg; Iron: 8mg; Zinc: 1mg

Avocado-Citrus Sherbet, page 239

CHAPTER TEN

DRINKS & DESSERTS

Blackberry Lemonade   222

Apple-Ginger Tea   223

Pomegranate & Celery Agua Fresca   224

Avocado-Coconut Milk Shake   226

Hibiscus-Lemongrass Tea   227

Coconut Horchata   228

Sparkling Parsley Green Tea with Lemon Ice Cubes   229

Chia Limeade   230

Coconut-Cauliflower Rice Pudding   231

Honey-Roasted Figs with Vegan Cheese   233

Baked Whole-Grain Churros with Dark Chocolate Sauce   234

Blackberry-Peach Crisp   236

Easy Fruit Sorbet   238

Avocado-Citrus Sherbet   239

BLACKBERRY LEMONADE

DAIRY-FREE, GLUTEN-FREE

SERVES **4** //*PREP TIME* **15 minutes** //*COOK TIME* **5 minutes**

For a refreshing change to the official drink of summer, add some sweet, juicy blackberries. The berries are a natural sweetener for the lemonade, and if they are sweet enough, there's no need to add sugar. This recipe lends itself well to strawberries and blueberries, too. Try any berry or mixture of berries you already have at home.

Zest of 4 lemons and juice of 6 lemons, plus more lemon slices for garnish

2 cups water, divided

¼ cup coconut sugar (see Tip)

½ cup fresh blackberries

Ice cubes, for serving

1 With a vegetable peeler or paring knife, remove the zest from 4 lemons. Set aside. Squeeze the juice from those 4 and from the remaining 2 lemons to yield 1 cup of juice.

2 In a large saucepan, bring 1 cup of water and the coconut sugar to a boil over high heat, stirring, until the sugar is dissolved. Remove from the heat and add the lemon zest, lemon juice, and remaining 1 cup of water. Let cool.

3 Puree the blackberries in a blender and stir the puree into the lemonade. Pour the lemonade through a fine-mesh sieve into a pitcher and chill in the refrigerator, covered, until very cold.

4 Serve the lemonade over ice in tall glasses, garnished with lemon slices.

Storage: The beverage can be kept in the refrigerator for up to 4 or 5 days.

Ingredient Tip: I use coconut sugar in this recipe for its wonderful flavor and lower glycemic index, but stevia, agave nectar, or honey are fine, too.

Per serving: Calories: 78; Total fat: <1g; Carbohydrates: 22g; Fiber: 3g; Protein: 2g; Calcium: 28mg; Vitamin D: 0mcg; Vitamin B12: 0mcg; Iron: 1mg; Zinc: <1mg

APPLE-GINGER TEA

DAIRY-FREE, GLUTEN-FREE

SERVES **4** *//PREP TIME* **10 minutes** *//COOK TIME* **10 minutes**

The aromatic combination of apples, ginger, and honey is both soothing and delicious. Although it's especially nice when served warm on a crisp fall day, this beverage can be enjoyed on a warm summer day by chilling it and serving it over ice cubes.

5 cups water

2 large apples, cored and cut into large wedges

4-inch piece fresh ginger, unpeeled and smashed

1 cinnamon stick, plus more for swizzling

Honey or agave nectar

1   Put the water, apples, ginger, and cinnamon stick in a large stockpot, cover, and bring to a boil over medium heat. Reduce the heat to low and simmer for 10 minutes.

2   Add the honey to taste and turn off the heat. Allow the tea to sit for about 5 minutes. Smash the apples against the side of the pan before straining. Taste and adjust the sweetener as needed, and serve warm with a cinnamon stick for stirring.

Storage: This recipe can be made in a larger batch, kept covered in the refrigerator, and reheated when ready to serve.

Ingredient Tip: This tea is also fabulous with pears or a combination of fruit.

Per serving: Calories: 60; Total fat: <1g; Carbohydrates: 16g; Fiber: 3g; Protein: <1g; Calcium: 7mg; Vitamin D: 0mcg; Vitamin B12: 0mcg; Iron: <1mg; Zinc: <1mg

POMEGRANATE & CELERY AGUA FRESCA

DAIRY-FREE, GLUTEN-FREE

SERVES **4** // *PREP TIME* **10 minutes**

These cool fruit waters are commonly found in Mexico; street vendors serve it in a barrel-shaped clear jar called a *vitrolero*. This presentation and preparation is growing in popularity in the United States as an alternative to sugary soda. There are as many different types of aguas as there are fruits, and I always have a big pot of it in my restaurant kitchen to cool off and stay hydrated during a hot, busy service.

2 cups pomegranate juice

2 celery stalks

Juice of 1½ limes, plus ½ lime, sliced, for garnish

¼ teaspoon ground cinnamon

2 cups ice, plus more for serving

Sweetener of your choice (optional)

1 Puree the pomegranate juice and celery in a blender and pass the mixture through a fine-mesh sieve.

2 Return the pomegranate-celery liquid to the blender along with the lime juice, cinnamon, and ice, and blend for 1 minute. Sweeten to taste.

3 Pour the beverage into glasses over ice and garnish with the lime slices.

Storage: The beverage can be kept in the refrigerator for up to 4 or 5 days.

Ingredient Tip: This recipe will work well with many varieties of fruit, so try it with pineapple, melon, or if you are lucky enough to come across them, fresh prickly pears. Just peel and cut the fruits into chunks and follow the same method.

Per serving: Calories: 75; Total fat: <1g; Carbohydrates: 19g; Fiber: 1g; Protein: <1g; Calcium: 26mg; Vitamin D: 0mcg; Vitamin B12: 0mcg; Iron: <1mg; Zinc: <1mg

AVOCADO-COCONUT MILK SHAKE

SERVES 2 //*PREP TIME* 5 minutes

Superfood avocados are often served as a dessert in Asian countries, topped with sweetened condensed milk. This refreshing tropical smoothie is a healthier take on the traditional dish, using light coconut milk instead. This beverage is a great use of leftover avocado that needs to be eaten before turning.

1 small ripe avocado, pitted, peeled, and sliced

¾ cup plain (or coconut) nonfat yogurt or non-dairy yogurt

½ cup light coconut milk, chilled

Juice of ½ lime

Pinch sea salt

1 Put the avocado, yogurt, coconut milk, lime juice, and salt in a blender and blend until smooth and frothy.

2 Drink immediately.

Ingredient Tip: Using coconut-flavored yogurt or coconut milk yogurt will enhance the coconutty taste and create a dairy-free concoction.

Per serving: Calories: 204; Total fat: 14g; Carbohydrates: 15g; Fiber: 5g; Protein: 7g; Calcium: 195mg; Vitamin D: 0mcg; Vitamin B12: 1mcg; Iron: 1mg; Zinc: 1mg

HIBISCUS-LEMONGRASS TEA

DAIRY-FREE, GLUTEN-FREE

SERVES **4** // *PREP TIME* **20 minutes** // *COOK TIME* **30 minutes**

This vibrant tea is my favorite home remedy for a cold because hibiscus is packed with vitamin C, and lemongrass is known as fever grass in Jamaica because it is believed to reduce fever. Wonderful when served hot, the tea can be also be served cold as a hot-weather refresher. When I'm feeling under the weather, I like to add a little fresh ginger for its added antibacterial effects.

1 quart water

3 stalks lemongrass, stemmed and chopped coarsely

1 cup dried hibiscus flower

Zest of 1 orange, plus more orange slices, for garnish

1 tablespoon honey or maple syrup

1   Pour the water and lemongrass into a medium saucepan over high heat and bring to a boil. Reduce the heat to low and simmer for 30 minutes.

2   Remove the saucepan from the heat, add the hibiscus flower and orange zest, and allow the mixture to steep for about 10 minutes.

3   Strain the tea through a fine-mesh sieve into a pitcher. Stir in the honey until combined.

4   Serve warm or chilled over ice, garnished with orange slices.

Ingredient Tip: Hibiscus is quite tart, so you will need to sweeten this a bit. I like to use honey or maple syrup, but any kind of sweetener will work.

Per serving: Calories: 64; Total fat: <1g; Carbohydrates: 17g; Fiber: 3g; Protein: 2g; Calcium: 226mg; Vitamin D: 0mcg; Vitamin B12: 0mcg; Iron: 2mg; Zinc: <1mg

COCONUT HORCHATA

DAIRY-FREE, GLUTEN-FREE

SERVES 4 to 6 //*PREP TIME* 20 minutes, plus overnight to soak //*COOK TIME* 10 minutes

Horchata is a rice-based drink that originated in the searing heat of Veracruz, Mexico, as an inexpensive refresher. Wildly popular in taquerias, it's simple to make this unique drink at home for taco Tuesday. It's especially nice with an added splash of light rum.

3 cups uncooked white rice

2 (4-inch) pieces cinnamon stick, plus more for garnish

4 cups hot water

15 blanched almonds

1 can (14-ounce) light coconut milk

1 cup sugar

1 cup cold water

1 lime, zest cut into long, wide strips

Ice cubes, for serving

6 to 8 fresh mint sprigs, for garnish

1   One day in advance, in a large bowl, combine the rice, crumbled cinnamon, and hot water. Cool, cover, and set aside overnight.

2   Heat a small sauté pan or skillet over medium heat and toast the almonds, swirling the skillet, until the almonds are golden, about 5 minutes. Remove from the heat and set aside in a bowl to cool.

3   Stir the almonds and coconut milk into the soaked rice. Working in batches, add the rice mixture to a blender and process until very smooth. Strain the batches through a medium-mesh sieve into a pitcher.

4   In a medium saucepan over low heat, stir together the sugar, cold water, and lime zest. Cook, stirring, until the sugar is just dissolved. Let cool and remove the lime zest.

5   Pour the cooled syrup into the pitcher and mix well. Cover and refrigerate until chilled.

6   When you're ready to serve, stir well and pour the horchata over ice cubes in tall glasses. Garnish with a mint sprig and a piece of cinnamon bark.

Ingredient Tip: If you don't like coconut, a similar version can be made by replacing the coconut milk with water or any kind of plant milk.

Per serving: Calories: 532; Total fat: 9g; Carbohydrates: 109g; Fiber: 2g; Protein: 8g; Calcium: 66mg; Vitamin D: 0mcg; Vitamin B12: 0mcg; Iron: 1mg; Zinc: <1mg

SPARKLING PARSLEY GREEN TEA
with LEMON ICE CUBES

DAIRY-FREE, GLUTEN-FREE

SERVES **4 to 6** //*PREP TIME* **20 minutes**

We all know that green tea is healthy, but why not double the antioxidant power by adding flavonoids and vitamin C–packed parsley as well? To make it extra special, keep some lemon ice cubes in the freezer to cool it down.

2 cups boiling water

2 green tea bags (decaf, if preferred)

1 small bunch parsley

Honey or agave nectar (optional)

16 ounces lemon-flavored sparkling water

Lemon ice cubes (see Tip), for serving

Mint sprigs, for garnish

1   In a medium bowl, pour the boiling water over the tea bags and parsley and let steep for 10 minutes. Strain into a pitcher and sweeten with honey (if using). Let cool.

2   Add the sparkling water and stir to combine.

3   Pour the mixture over lemon ice cubes in tall glasses and garnish with 1 or 2 mint sprigs.

Storage: The beverage can be kept in the refrigerator for up to 1 week.

Serving Tip: For lemon ice cubes, blend 2 or 3 diced whole lemons and 1 cup of water in a blender until smooth, pour the liquid into ice cube trays, and freeze. This technique works well with any kind of fruit for fun ice cubes to add to your tea or water.

Per serving: Calories: 7; Total fat: <1g; Carbohydrates: 1g; Fiber: 1g; Protein: <1g; Calcium: 21mg; Vitamin D: 0mcg; Vitamin B12: 0mcg; Iron: 1mg; Zinc: <1mg

CHIA LIMEADE

DAIRY-FREE, GLUTEN-FREE

SERVES **6 to 8** // *PREP TIME* **10 minutes**

The addition of liquid-absorbing chia seeds can mean that enjoying this beverage makes you feel fuller longer and curbs the appetite. This tart, delicious limeade is excellent with meals and as an energy-boosting afternoon pick-me-up. This is lovely with sweet Meyer lemons, when in season, or oranges and tangerines.

2 quarts cold water

Juice of 4 limes (key limes, if available), plus more lime slices, for garnish

¼ cup agave nectar, or more

¼ cup chia seeds

Ice cubes, for serving

Fresh sage sprigs, for garnish

1 In a large bowl, stir together the water, lime juice, and agave nectar.

2 Stir in the chia seeds and serve in tall glasses over ice, garnished with sage and lime slices.

Storage: The beverage can be kept in the refrigerator for up to 2 or 3 days.

Ingredient Tip: If you have access to key limes, by all means use them. They are so much sweeter than regular Persian limes. Key limes are also much smaller, so add a few more, accordingly.

Per serving: Calories: 91; Total fat: 2g; Carbohydrates: 17g; Fiber: 4g; Protein: 2g; Calcium: 58mg; Vitamin D: 0mcg; Vitamin B12: 0mcg; Iron: 0mg; Zinc: <1mg

COCONUT-CAULIFLOWER RICE PUDDING

DAIRY-FREE, GLUTEN-FREE

SERVES 4 //*PREP TIME* 15 minutes //*COOK TIME* 20 minutes

This creamy pudding is a delightful surprise. I love it with diced pineapple for a little extra sweetness. It is also a great way to sneak some veggies into an after-dinner dessert treat. This fabulous recipe is not just limited to dessert: try it as a healthy and hearty breakfast option, served warm or cold.

2 tablespoons coconut flakes (optional)

2 large heads cauliflower

1 cup unsweetened, boxed coconut milk (like Silk)

½ cup Butterless Butter (page 36) or coconut manna/butter

2 teaspoons maple syrup

2 teaspoons ground cinnamon

Pinch sea salt

1 tablespoon chia seeds

1 large egg or flax egg (see Tip)

1 tablespoon vanilla extract

Fresh or dried fruit, nuts, or seeds, for garnish

1   Place a small sauté pan or skillet over medium-low heat and toast the coconut (if using), swirling the skillet, until the coconut is golden, about 2 minutes. Remove from the heat and set aside to cool.

2   Cut the cauliflower heads in half and cut the florets into smaller pieces. Place the florets in a food processor and blend until the cauliflower resembles rice.

3   In a medium saucepan, stir together the cauliflower rice, coconut milk,
butterless butter, maple syrup, cinnamon, and salt. Bring the mixture to a boil over medium-high heat, reduce the heat to low, and simmer, stirring occasionally, until the cauliflower rice is tender, about 10 minutes.

4   In a medium bowl, stir together the chia seeds, egg, and vanilla. Slowly add ½ cup of the warm pudding mixture to the egg mixture, whisking thoroughly while pouring it in.

CONTINUED

5 Add the egg mixture back into the saucepan with the rest of the pudding. Simmer, stirring occasionally, for 5 minutes, until thickened. Remove the pudding from the heat and cool.

6 Serve warm, or cool in the refrigerator and serve cold. Top with the toasted coconut flakes, if using. Add other toppings, such as fresh or dried fruit, nuts, or seeds, as desired.

Storage: The rice pudding can be kept in an airtight container in the refrigerator for up to 4 days.

Substitution Tip: A flax egg is a substitute for a chicken egg that can be used for baking and other recipes that require an egg. They are simple to make: for 1 egg, combine 1 tablespoon flaxseed meal and 1½ tablespoons water and let sit for about 5 minutes to thicken.

Per serving: Calories: 332; Total fat: 22g; Carbohydrates: 26g; Fiber: 10g; Protein: 11g; Calcium: 238mg; Vitamin D: 1mcg; Vitamin B12: 1mcg; Iron: 2mg; Zinc: 1mg

HONEY-ROASTED FIGS
with VEGAN CHEESE

DAIRY-FREE, GLUTEN-FREE

SERVES 4 //*PREP TIME* **5 minutes** //*COOK TIME* **15 minutes**

If you like a cheese course after dinner or for entertaining guests, you will love this recipe. It also makes a great afternoon snack and a topping for a salad of bitter greens like frisée. I can't get enough of figs when they are in season. I'll eat them for breakfast, lunch, dinner, AND dessert. These are fantastic served over vanilla ice cream or frozen yogurt.

8 Mission figs, halved

1 tablespoon Butterless Butter (page 36)

2 tablespoons honey

Pinch ground cinnamon

Pinch sea salt

1 cup Dairy-Free Soft Cheese (page 33), for serving

8 crostini, for serving

1   Preheat the oven to 400°F.

2   Place the figs, cut-side up, in a baking dish.

3   Melt the butter in a small sauce-pan over low heat and whisk in the honey, cinnamon, and salt. Drizzle the hot honey butter over the figs

and roast them in the oven until soft and golden, about 12 minutes.

4   Divide the cheese among 4 serving dishes and top with the warm figs and sauce. Serve with the crostini on the side for dipping.

Ingredient Tip: Black figs are consistently the best figs on the market, always creamy and rich. They are available from early spring through early winter.

Per serving: Calories: 230; Total fat: 10g; Carbohydrates: 34g; Fiber: 3g; Protein: 1g; Calcium: 28mg; Vitamin D: 0mcg; Vitamin B12: <1mcg; Iron: 1mg; Zinc: <1mg

BAKED WHOLE-GRAIN CHURROS
with DARK CHOCOLATE SAUCE

DAIRY-FREE

SERVES **4** // *PREP TIME* **20 minutes** // *COOK TIME* **20 minutes**

Everyone loves this sweet fried Mexican treat. I began experimenting with healthier ways of making churros, and I now prefer this lighter baked version. The dark chocolate sauce is far superior to store-bought sauce and so easy to make. There is no excuse not to have it in the refrigerator at all times for all your dessert needs.

FOR THE CHURROS

Canola oil, for greasing the baking sheet

1 cup water

½ cup Butterless Butter (page 36)

6 tablespoons coconut sugar, divided

½ teaspoon sea salt

1 cup whole-wheat flour

1 flax egg (see Tip, page 232)

½ teaspoon vanilla extract

1 teaspoon ground cinnamon

FOR THE CHOCOLATE SAUCE

1 cup sugar

½ cup cold water

½ cup unsweetened cocoa powder

⅛ teaspoon kosher salt

1½ teaspoons vanilla extract

TO MAKE THE CHURROS

1   Preheat the oven to 425°F. Line a baking sheet with parchment paper and brush with a bit of oil.

2   In a medium saucepan, combine the water, butter, 2 tablespoons of coconut sugar, and salt, and bring to a boil over medium-high heat. Reduce the heat to low and simmer for about 10 minutes. Remove the saucepan from the heat and add the flour, stirring with a large wooden spoon until well blended.

3   In a small bowl, whisk together the flax egg and vanilla, then stir into the flour mixture, until completely incorporated.

4   Spoon the dough into a pastry bag with a large star tip. Squeeze the dough onto the baking sheet in 6-inch strips, leaving 2 inches between them.

5   Bake the churros for 10 minutes, or until golden brown.

6   In a small bowl, stir together the remaining 4 tablespoons of coconut sugar and the cinnamon. Sprinkle the warm churros with the cinnamon sugar.

7   While the churros are baking, in a small saucepan over medium heat, whisk together the sugar, water, cocoa powder, and salt. Bring to a boil, reduce the heat to low, and simmer for 30 seconds, stirring constantly. Remove from the heat, let cool slightly, and whisk in the vanilla.

8   Serve warm with the churros.

Storage: The chocolate sauce can be stored in an airtight container in the refrigerator for up to 2 weeks.

Make Ahead: Although you will want to eat these fresh out of the oven, if you are entertaining, you may want to prep ahead. They can be frozen either before or after baking. To freeze before baking, pipe the dough onto the baking sheet, wrap it gently in plastic, and freeze for several weeks. Baked, cooled churros can be wrapped in plastic and frozen for up to 1 month. To serve, thaw, uncovered, at room temperature, then reheat for about 10 minutes in a 350°F oven.

Per serving: Calories: 564; Total fat: 20g; Carbohydrates: 97g; Fiber: 8g; Protein: 7g; Calcium: 44mg; Vitamin D: <1mcg; Vitamin B12: <1mcg; Iron: 3mg; Zinc: 2mg

BLACKBERRY-PEACH CRISP

DAIRY-FREE

SERVES **6 to 8** // *PREP TIME* **15 minutes** // *COOK TIME* **30 minutes**

By now, you know that sweet-tart blackberries are my first choice in berries, but this crisp can be made with any berry or fruit. This summer version features ripe blackberries and peaches but is equally delicious prepared in cooler seasons with pears and cranberries. A crisp is one of the easiest desserts to make, and the payoff in flavor is huge.

FOR THE FILLING
6 ripe peaches, pitted and sliced

2 pints blackberries

1 teaspoon ground cinnamon

½ teaspoon sea salt

Pinch sugar

FOR THE STREUSEL
8 ounces Butterless Butter (page 36)

1 cup coconut sugar

8 ounces whole-wheat flour

1 teaspoon ground cinnamon

1 teaspoon sea salt

Ice cream or whipped cream, for serving

TO MAKE THE FILLING

1   In a medium bowl, combine the peaches, blackberries, cinnamon, salt, and sugar and toss until well mixed. Spread the fruit mixture in a large cast iron skillet and set aside.

TO MAKE THE STREUSEL

2   In a large bowl, mix together the butter, coconut sugar, flour, cinnamon, and salt with two forks until the ingredients start forming large crumbs.

3   Place the topping in the refrigerator to chill completely.

4   Preheat the oven to 325°F.

5   Evenly top the fruit with the streusel and bake for about 30 minutes, rotating halfway through, until the fruit is bubbling and the streusel is golden brown.

6 Transfer the crisp to a cooling rack, and cool slightly before serving.

7 Serve warm, topped with ice cream or whipped cream.

Storage: The crisp can be kept in an airtight container in the refrigerator for up to 1 week and in the freezer for up to 1 month.

Make Ahead: The streusel can be made 1 or 2 days ahead of baking the crisp and refrigerated until needed.

Per serving: Calories: 575; Total fat: 25g; Carbohydrates: 86g; Fiber: 12g; Protein: 8g; Calcium: 75mg; Vitamin D: <1mcg; Vitamin B12: <1mcg; Iron: 3mg; Zinc: 2mg

EASY FRUIT SORBET

DAIRY-FREE, GLUTEN-FREE

SERVES **4** //*PREP TIME* **10 minutes, plus 3 hours to freeze**

Cooling fruit sorbet is probably the most guilt-free of desserts, and it's inexpensive to make at home. Use your favorite seasonal fruits, or experiment and make a rainbow with several types of fruits. Just don't leave out the salt, because it keeps the sorbet scoopable.

3 cups ripe fruit of your choice, cut into chunks

½ teaspoon vanilla extract

¼ teaspoon sea salt

Sugar, as needed

1   Put the fruit, vanilla, and salt in a blender and blend until smooth. Taste for sweetness and add sugar, a little at a time, as desired.

2   Pour the mixture into a freezer-proof container with a flat bottom.

3   Cover and freeze until hard, about 3 hours.

Ingredient Tip: Xanthan gum is a natural stabilizer for ice creams and sorbets and can even be used as an egg replacement. It is found in health food stores, and if you find yourself making a lot of sorbet, you may want to invest in a container of it. Pectin is also a good choice: just add 1 teaspoon per quart of water to reduce ice crystallization for a smoother sorbet that lasts longer in the freezer.

Per serving using strawberries: Calories: 38; Total fat: <1g; Carbohydrates: 9g; Fiber: 2g; Protein: 1g; Calcium: 18mg; Vitamin D: 0mcg; Vitamin B12: 0mcg; Iron: 1mg; Zinc: <1mg

AVOCADO-CITRUS SHERBET

DAIRY-FREE, GLUTEN-FREE

SERVES 4 //*PREP TIME* 15 minutes, plus 2 hours to freeze //*COOK TIME* 5 minutes

Desserts made by blending avocados with sugar and lime juice are common in Latin America. In this sherbet, the richness of the avocado replaces the dairy in the recipe to give it a creamy texture with a zing of citrus flavor.

1 cup water

1 cup sugar

1 pinch salt

1 vanilla bean, split

4 ripe Hass avocados

½ cup freshly squeezed lime juice

1   In a medium saucepan, bring the water, sugar, and salt to a boil over medium-high heat. Reduce the heat to low and simmer until the sugar dissolves, about 5 minutes. Remove from the heat and scrape in the seeds from the vanilla bean. Add the vanilla pod, stirring to combine.

2   Cool, then remove the vanilla bean pod from the syrup and discard it or reserve it for another use.

3   Place the avocados in a blender or food processor and process until very smooth. Add the lime juice and vanilla syrup and blend until smooth.

4   Cool the mixture completely in the refrigerator and then process in an ice cream maker according to the manufacturer's directions. If you do not have an ice cream maker, spread the mixture out on a baking sheet and freeze until set, about 2 hours. Transfer the frozen mixture to a food processor and process until very smooth.

5   Transfer the sherbet to an airtight container and freeze for up to 1 month.

Variation Tip: The basic recipe can be used to make any kind of creamy fruit sorbet, such as orange, pineapple, and grapefruit sorbet.

Per serving: Calories: 428; Total fat: 21g; Carbohydrates: 64g; Fiber: 9g; Protein: 3g; Calcium: 22mg; Vitamin D: 0mcg; Vitamin B12: 0mcg; Iron: 1mg; Zinc: 1mg

MEASUREMENT CONVERSIONS

	US STANDARD	US STANDARD (OUNCES)	METRIC (APPROXIMATE)
VOLUME EQUIVALENTS (LIQUID)	2 tablespoons	1 fl. oz.	30 mL
	¼ cup	2 fl. oz.	60 mL
	½ cup	4 fl. oz.	120 mL
	1 cup	8 fl. oz.	240 mL
	1½ cups	12 fl. oz.	355 mL
	2 cups or 1 pint	16 fl. oz.	475 mL
	4 cups or 1 quart	32 fl. oz.	1 L
	1 gallon	128 fl. oz.	4 L
VOLUME EQUIVALENTS (DRY)	⅛ teaspoon	—	0.5 mL
	¼ teaspoon	—	1 mL
	½ teaspoon	—	2 mL
	¾ teaspoon	—	4 mL
	1 teaspoon	—	5 mL
	1 tablespoon	—	15 mL
	¼ cup	—	59 mL
	⅓ cup	—	79 mL
	½ cup	—	118 mL
	⅔ cup	—	156 mL
	¾ cup	—	177 mL
	1 cup	—	235 mL
	2 cups or 1 pint	—	475 mL
	3 cups	—	700 mL
	4 cups or 1 quart	—	1 L
	½ gallon	—	2 L
	1 gallon	—	4 L
WEIGHT EQUIVALENTS	½ ounce	—	15 g
	1 ounce	—	30 g
	2 ounces	—	60 g
	4 ounces	—	115 g
	8 ounces	—	225 g
	12 ounces	—	340 g
	16 ounces or 1 pound	—	455 g

	FAHRENHEIT (F)	CELSIUS (C) (APPROXIMATE)
OVEN TEMPERATURES	250°F	120°C
	300°F	150°C
	325°F	165°C
	375°F	190°C
	400°F	200°C
	425°F	220°C
	450°F	230°C

RESOURCES

The California Walnuts website is focused on a healthy lifestyle. It has tasty, nutritious, and easy recipes and a great newsletter with nutrition tips, recipes, and exercise and well-being articles: walnuts.org.

Food Matters TV has thousands of documentaries on healthy living, including cooking, mediation, exercise, and more: FMTV.com.

For online healthy food shopping, Thrive Market has thousands of wonderful products and amazing customer service, and it prides itself on keeping its prices low: thrivemarket.com.

Forks Over Knives is a great blog and website that has a beginner's guide to eating plant-based as well as a weekly meal-planning function: forksoverknives.com.

The New Health Rules by Frank Lipman is a simple guide to living well, with great advice for anyone who wants to be healthy, which is clear and easy to put into daily practice: amazon.com/New-Health-Rules -Whole-Body-Wellness -ebook/dp/B00N5BASDK.

T. Colin Campbell is the author of *Whole: Rethinking the Science of Nutrition*, and his organization's website is a great resource for all things plant-based: nutritionstudies.org/whole.

University of California, Davis School of Integrated Medicine's "Ultimate Resource Guide for Plant-Based Living": ucdintegrativemedicine .com/2015/03/the-ultimate -resource-guide-for-plant -based-living-2/#gs.4uzllt.

REFERENCES

American Cancer Society. "American Cancer Society Guideline for Diet and Physical Activity." Accessed May 5, 2020. cancer.org/healthy/eat-healthy-get -active/acs-guidelines-nutrition -physical-activity-cancer-prevention /summary.html.

American Heart Association. "Fruits and Vegetables Serving Sizes Infographic." Accessed May 5, 2020. heart.org/en/healthy -living/healthy-eating/add-color /fruits-and-vegetables-serving-sizes.

Hamblin, James. "Science Compared Every Diet, and the Winner Is Real Food." *The Atlantic.* March 24, 2014. theatlantic.com/health/archive /2014/03/science-compared -every-diet-and-the-winner-is-real -food/284595.

Harvard T.H. Chan School of Public Health. "Processed Foods and Health." Accessed May 2020. hsph.harvard.edu/nutritionsource /processed-foods.

Kassam, Shireen. "5 Surprising Benefits of a Plant-Based Diet." EcoWatch. March 25, 2020. ecowatch.com/plant-based -diet-health-benefits -2645576295.html?rebelltitem =3#rebelltitem3.

Kim, Hyunju, Laura E. Caulfield, Vanessa Garcia-Larsen, Lyn M. Steffen, Josef Coresh, and Casey M. Rebholz. "Plant-Based Diets Are Associated With a Lower Risk of Incident Cardiovascular Disease, Cardiovascular Disease Mortality, and All-Cause Mortality in a General Population of Middle-Aged Adults." *Journal of the American Heart Association* 8, no. 16 (2019). doi.org/10.1161/jaha.119 .012865.

Satija, Ambika, Shilpa N. Bhu-pathiraju, Eric B. Rimm, Donna Spiegelman, Stephanie E. Chiuve, Lea Borgi, Walter C. Willett, JoAnn E. Manson, Qi Sun, and Frank B. Hu. "Plant-Based Dietary Patterns and Incidence of Type 2 Diabetes in US Men and Women: Results From Three Prospective Cohort Studies." PLOS Medicine. Public Library of Science. Accessed May 5, 2020. journals.plos.org/plosmedicine /article?id=10.1371/journal.pmed .1002039.

US Department of Health and Human Services. "Dietary Guidelines for Americans." HHS.gov. January 26, 2017. hhs.gov/fitness/eat-healthy /dietary-guidelines-for -americans/index.html.

Yang, Ina. "To Shed Pounds, Going Vegetarian or Vegan May Help." NPR. July 29, 2015. npr.org/sections/thesalt /2015/07/29/426743443 /to-shed-pounds-going-vegetarian -or-vegan-may-help.

INDEX

A

Açai Breakfast Bowl, 87
Agave-Lime Vinaigrette, 64
Almond Yogurt, Fruit &
 Muesli Parfait, 83
Amaranth
 Maple Whole-Grain Hot Cereal, 91
Ancient Grain & Wild
 Mushroom Pilaf, 139
Animal rennet, 6
Apples, 19
 Almond Yogurt, Fruit &
  Muesli Parfait, 83
 Apple & Red Chile Chutney, 65
 Apple-Ginger Tea, 223
 Butternut Squash–Apple Soup with
  Chile Yogurt & Pepitas, 150–151
 Cabbage Soup with Apples
  & Thyme, 152
 Collard Greens with Pickled
  Apples & Walnuts, 144–145
 Fennel, Apple & Celery Salad, 132
 Green Grape Gazpacho, 157
Arugula
 Heirloom Tomato &
  Watermelon Salad, 130
 Lentil Salad with Caramelized
  Shallots & Feta, 127
 Pear, Arugula & Endive Salad with
  Candied Walnuts, 128–129
 Whole Roasted Cauliflower in
  Herb Salsa Verde, 208–209
Asparagus
 Kale, Frisée & Asparagus
  Salad with Toasted Pepita
  Vinaigrette, 125–126
 Lemon-Herb Red Quinoa, 147
Avocados, 20
 Avocado-Citrus Sherbet, 239
 Avocado-Coconut Milk Shake, 226

Avocado Milanesa Torta, 119–120
Avocados Rancheros, 77–78
Avocado Toast, 76
Beet Hummus Toast, 116
Best BLT, The, 112
Calabacitas Tacos, 186
Carrot Falafel with
 Zuccanoush, 193–194
Fresh, Chunky Guacamole, 41
Grains & Greens Bowl, 134
Spicy Vegan Sweet Potato Maki
 with Coconut Rice, 210–211
Vegan Breakfast
 Sando, 93–94
Vegan Spinach & Tofu
 Enchiladas, 178–179
Warm Pita with Hummus &
 Grilled Vegetables, 100–101
Zucchini Rolls with Spaghetti
 Squash & Quinoa, 212–213

B

Baked Vegetable Chips, 51
Baked Whole-Grain Churros
 with Dark Chocolate
 Sauce, 234–235
Balanced plate, 6
Bananas
 Açai Breakfast Bowl, 87
 Power Pancakes, 82
 Power Smoothie, 92
Barbecue Tofu Kebabs, 218–219
Barley
 Ancient Grain & Wild
  Mushroom Pilaf, 139
 Butternut Squash, Black Bean
  & Grain Chili, 195
Basic Vegetable Stock, 32
Basil
 Grains & Greens Bowl, 134

Green Tea Soba Noodles with
 Sesame Dipping Sauce, 200–201
Heirloom Tomato &
 Watermelon Salad, 130
Herb Vinaigrette, 69
Lemon-Herb Red Quinoa, 147
Lentil Salad with Caramelized
 Shallots & Feta, 127
Mediterranean Tomato &
 Eggplant Stew, 167–168
Pistou Soup, 165–166
Vegan Green Risotto with
 Broccoli, 182–183
Vegan Ricotta, Peach &
 Basil Panini, 105
Veggie Meatballs with Tomato
 Ragout, 176–177
Warm Pita with Hummus &
 Grilled Vegetables, 100–101
Whole Roasted Cauliflower in
 Herb Salsa Verde, 208–209
Beans, 4, 5, 16
 Avocado Milanesa Torta, 119–120
 Avocados Rancheros, 77–78
 Better Black Bean Burger,
  The, 98–99
 Butternut Squash & Lentil Chili, 160
 Butternut Squash, Black Bean
  & Grain Chili, 195
 Calabacitas Tacos, 186
 Garden Vegetable &
  Quinoa Soup, 169
 Greek Gigante Bean &
  Tomato Stew, 164
 Pistou Soup, 165–166
 Spinach Crêpes with Black
  Bean Sauce, 88–89
 Sweet Potato & Colorado
  Bean Hash, 90
 White Bean & Pasta Soup, 159

Bean sprouts
  Vegan Pad Thai, 206–207
Bee pollen, 17
Beets, 19
  Beet Hummus Toast, 116
  Better Black Bean Burger,
    The, 98–99
Berries, 19
  Açai Breakfast Bowl, 87
  Almond Yogurt, Fruit &
    Muesli Parfait, 83
  Blackberry Lemonade, 222
  Blackberry-Peach Crisp, 236–237
  PB & J, 103–104
  Power Pancakes, 82
  Vegan Breakfast Sando, 93–94
Best BLT, The, 112
Better Black Bean Burger,
  The, 98–99
Beverages
  Apple-Ginger Tea, 223
  Avocado-Coconut Milk Shake, 226
  Blackberry Lemonade, 222
  Chia Limeade, 230
  Coconut Horchata, 228
  Hibiscus-Lemongrass Tea, 227
  Pomegranate & Celery
    Agua Fresca, 224
  Power Smoothie, 92
  Sparkling Parsley Green Tea
    with Lemon Ice Cubes, 229
Biscuits & Vegetarian Redeye
  Gravy, 84–85
Blackberry Lemonade, 222
Blackberry-Peach Crisp, 236–237
Black-Eyed Pea & Baby
  Spinach Salad, 133
Bok choy
  Veggie Hot Pot, 170–171
Bowls
  Açai Breakfast Bowl, 87
  Grains & Greens Bowl, 134
  Sweet Potato & Lentil Bowl, 135–136
Breads
  Avocado Milanesa Torta, 119–120

Avocado Toast, 76
Beet Hummus Toast, 116
Best BLT, The, 112
Carrot Falafel with
  Zuccanoush, 193–194
Charred-Tomato Gazpacho, 155–156
Grilled Mushroom Cheesesteaks, 111
Guacamole Grilled Cheese, 115
PB & J, 103–104
Plant Meatball Marinara
  Hero, 117–118
Tofu Banh Mi, 108–109
Vegan Breakfast Sando, 93–94
Vegan Egg Salad Sando, 110
Vegan Pulled Pork
  Sandwiches, 106–107
Vegan Ricotta, Peach &
  Basil Panini, 105
Vegan Sloppy Joes, 113–114
Warm Pita with Hummus &
  Grilled Vegetables, 100–101
Broccoli
  Vegan Green Risotto with
    Broccoli, 182–183
  Vegan Macaroni & Cheese, 137–138
Brussels sprouts
  Brussels Sprouts with
    Chile & Mint, 141
  Vegan Brussels Sprout
    Caesar Salad, 124
Buffalo Cauliflower
  Steaks, 214–215
Butter, cultured, 19
Butterless Butter, 36
Butternut Squash &
  Lentil Chili, 160
Butternut Squash–Apple
  Soup with Chile Yogurt
  & Pepitas, 150–151
Butternut Squash, Black Bean
  & Grain Chili, 195

C

Cabbage, 19
  Cabbage & Veggie Lasagna, 187

Cabbage Soup with Apples
  & Thyme, 152
Sweet Potato & Lentil Bowl, 135–136
Calabacitas Tacos, 186
Capers
  Provençal Vegetable Tian, 216–217
  Vegan Caesar Dressing, 66
Caribbean Chard, Sweet Potato &
  Spicy Peanut Jumble, 204
Carrots, 19
  Basic Vegetable Stock, 32
  Carrot Falafel with
    Zuccanoush, 193–194
  Carrot, Ginger & Jalapeño Soup, 153
  Charred-Carrot Dip, 42–43
  Chickpea Soup with Black
    Kale, Harissa & Spiced
    Yogurt, 161–163
  Garden Vegetable &
    Quinoa Soup, 169
  Habanero Hot Sauce, 67
  Moroccan Veggie Tagine with
    Couscous, 196–197
  Pistou Soup, 165–166
  Sweet Potato & Lentil Bowl, 135–136
  Tofu Banh Mi, 108–109
  Veggie Hot Pot, 170–171
  White Bean & Pasta Soup, 159
  Zucchini Rolls with Spaghetti
    Squash & Quinoa, 212–213
Cauliflower
  Buffalo Cauliflower Steaks, 214–215
  Calabacitas Tacos, 186
  Cauliflower Crust Pizza, 205
  Coconut Cauliflower Rice, 142
  Coconut-Cauliflower Rice
    Pudding, 231–232
  Riced Cauliflower &
    Chickpea Pilaf, 202
  Sweet Potato & Lentil Bowl, 135–136
  Whole Roasted Cauliflower in
    Herb Salsa Verde, 208–209
Celery, 19
  Basic Vegetable Stock, 32
  Carrot, Ginger & Jalapeño Soup, 153

Fennel, Apple & Celery Salad, 132
Garden Vegetable &
    Quinoa Soup, 169
Pomegranate & Celery
    Agua Fresca, 224
Vegan Egg Salad Sando, 110
White Bean & Pasta Soup, 159
Charred-Carrot Dip, 42–43
Charred-Tomato Gazpacho,
    155–156
Cheese, 6
    Avocado Milanesa Torta, 119–120
    Avocados Rancheros, 77–78
    Buffalo Cauliflower Steaks, 214–215
    Butternut Squash, Black Bean
        & Grain Chili, 195
    Cabbage & Veggie Lasagna, 187
    Calabacitas Tacos, 186
    Cauliflower Crust Pizza, 205
    Dairy-Free Soft Cheese, 33
    Grilled Mushroom Cheesesteaks, 111
    Guacamole Grilled Cheese, 115
    Heirloom Tomato &
        Watermelon Salad, 130
    Honey-Roasted Figs with
        Vegan Cheese, 233
    Lentil Salad with Caramelized
        Shallots & Feta, 127
    Mediterranean Tomato &
        Eggplant Stew, 167–168
    Pistou Soup, 165–166
    Plant Meatball Marinara
        Hero, 117–118
    Provençal Vegetable Tian, 216–217
    Quinoa Fritters, 45–46
    Spaghetti with Braised Kale,
        Chile & Lemon, 180–181
    Spinach Crêpes with Black
        Bean Sauce, 88–89
    Vegan Breakfast Sando, 93–94
    Vegan Brussels Sprout
        Caesar Salad, 124
    Vegan Caesar Dressing, 66
    Vegan Green Risotto with
        Broccoli, 182–183

Veggie Meatballs with Tomato
    Ragout, 176–177
Chia seeds, 16
    Chia Limeade, 230
    Cocoa-Chia Waffles, 95
    Coconut-Cauliflower Rice
        Pudding, 231–232
    Peanut Butter Overnight Oats, 86
Chickpeas, 5, 16
    Beet Hummus Toast, 116
    Carrot Falafel with
        Zuccanoush, 193–194
    Chickpea Soup with Black
        Kale, Harissa & Spiced
        Yogurt, 161–163
    Crispy Cinnamon Chickpeas, 44
    Mediterranean-Style
        Hummus, 38–39
    Moroccan Veggie Tagine with
        Couscous, 196–197
    Riced Cauliflower &
        Chickpea Pilaf, 202
Chiles. See also Peppers
    Apple & Red Chile Chutney, 65
    Avocado Milanesa Torta, 119–120
    Fresh, Chunky Guacamole, 41
    Green Grape Gazpacho, 157
    Pico de Gallo, 61
    Pumpkin & Cashew Curry, 184–185
    Roasted Tomato Serrano
        Salsa, 60–61
    Thai-Inspired Peanut Sauce, 71
    Toasted-Pepita Dip, 40
    Vegan Pad Thai, 206–207
    Vegan Spinach & Tofu
        Enchiladas, 178–179
    Verde Cruda, 60
    Whole Roasted Cauliflower in
        Herb Salsa Verde, 208–209
Chocolate
    Baked Whole-Grain Churros with
        Dark Chocolate
        Sauce, 234–235
    Cocoa-Chia Waffles, 95
    Power Trail Mix, 47

Cilantro
    Black-Eyed Pea & Baby
        Spinach Salad, 133
    Caribbean Chard, Sweet Potato &
        Spicy Peanut Jumble, 204
    Carrot, Ginger & Jalapeño Soup, 153
    Chickpea Soup with Black Kale,
        Harissa & Spiced Yogurt, 161–163
    Fresh, Chunky Guacamole, 41
    Gingered Sweet Potato Mash, 146
    Herb Vinaigrette, 69
    Kale, Frisée & Asparagus
        Salad with Toasted Pepita
        Vinaigrette, 125–126
    Pico de Gallo, 61
    Roasted Tomato Serrano
        Salsa, 60–61
    Sweet Potato & Lentil Bowl, 135–136
    Toasted-Pepita Dip, 40
    Tofu Banh Mi, 108–109
    Vegan Pad Thai, 206–207
    Verde Cruda, 60
    Warm Pita with Hummus &
        Grilled Vegetables, 100–101
    Watercress, Jicama &
        Orange Salad, 131
Citrus, 19
Clean eating, 1
Cocoa-Chia Waffles, 95
Coconut
    Coconut Cauliflower Rice, 142
    Spicy Vegan Sweet Potato Maki
        with Coconut Rice, 210–211
Coconut milk
    Avocado-Coconut Milk Shake, 226
    Caribbean Chard, Sweet Potato &
        Spicy Peanut Jumble, 204
    Cocoa-Chia Waffles, 95
    Coconut Cauliflower Rice, 142
    Coconut-Cauliflower Rice
        Pudding, 231–232
    Coconut Curry Sauce, 72
    Coconut Horchata, 228
    Gingered Sweet Potato Mash, 146
    Non-Dairy Yogurt, 34

Coconut milk (*continued*)
  Pumpkin & Cashew Curry, 184–185
  Spicy Vegan Sweet Potato Maki
    with Coconut Rice, 210–211
Collard Greens with Pickled
    Apples & Walnuts, 144–145
Condiments, 17
  Apple & Red Chile Chutney, 65
  Eggless Mayonnaise, 37
  Flavored Oils, 56
  Flavored Vinegar, 57
  Fruit Mustard, 63
  Homemade Ketchup, 62
  Pickled Red Onions, 58
Corn
  Black-Eyed Pea & Baby
    Spinach Salad, 133
  Calabacitas Tacos, 186
  Corn Chowder, 158
  Creamless Creamed Corn, 143
  Grains & Greens Bowl, 134
  Warm Pita with Hummus &
    Grilled Vegetables, 100–101
Couscous, Moroccan Veggie
    Tagine with, 196–197
Creamless Creamed Corn, 143
Crispy Cinnamon Chickpeas, 44
Cucumbers
  Carrot Falafel with
    Zuccanoush, 193–194
  Charred-Tomato Gazpacho, 155–156
  Grains & Greens Bowl, 134
  Green Grape Gazpacho, 157
  Green Tea Soba Noodles with
    Sesame Dipping Sauce, 200–201
  Power Smoothie, 92
  Tofu Banh Mi, 108–109

D

Dairy-free
  Agave-Lime Vinaigrette, 64
  Almond Yogurt, Fruit &
    Muesli Parfait, 83
  Ancient Grain & Wild
    Mushroom Pilaf, 139

Apple & Red Chile Chutney, 65
Apple-Ginger Tea, 223
Avocado-Citrus Sherbet, 239
Avocado Toast, 76
Baked Vegetable Chips, 51
Baked Whole-Grain Churros with
    Dark Chocolate Sauce, 234–235
Barbecue Tofu Kebabs, 218–219
Basic Vegetable Stock, 32
Beet Hummus Toast, 116
Best BLT, The, 112
Better Black Bean Burger,
    The, 98–99
Blackberry Lemonade, 222
Blackberry-Peach Crisp, 236–237
Black-Eyed Pea & Baby
    Spinach Salad, 133
Brussels Sprouts with
    Chile & Mint, 141
Buffalo Cauliflower Steaks, 214–215
Butterless Butter, 36
Butternut Squash & Lentil Chili, 160
Butternut Squash–Apple Soup with
    Chile Yogurt & Pepitas, 150–151
Cabbage Soup with Apples
    & Thyme, 152
Calabacitas Tacos, 186
Caribbean Chard, Sweet Potato &
    Spicy Peanut Jumble, 204
Carrot Falafel with
    Zuccanoush, 193–194
Carrot, Ginger & Jalapeño Soup, 153
Charred-Carrot Dip, 42–43
Charred-Tomato Gazpacho, 155–156
Chia Limeade, 230
Cocoa-Chia Waffles, 95
Coconut Cauliflower Rice, 142
Coconut-Cauliflower Rice
    Pudding, 231–232
Coconut Curry Sauce, 72
Coconut Horchata, 228
Collard Greens with Pickled
    Apples & Walnuts, 144–145
Corn Chowder, 158
Creamless Creamed Corn, 143

Crispy Cinnamon Chickpeas, 44
Dairy-Free Soft Cheese, 33
Easy Fruit Sorbet, 238
Fennel, Apple & Celery Salad, 132
Flavored Oils, 56
Flavored Vinegar, 57
Fresh, Chunky Guacamole, 41
Fresh Tofu & Soy Milk, 28–29
Fruit Leather, 48–49
Garden Vegetable &
    Quinoa Soup, 169
Gingered Sweet Potato Mash, 146
Grains & Greens Bowl, 134
Greek Gigante Bean &
    Tomato Stew, 164
Green Grape Gazpacho, 157
Green Tea Soba Noodles with
    Sesame Dipping Sauce, 200–201
Habanero Hot Sauce, 67
Heirloom Tomato &
    Watermelon Salad, 130
Herb Vinaigrette, 69
Hibiscus-Lemongrass Tea, 227
Homemade Ketchup, 62
Honey-Roasted Figs with
    Vegan Cheese, 233
Jerk Tofu Steaks, 198–199
Kale Crisps, 52
Kale, Frisée & Asparagus
    Salad with Toasted Pepita
    Vinaigrette, 125–126
Lemon-Herb Red Quinoa, 147
Maple Whole-Grain Hot Cereal, 91
Mediterranean-Style
    Hummus, 38–39
Moroccan Veggie Tagine with
    Couscous, 196–197
Non-Dairy Yogurt, 34
Nut Milk, 35
Orange Vinaigrette, 70
PB & J, 103–104
Peanut Butter Overnight Oats, 86
Pear, Arugula & Endive Salad with
    Candied Walnuts, 128–129
Pickled Red Onions, 58

Pico de Gallo, 61
Pomegranate & Celery
     Agua Fresca, 224
Pomegranate Vinaigrette, 68
Power Pancakes, 82
Power Smoothie, 92
Power Trail Mix, 47
Pumpkin & Cashew Curry, 184–185
Riced Cauliflower &
     Chickpea Pilaf, 202
Roasted Tomato Serrano
     Salsa, 60–61
Salt & Pepper Tofu, 188
Sparkling Parsley Green Tea
     with Lemon Ice Cubes, 229
Spicy Tofu Scramble, 81
Spicy Vegan Sweet Potato Maki
     with Coconut Rice, 210–211
Sweet Potato & Colorado
     Bean Hash, 90
Sweet Potato & Lentil
     Bowl, 135–136
Thai-Inspired Peanut Sauce, 71
Toasted-Pepita Dip, 40
Tofu Banh Mi, 108–109
Turkish Eggplant Casserole, 191–192
Vegan Breakfast Sando, 93–94
Vegan Brussels Sprout
     Caesar Salad, 124
Vegan Caesar Dressing, 66
Vegan Egg Salad Sando, 110
Vegan Green Risotto with
     Broccoli, 182–183
Vegan Macaroni & Cheese, 137–138
Vegan Pad Thai, 206–207
Vegan Pulled Pork
     Sandwiches, 106–107
Vegan Ricotta, Peach &
     Basil Panini, 105
Vegan Sloppy Joes, 113–114
Vegan Spinach & Tofu
     Enchiladas, 178–179
Vegetable Shepherd's Pie, 189–190
Veggie Hot Pot, 170–171
Verde Cruda, 60

Warm Pita with Hummus &
     Grilled Vegetables, 100–101
Watercress, Jicama &
     Orange Salad, 131
White Bean & Pasta Soup, 159
Whole Roasted Cauliflower in
     Herb Salsa Verde, 208–209
Zucchini Rolls with Spaghetti
     Squash & Quinoa, 212–213
Dairy products, 4
Desserts
     Avocado-Citrus Sherbet, 239
     Baked Whole-Grain Churros with
          Dark Chocolate
          Sauce, 234–235
     Blackberry-Peach Crisp, 236–237
     Coconut-Cauliflower Rice
          Pudding, 231–232
     Easy Fruit Sorbet, 238
     Honey-Roasted Figs with
          Vegan Cheese, 233
Dips and spreads
     Charred-Carrot Dip, 42–43
     Eggless Mayonnaise, 37
     Fresh, Chunky Guacamole, 41
     Fruit Mustard, 63
     Mediterranean-Style
          Hummus, 38–39
     Pico de Gallo, 61
     Roasted Tomato Serrano
          Salsa, 60–61
     Toasted-Pepita Dip, 40
     Verde Cruda, 60
Dressings
     Agave-Lime Vinaigrette, 64
     Herb Vinaigrette, 69
     Orange Vinaigrette, 70
     Pomegranate Vinaigrette, 68
     Vegan Caesar Dressing, 66

E
Easy Fruit Sorbet, 238
Eggless Mayonnaise, 37
Eggplants
     Barbecue Tofu Kebabs, 218–219

Mediterranean Tomato &
     Eggplant Stew, 167–168
Provençal Vegetable
     Tian, 216–217
Turkish Eggplant Casserole, 191–192
Warm Pita with Hummus &
     Grilled Vegetables, 100–101
Eggs, 4, 20
     Avocados Rancheros, 77–78
     Kale, Frisée & Asparagus
          Salad with Toasted Pepita
          Vinaigrette, 125–126
     Spinach Crêpes with Black
          Bean Sauce, 88–89
Endive, Pear & Arugula Salad with
     Candied Walnuts, 128–129
Equipment, 21–24

F
Farro
     Grains & Greens Bowl, 134
Fats, 4
Fennel
     Fennel, Apple & Celery Salad, 132
     Mediterranean Tomato &
          Eggplant Stew, 167–168
Figs
     Fruit Mustard, 63
     Honey-Roasted Figs with
          Vegan Cheese, 233
Flavored Oils, 56
Flavored Vinegar, 57
Flaxseed, 17
     Maple Whole-Grain Hot Cereal, 91
Flexitarian diets, 2
Fresh, Chunky Guacamole, 41
Fresh Tofu & Soy Milk, 28–29
Frisée, Kale & Asparagus
     Salad, 125–126
Fruit Leather, 48–49
Fruit Mustard, 63
Fruits, 3, 7, 21. See also specific
     Easy Fruit Sorbet, 238
     Flavored Vinegar, 57
     Fruit Leather, 48–49

G

Garden Vegetable &
    Quinoa Soup, 169
Garlic, 20
Ginger, 20
  Agave-Lime Vinaigrette, 64
  Apple-Ginger Tea, 223
  Carrot, Ginger & Jalapeño Soup, 153
  Coconut Cauliflower Rice, 142
  Coconut Curry Sauce, 72
  Gingered Sweet Potato Mash, 146
  Green Tea Soba Noodles with
      Sesame Dipping Sauce, 200–201
  Jerk Tofu Steaks, 198–199
  Pumpkin & Cashew Curry, 184–185
  Spicy Vegan Sweet Potato Maki
      with Coconut Rice, 210–211
  Sweet Potato & Lentil Bowl, 135–136
  Thai-Inspired Peanut Sauce, 71
  Veggie Hot Pot, 170–171
  Zucchini Rolls with Spaghetti
      Squash & Quinoa, 212–213
Gluten-free
  Açai Breakfast Bowl, 87
  Agave-Lime Vinaigrette, 64
  Apple & Red Chile Chutney, 65
  Apple-Ginger Tea, 223
  Avocado-Citrus Sherbet, 239
  Avocado-Coconut Milk Shake, 226
  Avocados Rancheros, 77–78
  Baked Vegetable Chips, 51
  Barbecue Tofu Kebabs, 218–219
  Basic Vegetable Stock, 32
  Blackberry Lemonade, 222
  Black-Eyed Pea & Baby
      Spinach Salad, 133
  Brussels Sprouts with
      Chile & Mint, 141
  Buffalo Cauliflower Steaks, 214–215
  Butterless Butter, 36
  Butternut Squash & Lentil
      Chili, 160
  Butternut Squash–Apple Soup with
      Chile Yogurt & Pepitas, 150–151

Cabbage Soup with Apples
    & Thyme, 152
Calabacitas Tacos, 186
Caribbean Chard, Sweet Potato &
    Spicy Peanut Jumble, 204
Carrot, Ginger & Jalapeño Soup, 153
Cauliflower Crust Pizza, 205
Chia Limeade, 230
Chickpea Soup with Black
    Kale, Harissa & Spiced
    Yogurt, 161–163
Cocoa-Chia Waffles, 95
Coconut Cauliflower Rice, 142
Coconut-Cauliflower Rice
    Pudding, 231–232
Coconut Curry Sauce, 72
Coconut Horchata, 228
Collard Greens with Pickled
    Apples & Walnuts, 144–145
Corn Chowder, 158
Creamless Creamed Corn, 143
Crispy Cinnamon Chickpeas, 44
Dairy-Free Soft Cheese, 33
Easy Fruit Sorbet, 238
Eggless Mayonnaise, 37
Fennel, Apple & Celery
    Salad, 132
Flavored Oils, 56
Flavored Vinegar, 57
Fresh, Chunky Guacamole, 41
Fresh Tofu & Soy Milk, 28–29
Fruit Leather, 48–49
Gingered Sweet Potato Mash, 146
Grains & Greens Bowl, 134
Green Grape Gazpacho, 157
Habanero Hot Sauce, 67
Heirloom Tomato &
    Watermelon Salad, 130
Herb Vinaigrette, 69
Hibiscus-Lemongrass Tea, 227
Homemade Ketchup, 62
Honey-Roasted Figs with
    Vegan Cheese, 233
Jerk Tofu Steaks, 198–199
Kale Crisps, 52

Kale, Frisée & Asparagus
    Salad with Toasted Pepita
    Vinaigrette, 125–126
Lentil Salad with Caramelized
    Shallots & Feta, 127
Mediterranean-Style
    Hummus, 38–39
Mediterranean Tomato &
    Eggplant Stew, 167–168
Moroccan Mushroom Stew, 172–173
Non-Dairy Yogurt, 34
Nut Milk, 35
Orange Vinaigrette, 70
Pear, Arugula & Endive Salad with
    Candied Walnuts, 128–129
Pickled Red Onions, 58
Pico de Gallo, 61
Pomegranate & Celery
    Agua Fresca, 224
Pomegranate Vinaigrette, 68
Power Pancakes, 82
Power Smoothie, 92
Power Trail Mix, 47
Riced Cauliflower &
    Chickpea Pilaf, 202
Roasted Tomato Serrano
    Salsa, 60–61
Salt & Pepper Tofu, 188
Sparkling Parsley Green Tea
    with Lemon Ice Cubes, 229
Spicy Tofu Scramble, 81
Sweet Potato & Colorado
    Bean Hash, 90
Sweet Potato & Lentil
    Bowl, 135–136
Thai-Inspired Peanut Sauce, 71
Toasted-Pepita Dip, 40
Turkish Eggplant Casserole, 191–192
Vegan Brussels Sprout
    Caesar Salad, 124
Vegan Caesar Dressing, 66
Vegan Green Risotto with
    Broccoli, 182–183
Vegan Macaroni & Cheese, 137–138
Vegan Pad Thai, 206–207

Vegan Spinach & Tofu
    Enchiladas, 178–179
Vegetable Shepherd's
    Pie, 189–190
Verde Cruda, 60
Watercress, Jicama &
    Orange Salad, 131
Whole Roasted Cauliflower in
    Herb Salsa Verde, 208–209
Goji berries, 16
Grains, 3, 9. See also specific
Grains & Greens Bowl, 134
Grapes, 20–21
    Green Grape Gazpacho, 157
Greek Gigante Bean &
    Tomato Stew, 164
Green beans
    Pistou Soup, 165–166
Green Grape Gazpacho, 157
Green Tea Soba Noodles
    with Sesame Dipping
    Sauce, 200–201
Grilled Mushroom
    Cheesesteaks, 111
Guacamole Grilled Cheese, 115

H

Habanero Hot Sauce, 67
Health benefits, 10
Heirloom Tomato &
    Watermelon Salad, 130
Herbs, fresh, 20. See also specific
    Ancient Grain & Wild
        Mushroom Pilaf, 139
    White Bean & Pasta Soup, 159
Herb Vinaigrette, 69
Hibiscus-Lemongrass Tea, 227
Homemade Ketchup, 62
Homemade Seitan, 30–31
Honey-Roasted Figs with
    Vegan Cheese, 233
Hummus
    Beet Hummus Toast, 116
    Mediterranean-Style
        Hummus, 38–39

Warm Pita with Hummus &
    Grilled Vegetables, 100–101

I

Ingredient staples, 16–21

J

Jackfruit
    Vegan Pulled Pork
        Sandwiches, 106–107
Jerk Tofu Steaks, 198–199
Jicama, Watercress &
    Orange Salad, 131

K

Kale, 20
    Cabbage & Veggie Lasagna, 187
    Chickpea Soup with Black
        Kale, Harissa & Spiced
        Yogurt, 161–163
    Kale Crisps, 52
    Kale, Frisée & Asparagus
        Salad with Toasted Pepita
        Vinaigrette, 125–126
    Power Smoothie, 92
    Spaghetti with Braised Kale,
        Chile & Lemon, 180–181
Kitchen cleanse, 18

L

Lacto-ovo vegetarian diets, 2
Leeks
    Butternut Squash–Apple Soup with
        Chile Yogurt & Pepitas, 150–151
Legumes, 4, 8. See also specific
Lemongrass
    Hibiscus-Lemongrass Tea, 227
    Tofu Banh Mi, 108–109
Lemons
    Blackberry Lemonade, 222
    Lemon-Herb Red Quinoa, 147
    Spaghetti with Braised Kale,
        Chile & Lemon, 180–181
    Sparkling Parsley Green Tea
        with Lemon Ice Cubes, 229

Lentils, 5, 16
    Butternut Squash & Lentil Chili, 160
    Grains & Greens Bowl, 134
    Lentil Salad with Caramelized
        Shallots & Feta, 127
    Plant Meatball Marinara
        Hero, 117–118
    Sweet Potato & Lentil Bowl, 135–136
    Vegan Sloppy Joes, 113–114
    Vegetable Shepherd's Pie, 189–190
Lettuce
    Avocado Milanesa Torta, 119–120
    Best BLT, The, 112
    Vegan Spinach & Tofu
        Enchiladas, 178–179
    Warm Pita with Hummus &
        Grilled Vegetables, 100–101
Limes
    Agave-Lime Vinaigrette, 64
    Avocado-Citrus Sherbet, 239
    Chia Limeade, 230
    Pico de Gallo, 61
    Roasted Tomato Serrano
        Salsa, 60–61

M

Maple Whole-Grain Hot
    Cereal, 91
Marjoram
    Apple & Red Chile Chutney, 65
    Charred-Tomato Gazpacho, 155–156
    Whole Roasted Cauliflower in
        Herb Salsa Verde, 208–209
Mediterranean-Style
    Hummus, 38–39
Mediterranean Tomato &
    Eggplant Stew, 167–168
Milks, 20
Millet
    Ancient Grain & Wild
        Mushroom Pilaf, 139
    Maple Whole-Grain Hot Cereal, 91
Mint
    Almond Yogurt, Fruit &
        Muesli Parfait, 83

Mint (continued)
    Brussels Sprouts with
        Chile & Mint, 141
    Carrot Falafel with
        Zuccanoush, 193–194
    Charred-Carrot Dip, 42–43
    Chickpea Soup with Black
        Kale, Harissa & Spiced
        Yogurt, 161–163
    Coconut Horchata, 228
    Fennel, Apple & Celery Salad, 132
    Green Grape Gazpacho, 157
    Power Smoothie, 92
    Sparkling Parsley Green Tea
        with Lemon Ice Cubes, 229
    Zucchini Rolls with Spaghetti
        Squash & Quinoa, 212–213
Moroccan Mushroom
    Stew, 172–173
Moroccan Veggie Tagine with
    Couscous, 196–197
Mushrooms
    Ancient Grain & Wild
        Mushroom Pilaf, 139
    Better Black Bean Burger,
        The, 98–99
    Biscuits & Vegetarian
        Redeye Gravy, 84–85
    Grilled Mushroom Cheesesteaks, 111
    Moroccan Mushroom Stew, 172–173
    Vegan Pad Thai, 206–207
    Veggie Hot Pot, 170–171
    Veggie Meatballs with Tomato
        Ragout, 176–177

N

Non-Dairy Yogurt, 34
Noodles. See also Pasta
    Green Tea Soba Noodles with
        Sesame Dipping Sauce, 200–201
    Vegan Pad Thai, 206–207
    Veggie Hot Pot, 170–171
Nut Milk, 35
Nutritional needs, 2–4
Nuts, 4, 7–8, 17

Almond Yogurt, Fruit &
    Muesli Parfait, 83
Apple & Red Chile Chutney, 65
Better Black Bean Burger,
    The, 98–99
Caribbean Chard, Sweet Potato &
    Spicy Peanut Jumble, 204
Carrot Falafel with
    Zuccanoush, 193–194
Charred-Carrot Dip, 42–43
Coconut Horchata, 228
Collard Greens with Pickled
    Apples & Walnuts, 144–145
Dairy-Free Soft Cheese, 33
Fennel, Apple & Celery Salad, 132
Green Grape Gazpacho, 157
Lemon-Herb Red Quinoa, 147
Moroccan Veggie Tagine with
    Couscous, 196–197
Nut Milk, 35
Pear, Arugula & Endive Salad with
    Candied Walnuts, 128–129
Power Trail Mix, 47
Pumpkin & Cashew Curry, 184–185
Vegan Brussels Sprout
    Caesar Salad, 124
Vegan Green Risotto with
    Broccoli, 182–183
Vegan Macaroni & Cheese, 137–138
Vegan Pad Thai, 206–207

O

Oats, 17
    Almond Yogurt, Fruit &
        Muesli Parfait, 83
    Maple Whole-Grain Hot Cereal, 91
    Peanut Butter Overnight Oats, 86
    Plant Meatball Marinara
        Hero, 117–118
    Veggie Meatballs with Tomato
        Ragout, 176–177
Oils, 4, 17, 18
    Flavored Oils, 56
Onions, 20
    Barbecue Tofu Kebabs, 218–219

Basic Vegetable Stock, 32
Pickled Red Onions, 58
Oranges
    Carrot, Ginger & Jalapeño Soup, 153
    Hibiscus-Lemongrass Tea, 227
    Orange Vinaigrette, 70
    Toasted-Pepita Dip, 40
    Watercress, Jicama &
        Orange Salad, 131
    Whole Roasted Cauliflower in
        Herb Salsa Verde, 208–209

P

Pancakes
    Power Pancakes, 82
    Pumpkin Pancakes with
        Spiced Crema, 80
    Spinach Crêpes with Black
        Bean Sauce, 88–89
Pantry staples, 16–18
Parsley
    Basic Vegetable Stock, 32
    Carrot Falafel with
        Zuccanoush, 193–194
    Carrot, Ginger & Jalapeño Soup, 153
    Fennel, Apple & Celery Salad, 132
    Moroccan Mushroom Stew, 172–173
    Moroccan Veggie Tagine with
        Couscous, 196–197
    Pear, Arugula & Endive Salad with
        Candied Walnuts, 128–129
    Quinoa Fritters, 45–46
    Riced Cauliflower &
        Chickpea Pilaf, 202
    Sparkling Parsley Green Tea
        with Lemon Ice Cubes, 229
    Turkish Eggplant Casserole, 191–192
    Vegan Brussels Sprout
        Caesar Salad, 124
    Vegan Green Risotto with
        Broccoli, 182–183
    Veggie Meatballs with Tomato
        Ragout, 176–177
    Whole Roasted Cauliflower in
        Herb Salsa Verde, 208–209

Pasta
  Pistou Soup, 165–166
  Spaghetti with Braised Kale,
    Chile & Lemon, 180–181
  Vegan Macaroni & Cheese, 137–138
  White Bean & Pasta Soup, 159
PB & J, 103–104
Peaches
  Blackberry-Peach Crisp, 236–237
  Vegan Ricotta, Peach &
    Basil Panini, 105
Peanut butter
  Caribbean Chard, Sweet Potato &
    Spicy Peanut Jumble, 204
  PB & J, 103–104
  Peanut Butter Overnight Oats, 86
  Thai-Inspired Peanut Sauce, 71
Pear, Arugula & Endive Salad with
  Candied Walnuts, 128–129
Peas
  Grains & Greens Bowl, 134
Pepitas. See Pumpkin seeds
Peppers. See also Chiles
  Avocados Rancheros, 77–78
  Barbecue Tofu Kebabs, 218–219
  Black-Eyed Pea & Baby
    Spinach Salad, 133
  Butternut Squash & Lentil Chili, 160
  Butternut Squash, Black Bean
    & Grain Chili, 195
  Calabacitas Tacos, 186
  Caribbean Chard, Sweet Potato &
    Spicy Peanut Jumble, 204
  Carrot, Ginger & Jalapeño Soup, 153
  Charred-Tomato Gazpacho, 155–156
  Green Grape Gazpacho, 157
  Grilled Mushroom Cheesesteaks, 111
  Habanero Hot Sauce, 67
  Jerk Tofu Steaks, 198–199
  PB & J, 103–104
  Pico de Gallo, 61
  Pistou Soup, 165–166
  Provençal Vegetable Tian, 216–217
  Roasted Tomato Serrano
    Salsa, 60–61

Salt & Pepper Tofu, 188
Spicy Tofu Scramble, 81
Sweet Potato & Colorado
  Bean Hash, 90
Toasted-Pepita Dip, 40
Tofu Banh Mi, 108–109
Vegan Sloppy Joes, 113–114
Verde Cruda, 60
Warm Pita with Hummus &
  Grilled Vegetables, 100–101
Zucchini Rolls with Spaghetti
  Squash & Quinoa, 212–213
Pescatarian diets, 2
Pickled Red Onions, 58
Pico de Gallo, 61
Pineapple
  Power Smoothie, 92
Pistou Soup, 165–166
Plant-based milks, 20
Plant-forward diets, 1–2, 10
Plant Meatball Marinara
  Hero, 117–118
Pomegranate & Celery
  Agua Fresca, 224
Pomegranate arils
  Charred-Carrot Dip, 42–43
  Pomegranate Vinaigrette, 68
Potatoes. See also Sweet potatoes
  Barbecue Tofu Kebabs, 218–219
  Corn Chowder, 158
  Moroccan Veggie Tagine with
    Couscous, 196–197
  Pistou Soup, 165–166
  Vegan Macaroni & Cheese, 137–138
Power Pancakes, 82
Power Smoothie, 92
Power Trail Mix, 47
Processed foods, 11–12, 18
Protein, 5, 9–10
Provençal Vegetable Tian, 216–217
Pumpkin & Cashew
  Curry, 184–185
Pumpkin Pancakes with
  Spiced Crema, 80
Pumpkin seeds, 18

Butternut Squash–Apple Soup with
  Chile Yogurt & Pepitas, 150–151
Kale, Frisée & Asparagus
  Salad with Toasted Pepita
  Vinaigrette, 125–126
Power Trail Mix, 47
Toasted-Pepita Dip, 40
Watercress, Jicama &
  Orange Salad, 131

Q

Quinoa, 5, 17
  Better Black Bean Burger,
    The, 98–99
  Garden Vegetable &
    Quinoa Soup, 169
  Lemon-Herb Red Quinoa, 147
  Maple Whole-Grain Hot
    Cereal, 91
  Quinoa Fritters, 45–46
  Zucchini Rolls with Spaghetti
    Squash & Quinoa, 212–213

R

Radishes, 21
  Tofu Banh Mi, 108–109
  Vegan Spinach & Tofu
    Enchiladas, 178–179
Raisins
  Almond Yogurt, Fruit &
    Muesli Parfait, 83
  Moroccan Veggie Tagine with
    Couscous, 196–197
  Power Trail Mix, 47
Refrigerator staples, 19–21
Rice, 16
  Ancient Grain & Wild
    Mushroom Pilaf, 139
  Coconut Horchata, 228
  Spicy Vegan Sweet Potato Maki
    with Coconut Rice, 210–211
  Vegan Green Risotto with
    Broccoli, 182–183
Riced Cauliflower &
  Chickpea Pilaf, 202

Roasted Tomato Serrano
    Salsa, 60–61
Rye berries, 18

S

Sage
    Butternut Squash–Apple Soup with
        Chile Yogurt & Pepitas, 150–151
    Chia Limeade, 230
Salads
    Black-Eyed Pea & Baby
        Spinach Salad, 133
    Fennel, Apple & Celery Salad, 132
    Heirloom Tomato &
        Watermelon Salad, 130
    Kale, Frisée & Asparagus
        Salad with Toasted Pepita
        Vinaigrette, 125–126
    Lentil Salad with Caramelized
        Shallots & Feta, 127
    Vegan Brussels Sprout
        Caesar Salad, 124
    Watercress, Jicama &
        Orange Salad, 131
Salt & Pepper Tofu, 188
Sandwiches
    Avocado Milanesa Torta, 119–120
    Avocado Toast, 76
    Beet Hummus Toast, 116
    Best BLT, The, 112
    Better Black Bean Burger,
        The, 98–99
    Guacamole Grilled Cheese, 115
    PB & J, 103–104
    Plant Meatball Marinara
        Hero, 117–118
    Tofu Banh Mi, 108–109
    Vegan Breakfast Sando, 93–94
    Vegan Egg Salad Sando, 110
    Vegan Pulled Pork
        Sandwiches, 106–107
    Vegan Ricotta, Peach &
        Basil Panini, 105
    Warm Pita with Hummus &
        Grilled Vegetables, 100–101

Sauces
    Coconut Curry Sauce, 72
    Habanero Hot Sauce, 67
    Homemade Ketchup, 62
    Pico de Gallo, 61
    Roasted Tomato Serrano
        Salsa, 60–61
    Thai-Inspired Peanut Sauce, 71
    Verde Cruda, 60
Scallions, 21
Seeds, 4
Seitan, Homemade, 30–31
Serving sizes, 3–4, 6
Sesame seeds, 18
    Charred-Carrot Dip, 42–43
    Green Tea Soba Noodles with
        Sesame Dipping Sauce, 200–201
    Heirloom Tomato &
        Watermelon Salad, 130
    Spicy Vegan Sweet Potato Maki
        with Coconut Rice, 210–211
Shallots, Caramelized & Feta,
    Lentil Salad with, 127
Soups. See also Stews
    Basic Vegetable Stock, 32
    Butternut Squash & Lentil Chili, 160
    Butternut Squash–Apple Soup with
        Chile Yogurt & Pepitas, 150–151
    Butternut Squash, Black Bean
        & Grain Chili, 195
    Cabbage Soup with Apples
        & Thyme, 152
    Carrot, Ginger & Jalapeño
        Soup, 153
    Charred-Tomato Gazpacho, 155–156
    Chickpea Soup with Black
        Kale, Harissa & Spiced
        Yogurt, 161–163
    Corn Chowder, 158
    Garden Vegetable &
        Quinoa Soup, 169
    Green Grape Gazpacho, 157
    Pistou Soup, 165–166
    Veggie Hot Pot, 170–171
    White Bean & Pasta Soup, 159

Soybeans
    Fresh Tofu & Soy Milk, 28–29
Spaghetti with Braised Kale,
    Chile & Lemon, 180–181
Sparkling Parsley Green Tea with
    Lemon Ice Cubes, 229
Spices, 17
Spicy Tofu Scramble, 81
Spicy Vegan Sweet Potato Maki
    with Coconut Rice, 210–211
Spinach
    Black-Eyed Pea & Baby
        Spinach Salad, 133
    Garden Vegetable &
        Quinoa Soup, 169
    Moroccan Mushroom Stew, 172–173
    Power Smoothie, 92
    Spinach Crêpes with Black
        Bean Sauce, 88–89
    Vegan Spinach & Tofu
        Enchiladas, 178–179
Spinach Crêpes with Black
    Bean Sauce, 88–89
Squash, 21. See also Zucchini
    Butternut Squash & Lentil Chili, 160
    Butternut Squash–Apple Soup with
        Chile Yogurt & Pepitas, 150–151
    Butternut Squash, Black Bean
        & Grain Chili, 195
    Calabacitas Tacos, 186
    Pistou Soup, 165–166
    Provençal Vegetable Tian, 216–217
    Zucchini Rolls with Spaghetti
        Squash & Quinoa, 212–213
Stews
    Greek Gigante Bean &
        Tomato Stew, 164
    Mediterranean Tomato &
        Eggplant Stew, 167–168
    Moroccan Mushroom Stew, 172–173
    Moroccan Veggie Tagine with
        Couscous, 196–197
    Pumpkin & Cashew Curry, 184–185
Sunflower seeds, 18
    Grains & Greens Bowl, 134

Power Trail Mix, 47
Sweet potatoes, 20
   Baked Vegetable Chips, 51
   Caribbean Chard, Sweet Potato &
      Spicy Peanut Jumble, 204
   Gingered Sweet Potato Mash, 146
   Moroccan Veggie Tagine with
      Couscous, 196–197
   Spicy Vegan Sweet Potato Maki
      with Coconut Rice, 210–211
   Sweet Potato & Colorado
      Bean Hash, 90
   Sweet Potato & Lentil Bowl, 135–136
   Vegetable Shepherd's Pie, 189–190
Swiss chard
   Caribbean Chard, Sweet Potato &
      Spicy Peanut Jumble, 204
   Pistou Soup, 165–166

T

Tahini
   Carrot Falafel with
      Zuccanoush, 193–194
   Charred-Carrot Dip, 42–43
   Mediterranean-Style
      Hummus, 38–39
Tempeh, 5
   Avocado Milanesa Torta, 119–120
   Best BLT, The, 112
   Kale, Frisée & Asparagus
      Salad with Toasted Pepita
      Vinaigrette, 125–126
   Vegan Breakfast Sando, 93–94
Thai-Inspired Peanut Sauce, 71
Thyme
   Basic Vegetable Stock, 32
   Cabbage Soup with Apples
      & Thyme, 152
   Chickpea Soup with Black
      Kale, Harissa & Spiced
      Yogurt, 161–163
   Jerk Tofu Steaks, 198–199
   Lemon-Herb Red Quinoa, 147
   Mediterranean Tomato &
      Eggplant Stew, 167–168

   Moroccan Mushroom Stew, 172–173
   Provençal Vegetable Tian, 216–217
   Turkish Eggplant Casserole, 191–192
   Vegetable Shepherd's Pie, 189–190
Toasted-Pepita Dip, 40
Tofu, 5
   Barbecue Tofu Kebabs, 218–219
   Fresh Tofu & Soy Milk, 28–29
   Jerk Tofu Steaks, 198–199
   Salt & Pepper Tofu, 188
   Spicy Tofu Scramble, 81
   Tofu Banh Mi, 108–109
   Vegan Breakfast Sando, 93–94
   Vegan Egg Salad Sando, 110
   Vegan Pad Thai, 206–207
   Vegan Ricotta, Peach &
      Basil Panini, 105
   Vegan Spinach & Tofu
      Enchiladas, 178–179
   Veggie Hot Pot, 170–171
Tofu Banh Mi, 108–109
Tomatillos
   Green Grape Gazpacho, 157
   Verde Cruda, 60
Tomatoes
   Avocado Milanesa Torta, 119–120
   Barbecue Tofu Kebabs, 218–219
   Best BLT, The, 112
   Butternut Squash & Lentil Chili, 160
   Butternut Squash, Black Bean
      & Grain Chili, 195
   Caribbean Chard, Sweet Potato &
      Spicy Peanut Jumble, 204
   Carrot Falafel with
      Zuccanoush, 193–194
   Charred-Tomato Gazpacho, 155–156
   Fresh, Chunky Guacamole, 41
   Garden Vegetable &
      Quinoa Soup, 169
   Grains & Greens Bowl, 134
   Greek Gigante Bean &
      Tomato Stew, 164
   Habanero Hot Sauce, 67
   Heirloom Tomato &
      Watermelon Salad, 130

   Mediterranean Tomato &
      Eggplant Stew, 167–168
   Moroccan Veggie Tagine with
      Couscous, 196–197
   Pico de Gallo, 61
   Pistou Soup, 165–166
   Provençal Vegetable Tian, 216–217
   Roasted Tomato Serrano
      Salsa, 60–61
   Spicy Tofu Scramble, 81
   Sweet Potato & Colorado
      Bean Hash, 90
   Toasted-Pepita Dip, 40
   Turkish Eggplant Casserole, 191–192
   Vegan Breakfast Sando, 93–94
   Veggie Meatballs with Tomato
      Ragout, 176–177
   Warm Pita with Hummus &
      Grilled Vegetables, 100–101
   White Bean & Pasta Soup, 159
Tortillas
   Avocados Rancheros, 77–78
   Calabacitas Tacos, 186
   Vegan Spinach & Tofu
      Enchiladas, 178–179
Tubers, 8–9
Turkish Eggplant Casserole,
   191–192

V

Vegan Breakfast Sando, 93–94
Vegan Brussels Sprout
   Caesar Salad, 124
Vegan Caesar Dressing, 66
Vegan diets, 2
Vegan Egg Salad Sando, 110
Vegan Green Risotto with
   Broccoli, 182–183
Vegan Macaroni & Cheese, 137–138
Vegan Pad Thai, 206–207
Vegan Pulled Pork
   Sandwiches, 106–107
Vegan Ricotta, Peach &
   Basil Panini, 105
Vegan Sloppy Joes, 113–114

Vegan Spinach & Tofu
Enchiladas, 178–179
Vegetables, 3, 7. *See also specific*
Flavored Vinegar, 57
Vegetable Shepherd's Pie, 189–190
Vegetable Shepherd's Pie, 189–190
Vegetarian diets, 2, 10
Veggie Hot Pot, 170–171
Veggie Meatballs with Tomato
Ragout, 176–177
Verde Cruda, 60
Vinegars, 16–17, 18
Flavored Vinegar, 57

W

Warm Pita with Hummus &
Grilled Vegetables, 100–101
Watercress, Jicama &
Orange Salad, 131
Watermelon & Heirloom
Tomato Salad, 130

Wheat berries
Ancient Grain & Wild
Mushroom Pilaf, 139
White Bean & Pasta Soup, 159
Whole foods, 6–10
Whole Roasted Cauliflower in
Herb Salsa Verde, 208–209

Y

Yogurt
Açai Breakfast Bowl, 87
Almond Yogurt, Fruit &
Muesli Parfait, 83
Avocado-Coconut Milk Shake, 226
Butternut Squash–Apple Soup with
Chile Yogurt & Pepitas, 150–151
Butternut Squash, Black Bean
& Grain Chili, 195
Chickpea Soup with Black
Kale, Harissa & Spiced
Yogurt, 161–163

Dairy-Free Soft Cheese, 33
Green Grape Gazpacho, 157
Moroccan Mushroom
Stew, 172–173
Non-Dairy Yogurt, 34
Vegan Caesar Dressing, 66
Vegan Spinach & Tofu
Enchiladas, 178–179

Z

Zucchini
Calabacitas Tacos, 186
Carrot Falafel with
Zuccanoush, 193–194
Pistou Soup, 165–166
Provençal Vegetable
Tian, 216–217
Warm Pita with Hummus &
Grilled Vegetables, 100–101
Zucchini Rolls with Spaghetti
Squash & Quinoa, 212–213

ACKNOWLEDGMENTS

I've been passionate about cooking and introducing people to healthy eating through my restaurants and cooking classes for many years, and I consider it an essential part of my mission as a chef. I am thrilled to be able to share my knowledge in a cookbook. This book is more than just a chef who is crazy about nutritious food and a stack of recipes. I consider all my work a collaboration between me and my chefs, cooks, dishwashers, front-of-the-house staff, vendors, and customers. I'd be nowhere without this extension of my family's encouragement, support, loyalty, and, most importantly, feedback and ideas.

My immediate family, father Russ, mother Charlene, and sister Holly, have always been there with their enthusiasm and sometimes financial support, without which I would not have had the courage to open my own business.

I'd also like to thank my wonderful group of close friends who allow me to escape the stress of the restaurant kitchen by sharing vacations, meals, and millions and millions of laughs with me. I don't want to make the mistake of leaving any friends out because I'm lucky to have so many. I'll just say, you know who you are.

Finally, I'd like to thank the team at Callisto Media for granting me the opportunity to bring to life a dream book after years spent in my musings. Especially David Lytle and Michelle Anderson, for patiently helping me put my thoughts to paper in a way that others will want to read, cook from, and find useful in improving their health in a delicious way.

ABOUT THE AUTHOR

Ivy Stark found her passion for food early on, growing up in Boulder, Colorado, when she was first exposed to fine dining through her father, who worked in luxury hotel management. Stark was the executive chef of the highly popular Mexican restaurant Dos Caminos in New York City, where she earned national recognition and ranked as one of New York's top chefs. It was there that she wrote her first book, *Dos Caminos Mexican Street Food: 120 Authentic Recipes to Make at Home*, followed by *Dos Caminos Tacos*. In 2019, Stark took the giant leap of opening her own restaurants: BKLYNwild, serving vegan and vegetarian food, and Mexology, serving fresh, creative Mexican food, both located in the vibrant, arts-centered DUMBO neighborhood in Brooklyn. When she's not in the kitchen, Stark devotes her time to various culinary boards and charities such as City Harvest, Meals on Wheels, and C-CAP. She has appeared on *Today* and *Good Morning America*, in addition to multiple appearances on Food Network as a judge on *Beat Bobby Flay*. In her spare time, Stark enjoys skiing, running, baseball, and hanging out with her dogs Frida and Diego in Brooklyn.

CPSIA information can be obtained
at www.ICGtesting.com
Printed in the USA
JSHW012344220820
7401JS00006B/11

CPSIA information can be obtained
at www.ICGtesting.com
Printed in the USA
JSHW012344220820
7401JS00006B/11

9 781646 118847